ADVANCE PRAISE FOR

The End of Protest

"Micah White gives us a bird's-eye view of the ever-shifting battle field of dynamic social change. New wars require new arts to be successful."

LUPE FIASCO, rapper and hip-hop artist

"Micah is a systems genius and the moral voice of a thinking generation. His points are simple, true and astounding."

ROSEANNE BARR, actor

"Within the context of his experience with the Occupy movement, Micah White bravely challenges the current protest-rut in which many social justice activists find themselves. His critique of modern social movements challenges activists to progress to the next level, while leaving us hopeful that the revolution for a better world is already upon us."

PAM PALMATER, Mi'kmaw lawyer, professor and Idle No More spokesperson & educator

"*The End of Protest* is an engrossing historical document, call to arms, guide, and self-critical look at the Occupy movement from one of its co-founders. It traces the history of protest in the North and offers a new vision, tactics and strategy for a peaceful revolution through a horizontal, mundialist movement. An inspiring must-read for any activist."

CARMEN AGUIRRE, author of *Mexican Hooker #1* and *Something Fierce*, winner of Canada Reads

"Micah White issues an impassioned clarion call for activists to reinvent protest—a format that that has been so utterly devitalized, it has lost its bite and power to impel change. White makes his case by drawing on decades of personal experience and the historical record, and what springs forth from these pages is an eminently readable playbook packed with wisdom and practical advice for resuscitating the power of dissent in the twenty-first century."

GABRIELLA COLEMAN, author of
Hacker, Hoaxer, Whistleblower, Spy

"*The End of Protest* is an informative and inspiring book for activists of any and every stripe. White's emphasis on 'mental environmentalism,' as he puts it, is brilliant."

ALEX EBERT, lead singer of
Edward Sharpe and the Magnetic Zeros

"Micah White is a *strategist*, a new breed of revolutionary. He knows that resistance isn't so much about what you do as who you *are*: it cuts right inside you, into your very Being, into your belief systems, into your democratic hopes, into your anti-corporate desires, into your whole mental environment. This is *Rules for Radicals* for the World Party—the one yet to be."

ANDY MERRIFIELD, author of
The Wisdom of Donkeys and *Magical Marxism*

"Micah White argues convincingly that established modes of protest are outdated and sketches the outlines for how activists can and must innovate. His book is a love letter to activists of the future."

MICHAEL HARDT, co-author of the Empire trilogy
(*Empire*, *Multitude*, *Commonwealth*) as well as *Declaration*

"Fearlessly lucid, radically open-minded, Micah White puts protest back where it belongs—among the greatest forces ever to shape history. Then he exposes a protest culture just as jaded as the structures it seeks to overthrow, and as desperately in need of 'ruthless innovation.' Many books tell us *why* we should protest; this book tells us *how*."

J.B. MacKINNON, author of *The Once and Future World*

"President Kennedy said, 'Those who make peaceful revolution impossible make violent revolution inevitable.' One of the most urgent existential questions of our time is how to respond to that supposition. In *The End of Protest,* Micah White guides the conversation by combining an expansive grasp of history and political philosophy with a thrilling sense of future possibility."

MARIANNE WILLIAMSON, author of *A Return to Love*

"Micah White offers us a deeply honest, courageous and ultimately optimistic view of how people can make a far better world—and why we're not there yet. The book is so packed with insights and ideas that you're bound to agree with some and question others. But you will be challenged and you will get smarter. This book is much needed fuel for a people's compassionate revolution."

JONAH SACHS, author of *Winning the Story Wars*

"*The End of Protest* is nothing less than a new paradigm for resistance. It will be sure to initiate a heated and necessary debate about how to confront oppression, and what constitutes victory."

DOUGLAS RUSHKOFF, author of *Throwing Rocks at the Google Bus* and *Present Shock*

micah white

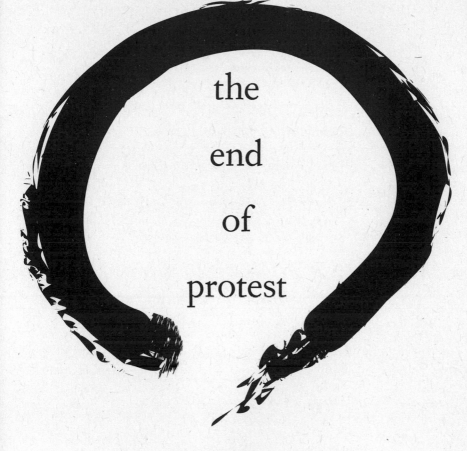

the end of protest

a new playbook for revolution

Alfred A. Knopf Canada

PUBLISHED BY ALFRED A. KNOPF CANADA

 Published in 2016 by Alfred A. Knopf Canada, a division of Penguin Random House Canada Limited. Distributed by Penguin Random House Canada Limited, Toronto.

www.penguinrandomhouse.ca

Library and Archives Canada Cataloguing in Publication

White, Micah, 1982– , author
The end of protest : a new playbook for revolution / Micah White.

Includes bibliographical references and index.
Issued in print and electronic formats.

ISBN 978-0-345-81004-5
eBook ISBN 978-0-345-81006-9

1. Social movements. 2. Social change. I. Title.

HM881.W45 2016 303.48'4 C2015-905784-1

Text and cover design by Terri Nimmo

Cover image: © Ho Yeow Hui / Shutterstock.com (also used in interior)

Printed and bound in the United States of America

2 4 6 8 9 7 5 3

For Chiara: your light has transformed me.

And to those who never protest the same way twice,

thank you.

Being a revolutionary is like being in love. The characteristic of people in love is that they do not believe that anybody else in their lifetime has also been in love. So they do not learn from other people's mistakes and repeat all the same errors.

PAUL N. ROSENSTEIN-RODAN, ECONOMIST, 1974

CONTENTS

PART THREE: TOMORROW

CONCLUSION

All day, all week, Occupy Wall Street!

LUPE FIASCO, AMERICAN RAPPER, 2011

PREFACE

> "All right, you ninety thousand redeemers, rebels and radicals out there . . . On September 17, we want to see twenty thousand people flood into Lower Manhattan, set up tents, kitchens, peaceful barricades and occupy Wall Street for a few months."

With this wild wish, a global uprising was unleashed. The clamour was tremendous, the mood contagious. For a few magical weeks in 2011, the Occupy Wall Street meme spread from city to city, financial district to public park: Occupy Toronto, Occupy Oakland, Occupy Vancouver, Occupy London, Occupy Sydney . . . People's encampments sprang up in 951 cities across eighty-two countries. For many it was an all-consuming experience; the event was in them and they were the event. Participants started losing their fear, jeopardizing the status quo, quitting their jobs and *living without dead time*—fully awake in the moment. Occupy celebrated people for becoming authentic and sharing themselves. Unleashing humanity's collective creativity was the essence of our movement.

Occupy Wall Street was a *political miracle,* a rupture moment that redefined reality, pushed the limits of possibility and transformed participants into their best and truest selves. Without leaders, we all became leaders. Beautiful ideas did not have to wait for approval. If someone desired to create a people's library, she or he was encouraged, and book donations flowed in. If another wanted to organize a march, that person was empowered and people joined the action. Thousands of hungry people were fed by the movement's free kitchens. People were attracted because our encampments were a space outside the normal rules of hierarchical consumer society. For many, Occupy provided the first experience of radical democracy; the freedom was intoxicating.

A better world seemed imminent and already manifesting. The border between ironic detachment and ardent hope had finally been breached.

With revolution seemingly within reach, amid the vertigo-inducing fever of a social uprising, it is easy to forgive our naivety.

In the end, the encampments were evicted with paramilitary force. Occupy evaporated, and normalcy returned to financial districts worldwide. And yet nothing will ever be as it was before the people tasted the power of a global social movement.

Asked to explain why our movement vaporized, Edward Snowden, the National Security Agency whistleblower, asserted that Occupy revealed the limits of our conception of protest: "Occupy Wall Street had such limits because the local authorities were able to enforce, basically in our imaginations, an image of what proper civil disobedience is—one that is simply ineffective."[1] Snowden is right to blame authorities for developing counter-tactics that constrain protesters to ineffective, performative and symbolic acts. These counter-tactics include requiring protest permits, encouraging organizers to work with authorities on orchestrating pre-planned voluntary arrests, establishing so-called free speech zones in areas where being heard is impossible, or forcing protesters to keep moving on sidewalks rather than block traffic. These counter-tactics were developed to neutralize the effectiveness of activism, and they work to prevent protests from achieving social change.

Snowden is also right to suggest that contemporary activists must share the blame for their role in perpetuating failed protest behaviours and outdated social change theories. All too often, protesters recycle tactics that have been overused for decades and are simply destined to fail today. Authorities encourage these nostalgic protest rituals because they follow a predictable script that is easy to control. These tactics may have worked in the past, but times have changed. Now we succumb to a vague theory of social change, as the activist Peter Gelderloos once put it, in which we "protest, protest, protest, and eventually the 'people' will rise up, the state will crumble, or something like that."[2] The first step toward creating positive social change is to take responsibility for the failure of the "protest, protest, protest" paradigm. This process begins from the acknowledgement that contemporary protest is broken and the willingness to fix it.

The only way to fix a broken paradigm is to replace it with a new paradigm. Occupy was a gift to activists across the world who are now searching for the next paradigm of social activism. The event was a wake-up call to break the script of contemporary protest and rethink the principles of achieving social change through collective action. Above all, the lesson of our movement was to embrace the challenge that each generation of revolutionaries has had to overcome: to discover the new form of protest that is effective in the present historical moment.

> A revolution is not a spectacle! There are no spectators! Everyone participates whether they know it or not.
>
> THE WEATHER UNDERGROUND, 1968

INTRODUCTION: YOU ARE NEEDED

You may long for the protest to end all protests, a final revolution that eradicates injustice and transforms society. You dream of a better world in which protest is no longer necessary. You wish to make protest effective so that the ideals you hold become manifest. For you the end of protest is a consummation of activism, the completion of your work and objective of your struggle. You understand that the end of protest is in itself revolution.

This book will offer you tools for hastening social transformation. Recognizing that protest is one tool among many for creating social change, grab what works and discard the rest.

And if you are threatened by revolution, fearing or disdaining movements like Occupy, and you've come to this book from a desire to end protest—to foreclose dissent—know that this book is for you, too. Uprisings always need people who convert to the cause from positions of power: police who switch sides, insiders who become whistleblowers, and politicians who heed the people's demands. You may oppose us today but you will join us tomorrow. Our movement is even stronger when it includes the converted, who understand the errors of the old world because they embodied them.

You may be skeptical of those who take to the streets, considering them reckless. They seem to have nothing to lose, and you have worked so hard to achieve your position, wealth and prestige. You may not sympathize with their anger. You may believe that good society ought to have few disruptions. True, many aspects of upheaval are unpleasant. Revolutions are sometimes violent and always have unintended consequences. "In a society such as ours," writes Herbert Marcuse, a leading twentieth-century social theorist and philosopher, "in which pacification has been achieved up to a certain point, it appears crazy at first to want revolution. For we have whatever we want." He continues with a prescription: "[T]he aim here is to transform the will itself, so that people no longer want what they now want."[3] You desire the end of protest, but the fulfilment of your desire would be disastrous for you.

The lack of protest is perilous for society. Protest is a symptom of the need for social change, and the people in the streets are harbingers of greater democracy. The absence of effective protest is a warning sign of impending civil strife. Whether you support or suppress protesters, history shows that dissent is necessary for social growth and collective renewal. Revolution grants us the social freedom essential for humans to break old habits and reach their true collective potential.

PART ONE

TODAY

When things reach the end
they return again to the beginning.

T'AI KUNG, *The Six Secret Teachings*,
C. 475–221 BC

In all conduct of war the unexpected and chance play a large role, and the mastering of this dark element of uncertainty through decisiveness is one of the most important qualities of the commander.

HANS DELBRÜCK, *History of the Art of War, Volume IV: The Dawn of Modern Warfare*, 1920

I.

THE BIRTH OF OCCUPY

Several years before Occupy Wall Street, a steadily increasing number of protests worldwide demanded greater democracy, economic equality and political representation. Financial collapse, and the subsequent rise in food prices brought on by crop failures partially due to climate change, kicked off a doubling of protests with an identifiable grievance or explicit demand, from 59 in 2006 to 80 in 2008 and 153 in 2011, the year of Occupy.[4] The size of protests grew dramatically, too. Those years saw the largest protests in human history: thirty-seven demonstrations drew more than a million participants between 2006 and 2013. In 2010, 3.5 million people protested in France against raising the minimum retirement age, and 3 million took to the streets in Portugal to oppose austerity measures in the nation's first general strike in twenty-two years. Massive social mobilization of dissent occurred in Brazil. And an astonishing 100 million workers in India went on strike on February 20, 2013, to demand lower prices, more jobs, greater investment in public sector enterprises and improved labour rights.

The cycle of revolt that eventually led to Occupy Wall Street began in Tunisia on December 17, 2010, when Mohamed Bouazizi, a twenty-six-year-old street vender, set himself on fire to protest the humiliating treatment he received from a police officer who confiscated his fruit cart. Bouazizi went to the governor to demand that his wares be returned. When the governor refused to see him, Bouazizi stood in the street, doused himself with gasoline and self-immolated while shouting, "How do you expect me to make a living?" His political suicide unleashed the pent-up rage of a people who had been suffering under a regime that used, as one U.S. State Department report observes, "intimidation, criminal investigations, the judicial system, arbitrary arrests, residential restrictions, and travel controls to discourage criticism."[5] Bouazizi's death triggered immediate and widespread demonstrations, toppling the autocratic government of Ben Ali in Tunisia and igniting the Arab Spring, a period of popular unrest that spread to Algeria, Egypt, Yemen, Bahrain, Libya and nearly all Arab countries.

Bouazizi's self-immolation inspired activists in Algeria and Mauritania to express their dissent in the same dramatic way. Then, on January 18, the Arab Spring spread to Cairo, when an Egyptian self-immolated in front of parliament and five other attempts followed. A week later, tens of thousands of Egyptians gathered in Cairo's Tahrir ("Liberation") Square, in front of the Mogamma, a massive centralized government administration building, for a "Day of Rage" against police brutality and thirty years of oppressive rule by Hosni Mubarak. I had lived near Tahrir Square for several months in the years prior to this uprising. I remembered the level of police repression that existed back then, and seeing pictures of protesters swarming the streets I immediately understood that this was a historic revolutionary moment. Egyptian protesters established a permanent pro-democracy encampment in Tahrir Square. The world watched as civilians publicly demanded Mubarak's abdication, defending themselves against gunfire and thugs sent by the regime. When Mubarak finally stepped down on February 11, another wave of protest was unleashed across the world. The people, emboldened by success, saw that dramatic change was possible.

On May 15, anti-austerity protests spread to fifty-eight cities across Spain. Fifty thousand gathered in Madrid to demand direct, participatory democracy. Inspired by the Tahrir Square Uprising, activists in the 15-M Movement pioneered the *acampadas* ("camping") tactic of setting up consensus-based general assemblies in the public squares. The people articulated their demand for real democracy by displaying a new form of autonomous self-organization. Group discussion, open assemblies and fluid consensus worked to resolve complex questions.

These new forms of collective protest that were invented in Tunisia, Egypt and Spain were unified in Occupy Wall Street and replicated globally. It was cognitariat youth, highly educated and hyper-connected, who spread the tactics from city to city. A global youth network coalesced. Online social networks disseminated the call for offline action. Camping in public was officially frowned upon, if not openly forbidden, and repeating these new social behaviours granted us a way to express our dissent.

Witnessing dictators being toppled and the birth of vibrant democratic assemblies abroad, many activists yearned to import the revolution into the United States and Canada. Kalle Lasn and I succeeded. Our wish for twenty thousand people to flood into Lower Manhattan miraculously came true. Our #OCCUPYWALLSTREET meme turned out to be highly contagious, ricocheting from Wall Street to financial districts worldwide.

Kalle is the founder of *Adbusters*, the Canadian culture jamming magazine and international activist website, and I am a lifelong activist who had been working as an editor at the magazine for five years. I first started reading *Adbusters* when I was a rebellious fourteen-year-old; working with Kalle was my dream job. In the year leading up to Occupy, Kalle and I had become exceptionally close collaborators. The *Adbusters* office was based in Vancouver, British Columbia, and I lived in Berkeley, California. Our collaboration was conducted through email and over the phone.

The year before Kalle and I created the Occupy Wall Street idea, we had tried to launch a global week of action aimed at consumerism, calling it a Carnivalesque Rebellion. We devoted the ninety-second issue of *Adbusters* to advocating for a series of protests beginning on November 22, 2010, with a new campaign, #NOSTARBUCKS. This boycott of corporate coffee was to continue through the pre-existing anti-consumerist holiday Buy Nothing Day, celebrated on the Black Friday after Thanksgiving and the beginning of the Christmas shopping season in the United States, Canada, the U.K. and elsewhere. Calling on the mood of carnivalesque playfulness was our attempt to channel the spirit of the antiglobalization movement's inaugural protest, the Carnival Against Capital held on June 18, 1999, in London. The Carnivalesque Rebellion was also our earliest experiment with using Twitter hashtags to launch an offline action. Kalle and I and the rest of *Adbusters* put our full energy, faith and creativity into catalyzing the week of action. We sincerely believed a revolutionary moment was within reach. We were wrong. The Carnivalesque Rebellion was a flop, and the protest fizzled with a few insignificant actions that didn't catch on. Even that year's Buy Nothing Day was nothing special. Our failure was humbling. However, rather than be discouraged, I became convinced that our idea for a contagious action spread through a hashtag was simply ahead of its time. We failed because we were too early. I remember feeling that Kalle and I were living in the future of activism and being confident that if we tried again the people might catch up. We learned from the failure of the Carnivalesque Rebellion and repeated the effort in 2011. This time, inspired by the Arab Spring and spinoff uprisings, we took a pre-existing tactic—occupation—and transposed it to new terrain: the world's financial districts.

Along with Tahrir Square and the *acampadas*, the origins of the tactic behind Occupy Wall Street are the student occupations that swept universities in London, New York City, Berkeley and dozens of cities in 2009. I carefully watched these events unfold in person in Berkeley and from afar. Writing for *Adbusters*, I celebrated the student occupations as a potential sign of a coming revolutionary moment. During the wave of occupations, students would take over campus classrooms and auditoriums in political protest. In the U.K., occupation began as a way to force universities to take a public stand against Israel's then-ongoing bombing of Gaza during three weeks of war in 2008–2009. Later occupations became a general method of protesting against tuition hikes. As the tactic spread to New York's New School and California's public universities it lost its focus, and the popular slogan "Demand Nothing! Occupy Everything!" emerged. I was present at the occupation of Wheeler Hall at the University of California, Berkeley in November 2009. Watching the students trapping themselves in a top-floor classroom and shouting impossible-to-hear words to the crowd of spectators below, I first had the idea to transpose the tactic of occupation to public space. Cloistered in classrooms, the occupations were too easy to ignore. They felt desperate and cliquish, not magical and inclusive. I remember thinking that the occupation tactic would be more beautiful and effective if it were applied to parks rather than classrooms. Two years later, following the failure of the Carnivalesque Rebellion, Kalle and I turned the occupation tactic into Occupy Wall Street.

We released the idea of Occupy Wall Street on July 13, 2011, with a two-page tactical briefing and a surrealist poster of a ballerina balanced on the Wall Street Bull, a famous public sculpture near the financial district. Floating above the ballerina was a tantalizing question—"What is our one demand?" In the smoky background, militant protesters linked arms and seemed to move toward the viewer. The ballerina-and-bull poster was inspired by a photograph by the conceptual artist Joan Fontcuberta purporting to show a mujahedeen balancing atop a donkey in Afghanistan. The image was a hoax, but Kalle was captivated by the fearless, playful, revolutionary joy that Fontcuberta's photograph conveyed. Kalle transposed the concept, and the iconic poster for Occupy was born. We sent the call for Occupy to our *Adbusters* network, a list of ninety thousand email addresses, and printed it in 40,524 copies of the ninety-seventh issue of the magazine.* To give the campaign a late boost, the Occupy Wall Street issue of *Adbusters* was timed to appear on newsstands just weeks prior to the September 17 launch—a date chosen because it was Kalle's mother's birthday.

The core message of our tactical briefing was that a new form of protest—the synthesis of the Tahrir Square tactic of public-space occupation and the consensual general assembly model of Spain's *acampadas*—would finally allow Americans to break the stranglehold of "the greatest corrupter of our democracy: Wall Street, the financial Gomorrah of America."[6] Although our meme was targeted at New York City, Kalle and I called for solidarity protests in financial districts worldwide. To disseminate this tactical innovation, we wrote in the tactical briefing,

> The spirit of this fresh tactic, a fusion of Tahrir with the *acampadas* of Spain, is captured in this quote [from Raimundo Viejo, a political theorist and activist associated with the 15-M Movement in Spain]: "The antiglobalization movement was

* At least twenty thousand of those addresses were old and bounced. Although I cannot know for certain, I estimate that only five to seven thousand individuals actually read the original email. Roughly 15,670 copies of the Occupy issue of *Adbusters* were sold on newsstands.

> the first step on the road. Back then our model was to attack the system like a pack of wolves. There was an alpha male, a wolf who led the pack, and those who followed behind. Now the model has evolved. Today we are one big swarm of people."

We urged readers to "bring tent," to hold an assembly and "incessantly repeat one simple demand in a plurality of voices." We reminded *Adbusters* readers that Egypt's Hosni Mubarak was forced to step down because the crowd in Tahrir spoke in unison. We called for an occupation of Wall Street with an open assembly where the people's one demand would be decided. The soul of *Adbusters* is anti-corporate and anti-consumerist. Our purpose in launching Occupy was the creation of a mass protest that could reverse the recent U.S. Supreme Court's Citizens United ruling (2010) that granted corporations and labour unions the right to spend unlimited amounts of money influencing elections. In the United States, the electoral candidate who spends the most on their campaign wins the election 90 percent of the time. If money determines electoral victory and corporations and unions are able to give unlimited amounts of money, then it is clear that elections are no longer being decided by the people. We proposed in our tactical briefing that the best demand for protesters might be that "Barack Obama ordain a Presidential Commission tasked with ending the influence money has over our representatives in Washington." The tactical briefing captured the imagination of activists. A swarm of five thousand people responded to our call on the first day of Occupy Wall Street.

This email that sparked Occupy was written over phone calls between Kalle, at *Adbusters* headquarters in Vancouver, and me, at my home office in Berkeley. We were hoping for a protest on Wall Street, thousands of miles away, and the only way to make it happen would be to release the meme to activists in the New York area. Kalle understands social media tactics but does not directly use social media; it was my responsibility to spread the meme online. On July 4, nine days before the tactical briefing was officially released, I became the first person to use the hashtag #OCCUPYWALLSTREET on Twitter when I sent a tweet from the *Adbusters* account calling for Americans to "dream of insurrection against corporate rule." I then posted the call on Reddit, in political forums on the anonymizing Tor deep web and on activist websites of the Anonymous movement. I emailed every activist I knew. I also registered @OccupyWallStNYC, the movement's first Twitter account. Within twenty-four hours of our tactical briefing, the Occupy idea was taken up by Justine Tunney, a computer programmer and active participant in Reddit's anarchism forum. Justine registered OccupyWallSt.org and began coding the website that ultimately became the movement's hub. I knew instantly that Occupy Wall Street was going to take off because Justine and the other founding Zuccottis (the name given to the first Occupiers in Zuccotti Park) did not wait for *Adbusters*' approval or guidance. Instead, they seized the meme and held weekly organizing meetings in Tompkins Square Park, deciding how the movement should unfold. About two hundred people attended these early meetings and became the first founders of Occupy Wall Street. I was inspired by their initiative. And from my past activist experience, I knew that it was a very good sign that the protest meme was already slipping outside the creators' control.

A month before the occupation, the Occupy Wall Street meme began to attract significant underground attention. Anonymous released a video communiqué endorsing Occupy Wall Street. Their video borrowed language from our tactical briefing and swiftly garnered 100,000 views on YouTube. I tweeted at the American rapper Lupe Fiasco, and he surprised me by embracing the action, promoting it to his one million Twitter followers. Lupe, who later donated substantial resources to Occupy in New York City and Chicago, also created the signature chant of our movement: "All Day, All Week, Occupy Wall Street!" Meanwhile, activists in Milan, Valencia, Lisbon, Athens, Madison, Amsterdam, Los Angeles, Israel and beyond vowed to hold solidarity protests. Despite the excitement, the large non-profits, unions and well-known American activists, like the filmmaker Michael Moore who was bombarded with hundreds of tweets asking for support in a concerted effort prior to September 17, ignored the meme and refused to endorse it prior to the launch. Only after the rebellion was a sensation, in the second week of the occupation, did many of these people and organizations jump on board.

When Occupy started in 2011, Kalle was a sixty-nine-year-old Estonian-born Canadian citizen and I was a twenty-nine-year-old American activist. I was similar in age and culture to the urban youth who began organizing Occupy Wall Street, and from the beginning I became the bridge between *Adbusters* and the Zuccottis in New York City. A week before the encampment was founded, I handed over control of the @OccupyWallStNYC Twitter account to Marisa Holmes, an activist filmmaker who became a crucial member of the facilitation team. At the time, the Twitter account had around 6,000 followers. It grew to over 150,000 within weeks. I spoke on the phone with Occupy founders and participated in their email discussions. Kalle insisted that we turn down all television interviews, which I did, and I also refused most newspaper interviews. Instead, I identified the local activists *Adbusters* could trust and directed journalists to them. After debriefing with Kalle, I would occasionally offer advice to the Zuccottis. Although I spoke with the founders frequently, *Adbusters* could not control the movement and did not try to. We could only hope to shape its direction through the thirty tactical briefings we wrote during the movement.

Five thousand activists showed up at noon on Saturday, September 17, and around three hundred slept in Zuccotti Park that first night after vowing to hold the encampment until their as-yet-undetermined demands were met.

From the beginning, Occupy Wall Street was a beautiful event. A sense of community permeated the assemblies. Free kitchens provided superb daily meals to thousands of Occupiers. "I was struck by the organization of the space: paths were clear, tents were neatly covered in tarps, folks were singing in one corner dedicated to song and spirit, delicious looking pizzas were being served for dinner, there were people staffing a media relations tent, and a library with books for loan and reference organized in rows inside waterproof containers," remembers one participant.[7] Occupy was a total experience. People who went down to Zuccotti to see what was happening were often drawn in and became active participants in a protest movement for the first time. Walking past our assemblies, curious onlookers easily got pulled in by our energy. Middle-class people set up encampments and started feeding the destitute homeless. Rabble-rousers led disruptive actions. New ways of circumventing police restrictions, such as bike generators to power the encampments and communication apps to self-organize, emerged. Radical ideas were floated and taken up spontaneously. For the first time in decades, politicians were forced to respond to a clamorous democracy.

History wasn't made, however, until a series of unexpected incidents occurred. And this is a general law of rebellion.

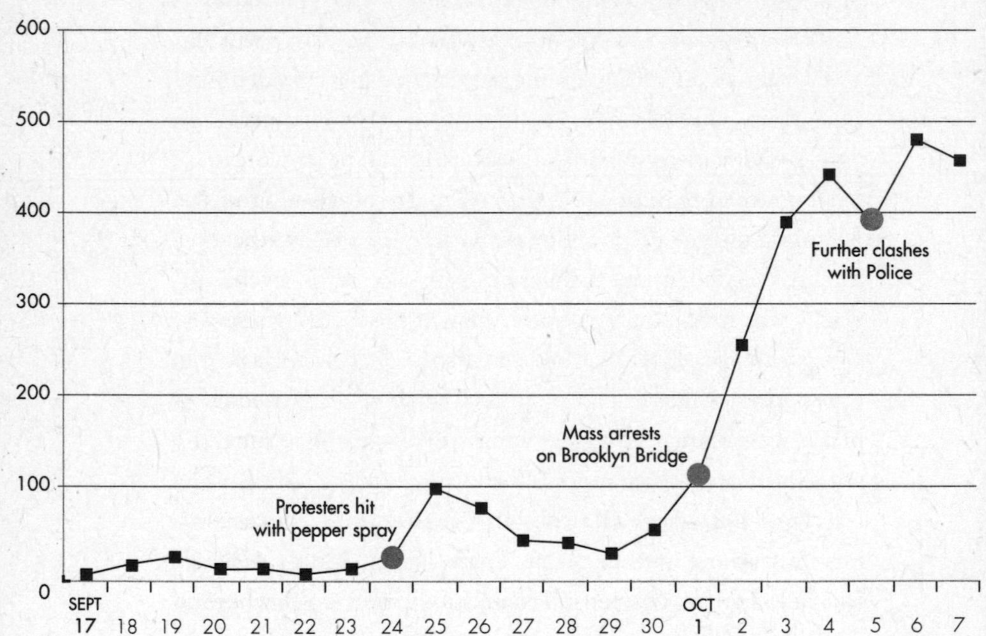

Occupy Wall Street was largely ignored until a series of unexpected events, beginning with the pepper-spraying incident, propelled the movement into international renown. Revolutions often emerge from flukes rather than from carefully planned actions.

Revolutions rarely emerge from a carefully planned action; more often a fluke event or accidental act instigates the uprising—or, rather, the planned actions create an opportunity for chance to intervene. In 1927 an early theorist of revolution and Episcopal priest, Lyford P. Edwards, was a prescient observer: "the outbreak of revolution is commonly signalled by some act, insignificant in itself, which precipitates a separation of the repressors and their followers from the repressed and their followers," he writes.[8] In the case of Occupy Wall Street, the first fluke came during a pre-planned *snake march** near Union Square on September 24, 2011. As the march neared East Twelfth Street, a police officer pepper-sprayed two women, who fell to their knees and screamed in pain. The incident was caught on video from multiple angles by bystanders and rebroadcast nationwide by the political comedian Jon Stewart, who mocked NYPD Deputy Inspector Anthony Bologna, the offending police officer. The mood was relatively lighthearted until the second fluke: the October 1 mass arrest of seven hundred Occupiers on the Brooklyn Bridge. As the news spread worldwide, so did the Occupy tactic. Within four days, the number of news articles per day about Occupy increased fourfold from one hundred to four hundred.[9] At the same time, the number of encampments increased exponentially.

The global spread of Occupy felt organic because it was foretold. It was built into the meme. From the beginning, *Adbusters* had called for occupations in financial districts everywhere to

---

* A snake march occurs when protesters disrupt the flow of streets by marching into the direction of traffic or among cars rather than in an orderly or permitted manner. It is an urban protest tactic developed during the antiglobalization movement.

underline the point that the influence of money was strangling democracies worldwide. After the mass arrest, encampments formed in financial districts in San Francisco, London, Vancouver and several hundred other cities. Local activists joined the wider movement by appending the name of their city to the word Occupy. Each occupation had its own flair while maintaining a shared ideal of participatory, consensual democracy. During the height of our movement, every protest called itself Occupy. To be taken seriously, one needed only use the meme. And the movement spread more quickly because few people knew the origin of the idea. For most participants, Occupy simply appeared out of nowhere, making it easier for them to take ownership of the meme. (In fact, the first in-depth article to explore the origins of Occupy Wall Street, based on interviews with both Kalle and me, wasn't published until after the Occupiers were evicted from Zuccotti Park.)[10]

In our first tactical briefing, *Adbusters* had called for Occupy Wall Street to demand a presidential commission on ending the influence of money on democracy. Although getting money out of politics became a core rallying point for the wider movement, the general assembly in Zuccotti disregarded our specific suggestion for one demand. Occupy was owned by its participants. It spread into the cultural imagination and became a shared tool for achieving social change on a variety of issues.

People learned that by invoking Occupy their protests would quickly attract eager participants and curious media attention. Eventually anything from protesting development near Berkeley (Occupy the Farm) to providing hurricane disaster relief (Occupy Sandy) could be a part of the Occupy umbrella. Building from fluke events to become the lingua franca for a variety of passions and causes, our new social protest behaviour had gained history-making weight.

> Do not renew an attack along the same line (or in the same form) after it has once failed.
>
> B.H. LIDDELL HART, *Strategy*, 1954

2.

A CONSTRUCTIVE FAILURE

News of innovative tactics brings revolt. People everywhere saw that occupying space and holding assemblies was a way to be heard, so they occupied or supported those who did. Protesters worldwide adopted the behaviours of Occupy Wall Street, the twinkle fingers to signal consent and the people's microphone—a tactic of chanting in unison to boost our voices by repeating the words of the person who was speaking that was first used by anti-nuclear activists in the 1980s and antiglobalization protesters in the 1990s to overcome police prohibition on amplified sound—and turned them into ritualized acts because everyday people believed participation in this disruptive social movement was worth the risk of arrest and, this time, just might work to change the status quo.

In the final analysis, Occupy's success came from a profound, overriding and widely shared conviction that *this* was it—the mass social movement that would change everything. This belief turned out to be founded on a number of unquestioned assumptions about how to shift political reality. We believed that nominally democratic governments would be swayed by a historic event that was *mass*, *urban*, *non-violent* and *unified*. These four characteristics had dominated the theory and practice of revolution for decades, especially after the revolutionary waves of 1989 that toppled Communism in Poland, Hungary, East Germany, Bulgaria, Czechoslovakia and Romania. In our inaugural tactical briefing, Kalle and I had articulated this assumption with a story of how an occupation of Wall Street could lead to fundamental change. "If we hang in there, twenty-thousand strong, week after week against every police and National Guard effort to expel us from Wall Street, it would be impossible for Obama to ignore us. Our government would be forced to choose publicly between the will of the people and the lucre of the corporations." In other words, we maintained a theatrical view of activism that treats public space as the stage for a political spectacle. We assumed that the United States would be unable to use force against non-violent democracy protesters without eventually capitulating to our demands because the eyes of the international community would be on our political performance. As one popular protest chant puts it, "The whole world is watching!" Kalle and I—and many activists who flocked to the encampments—believed that if the world watched the Occupiers maintain their dignity and demands in the face of police brutality, the movement would win . . . just as it had seemed to win in Tunisia and Egypt. The first part of our story came true. Occupiers overcame extreme adversity to keep the movement alive. Ultimately, over seven thousand participants in Occupy were arrested in the United States, and many people experienced serious injuries and broken bones caused by police violence. Police brutality was particularly rampant against Occupiers in Oakland, California, where numerous complaints were filed against authorities. In one complaint from October 25, for example, a protester alleged, "Officers found a person alone, beat him, and broke his knee."[11] But the second part of our story of change, the faith that brutal repression of dignified Occupiers would backfire against the United States, proved to be wrong.

Occupy Wall Street was a *constructive failure* but not a *total failure*. Occupy demonstrated the efficacy of using social memes to quickly spread a movement, shifted the political debate on the fair distribution of wealth, trained a new generation of activists who went on to be the base for movements ranging from campus fossil fuel divestment to Black Lives Matter protests. Occupy launched many local projects that will have lasting small-scale impact. Occupy buoyed many institutional activist organizations that were able to materially profit from the renewed interest in protest. All of these are signs that our movement was culturally influential. It may be comforting to believe that Occupy splintered into a thousand shards of light. However, an honest assessment reveals that Occupy Wall Street failed to live up to its revolutionary potential: we did not bring an end to the influence of money on democracy, overthrow the corporatocracy of the 1 percent or solve income inequality. If our movement did achieve successes, they were not the ones we'd intended. When victory eluded Occupy, a world of activist certainties fell apart.

I call Occupy Wall Street a constructive failure because the movement revealed underlying flaws in dominant, and still prevalent, theories of how to achieve social change through collective action. Occupy set out to "get money out of politics," and we succeeded in catalyzing a global social movement that tested all of our hypotheses. The failure of our efforts reveals a truth that will hasten the next successful revolution: the assumptions underlying contemporary protest are false. Change won't happen through the old models of activism. Western democracies will not be swayed by public spectacles and mass media frenzy. Protests have become an accepted, and therefore ignored, by-product of politics-as-usual. Western governments are not susceptible to international pressure to heed the protests of their citizens. Occupy's failure was constructive because it demonstrated the limitations of contemporary ideas of Protest. I capitalize *p* to emphasize that the limitation was not in a particular tactic but rather in our concept of Protest, or our theory of social change, which determined the overall script. Occupy revealed that activists need to revolutionize their approach to revolution.

Failure can be liberating. Defeat detaches us from a theory of revolution that is no longer effective, reopening the possibility of true change. "For a revolutionary," writes Régis Debray, professor of philosophy and associate of Che Guevara, "failure is a springboard. As a source of theory it is richer than victory: it accumulates experience and knowledge."[12] Opportunities to test the fundamental principles of activism are as rare as revolutionary moments. In North America, activists had to wait eight years, following the defeat of the anti–Iraq War movement, for a social movement that would test our assumptions on a planetary scale. The anti–Iraq War movement collapsed after its global march on February 15, 2003, the largest synchronized protest in human history, failed to sway President Bush and Prime Minister Blair to halt the pre-emptive war on Iraq. Activists in 2003 believed that if millions of people around the world said no in unison on a single day, war would be impossible. Like Occupy, the anti-war movement vaporized when the theory of social change underlying the movement—that governments will bend if millions of people assemble in the streets, march and make a single demand—was proven ineffective.

In politics as in war
the lost moment never returns.

NAPOLEON, 1815

3.

THE LOST MOMENT

The end of Occupy Wall Street was nigh very soon after the start of our movement. Winter was coming, and the public mood was shifting. For two weeks, an influx of apolitical drug users had been flooding Zuccotti and altering the dynamics of the encampment. A journalist for the *New York Daily News* reported that aggressive vagrants were being sent to Occupy by New York police in a strategy to exploit the movement's open structure: "Two different drunks I spoke with last week told me they'd been encouraged to 'take it to Zuccotti' by officers who'd found them drinking in other parks, and members of [Occupy's] community affairs working group related several similar stories they'd heard while talking with intoxicated or aggressive new arrivals."[13] Rumours (some true and some false) of sexual violence, disease and dangerous disorder in the encampments began circulating. In Vancouver, for example, an Occupier died in her tent from a heroin and cocaine overdose. And in Oakland, a man was fatally shot near the Occupy encampment. While a few Occupiers insisted that the Zuccotti encampment in Lower Manhattan could last forever, it was clear to Kalle and me that the momentum was slowing. "Hope thwarted is in danger of turning sour, patience exhausted becoming anger, militant nonviolence losing its allure," we wrote in our eighteenth tactical briefing on November 14. *Adbusters* suggested that Occupiers declare victory, throw a party, voluntarily disband and prepare to bounce back in the spring. The timing was eerie.

At 1:00 a.m. on November 15, Mayor Bloomberg carried out a paramilitary raid on Zuccotti Park, our movement's birthplace. The surprise attack began with a total media blackout. The airspace above was closed to news helicopters. The encampment was surrounded by armoured police, illuminated by floodlights and hit with tear gas. No one was allowed in. Credentialed journalists who tried to enter were forced back; seven reporters were arrested. One hundred and fifty Occupiers were arrested, too. Everything in the park, including five thousand books from the people's library, was confiscated or destroyed. The police deployed a Long Range Acoustic Device, the infamous "sound cannon" best known for its military use against Somali pirates and Iraqi insurgents.[14]

The eviction in Lower Manhattan was effective, and it was no coincidence that evictions spread immediately. Five days before Zuccotti was dismantled, police coordinated nationwide conference calls with mayors from eighteen cities.[15] An eviction script was developed to counter the tactics of Occupy.

Mayors learned to announce an impending eviction, to give Occupiers a firm deadline so that the people would gather to defend the encampment. Authorities would then let the deadline expire so that protesters were exhausted by the state of tension and readiness. Many protesters would return home believing that the crisis had passed. At that point, the police would strike and complete the eviction using maximum force. The counter-revolutionary tactics developed by Bloomberg and others were quickly deployed in city after city. The crackdown was coordinated at the highest levels of U.S. law enforcement: the Federal Bureau of Investigation, the Joint Terrorism Task Force and the Department of Homeland Security.[16] At the same time in Canada, the Integrated Terrorism Assessment Centre, a division of the Canadian Security Intelligence Service normally tasked with counter-terrorism, was monitoring Occupy protests in the country.[17] Within a week, most of the movement's encampments across the world were gone.

Eight days after the Zuccotti eviction, Occupy supporters interrupted a speech by President Barack Obama. The president was speaking about jobs at a high school in Manchester, New Hampshire, when the Occupiers shouted the signature "Mic check!" In unison, they directly pleaded for an end to the crackdown on Occupy. Before their message was fully delivered, they were silenced and removed from the room. The president pacified the crowd. He publicly acknowledged Occupy Wall Street for the first time. "[For] a lot of the folks who've been down in New York and all across the country in the Occupy movement, there is a profound sense of frustration, there's a profound sense of frustration about the fact that the essence of the American dream, which is that if you work hard, if you stick to it that you can make it, feels like that's slipping away," the president said, before returning to the teleprompter script.[18] But the Occupiers were tenacious and strategic. Once Obama finished his speech and was greeting the audience, protester Ryan Hirsch slipped a message into his palm.

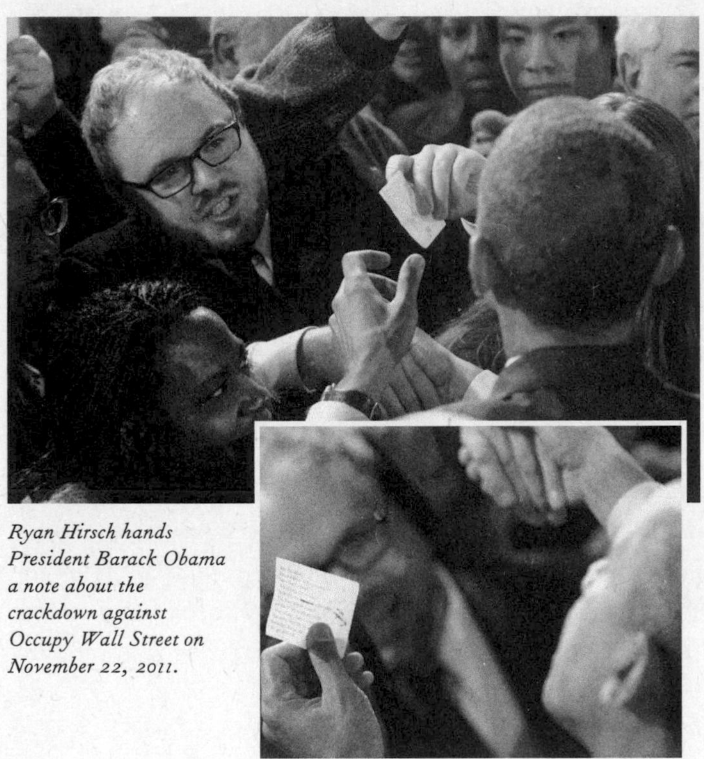

Ryan Hirsch hands President Barack Obama a note about the crackdown against Occupy Wall Street on November 22, 2011.

The second photograph shows President Obama silently reading the following note as Hirsch gazes at his reaction: "Mr. President: Over 4,000 peaceful protesters have been arrested. While bankers continue to destroy the economy with impunity. You must stop the assault on our 1st amendment rights. Your silence sends a message that police brutality is acceptable. Banks got bailed out. We got sold out." This action proved an important point: the highest elected representative could not now deny knowing about the suppression of America's greatest democracy movement in half a century. Obama remained silent. The evictions continued and the movement never recovered. Some encampments persisted, and the Zuccottis tried unsuccessfully to occupy a new space on December 17. But the grand General Strike meant to revive the movement on May 1, 2012, fizzled. It was obvious we had lost: the bankers weren't going to be arrested and the influence of money on democracy wasn't going to be halted. The decisive moment had passed.

> The habitual tactics of marching, holding signs, and establishing temporary autonomous zones risk becoming comforting substitutes for effective success.
>
> NICK SRNICEK AND ALEX WILLIAMS,
> *Accelerate: Manifesto for an Accelerationist Politics*, 2013

4.

THE END OF PROTEST

Occupy Wall Street marks the end of protest as we've known it and the beginning of a fundamentally different approach. We achieved a global movement that fulfilled all the most difficult requirements that the citizenry of democracies have been told were prerequisites for political change. Occupy was mass, modern, secular (with a universalist spirituality) and overwhelmingly non-violent during its peak. It included people from across the political spectrum, which the sociologist Thomas Greene explains as necessary: "Revolutionary movements do not succeed where only the workers are mobilized, or only the peasants, or only the middle classes. They succeed only when a critical mass of most or all of the major classes in the society is mobilized in the revolutionary process."[19] Our movement articulated the will of the governed.

We spoke publicly in unison, declaring *We are the 99 percent* and rallied mostly around a primary demand: *Stop the influence of corporate money on our elections!* Occupy was nearly a textbook example of a movement that should work—and for a few beautiful weeks, nearly everyone believed it would. And then we were defeated.

Activism is in crisis. Occupy was the strongest, most sophisticated and broadly based social movement in fifty years—and yet we were completely unable to sway the balance of power. The lesson of Occupy's constructive failure goes deeper than our inability to overcome the violence that was deployed against us. It is true that police departments have been militarized at an alarming rate in recent years. In the United States, for example, over $5 billion worth of surplus military equipment—helicopters, night vision goggles, assault rifles, armoured vehicles and more—has been transferred to state and local police through a Department of Defense program known as 1033. In Canada, a similar program known as the Directorate Disposal, Sales, Artefacts and Loans, a division of the Department of National Defence, has also transferred military gear, including "rolling fortress" armoured vehicles to municipalities.[20] It is disturbing that governments are using military equipment to suppress democracy protests but it is not a new phenomenon. Activists have always had to overcome well-equipped police and advanced crowd-control techniques. This is particularly true in the years since the World Trade Organization protests in Seattle in 1999 and the G20 protests in Toronto in 2010. Armoured police supported by tanks and equipped with tear gas, sound grenades and truncheons have rendered contemporary urban protest tactics ineffective for now, but new and effective tactics are guaranteed to emerge.

The deeper lesson of the defeat of Occupy is that Western governments are not required to comply with their people's demands, even if those demands are articulated by a historic social movement backed by millions of people in the streets. We have been acting as if the people have sovereignty over their governments when they act collectively. Now it is clear that the people's sovereignty has been lost. We were wrong to believe that bigger and bigger street protests could force prime ministers and presidents to heed the wishes of the people. Activism, it turns out, has been chasing an illusion.

The repertoire of protest tactics that contemporary activists rely on—like marching and similar kinds of disruptive public behaviours—were designed to influence twentieth-century democracies. They were designed to influence elected representatives who had to listen to their constituents. But the breakdown of that paradigm has happened. With the failure of Occupy we learned instead that these ritualized public spectacles of tens of thousands in the streets are only effective when applied against autocratic regimes that are vulnerable to international pressure. It seems that popular protest functions only when it is aligned with the pre-existing Western geopolitical agenda. That is why secular youth protesting in Egypt were used to justify regime change at the same time as demographically similar protesters in the United States were suppressed. Or why the United States will issue a statement expressing "serious concerns about the reports of excessive use of force by police" in Istanbul while ignoring the same forceful countertactics when deployed to quell domestic unrest.[21] The media images of people in the streets served to justify the overthrow of leaders of non-democratic regimes, like Tunisia's Ben Ali and Egypt's Mubarak, who succumbed to international pressure to heed the wishes of their people, but they failed to sway Prime Minister Stephen Harper and President Obama. This contradiction between seeming to encourage democracy protests abroad while repressing democracy protests at home has led military analysts in Russia to accuse Western governments of deploying social movements, or so-called colour revolutions, as a new form of warfare to destabilize opponents.[22]

At first, and superficially, the revolution in Egypt appeared to be a success, but three years after the fall of Mubarak it became clear that the people who protested in Tahrir Square did not gain greater democracy: another authoritarian pro-Western military leader has ascended to power and passed a draconian anti-protest law that prohibits public gatherings of more than ten people without prior government approval. Democracy protesters are now routinely killed—seventeen were murdered across Egypt on the fourth anniversary of the Tahrir Square Uprising—without significant international outcry.[23]

Protest is broken and the people know it worldwide. As the activist and filmmaker Astra Taylor puts it, "We've had some of the biggest marches and protests in public outpourings in history in the last fifteen years, and it doesn't just magically have a political consequence."[24]

The failure of contemporary activism is good news. The ingredients for global revolution are now here. Democracy functions because its citizenry believes that protest, if performed properly and when no other redress is available, is effective. The possibility of revolution keeps politicians beholden to the people. Without our faith in the assumption that elected representatives can be ousted by a collective uprising, and without our elected representatives' fear that protests can end their political career, democracy would be tyranny.

If social change through collective protest is impossible, democracy has been negated. The defeat of Occupy Wall Street, a once-in-a-generation uprising, was also the end of our illusion of democracy. A generation's faith in the legitimacy of representative democracy was shaken when the people's encampments, a manifestation of participatory democracy, were evicted and our demands ignored. And the legitimacy of contemporary activism was shattered too. It is too easy to blame the police. Activists must also acknowledge our role in the defeat: the theories guiding our methods of protest were faulty. The spirit of *Adbusters*' initial tactical briefing was beautiful and inspiring, but the hypothesis that a people's assembly could end the influence of money in democracy just as it had deposed autocrats in Tunisia and Egypt proved inaccurate. Likewise, an adherence to the ideology of prefigurative anarchism, the notion that the people must build the world we want to live in rather than make demands of the existing reality, blinded many founding Occupiers in New York City. The refusal, and inability, to reach consensus on "our one demand" and develop complex decision-making procedures meant that the movement could never move toward legitimate sovereignty, political negotiation and a transfer of power—a naive mistake. Stuck between two competing theories of revolution—performative public protests designed to sway global opinion versus the creation of autonomous spaces that manifest popular sovereignty—we failed to realize that both approaches were false.

The *Adbusters* tactical briefing was a long shot, a gamble that succeeded because we were willing to risk it all. Time was ripe and our wish was granted. We conjured a social movement par excellence. And for twenty-eight days the storm was perfect. A one-in-a-million lightning strike. Occupy's existence tested everything our generation had been taught about activism. Occupy interrogated the relationship between everyday people and their elected government. We hypothesized that we live in a representative, responsive democracy that ultimately bows, out of self-restraint, to the demands of the people. We believed that the people could gain sovereign protection from police repression by enacting collective, consensual democracy. We thought no government could resist the united chorus of its citizens expressing themselves with democratic fervour. That was the meaning of democracy. Not anymore. When our encampments were smashed and our momentum was reversed, many people blamed the police or the corporatocracy or the Occupiers or fell back into unquestioning cynicism. Instead, the assumptions we held about activism and how to achieve political change were to blame.

Activists have not been passive. For decades, we have tried every tactic to shift the course of our governments. We have voted, written editorials and manifestos, donated money, held signs, protested in marches, blocked streets, shared links, signed petitions, held workshops, knitted scarves, learned to farm, turned off the television, programmed apps, engaged in direct action, committed vandalism, launched legal challenges against pipelines . . . and occupied the financial districts. All this has been for naught. A new approach to activism and a new kind of protest are desperately needed.

Occupy inaugurated the end of protest, a period in which activism must be reinvented—realigned with its spiritual calling—to be effective once again. The end of protest is a natural part of the cycle of social change. And I suspect it won't be long before a novel form of social activism breaks out once again. Until then, ineffective protests will continue (every social earthquake, like Occupy, has its aftershocks), but these isolated events won't spiral into revolution or shift the course of history. Rather, they will follow a predictable pattern that the police are well prepared to control. Or they will chase after misguided goals, such as larger crowds in the streets, that are irrelevant to the likelihood of revolutionary social change.

The end of protest heralds the coming transformation of activism: a time when the tactics used, and the underlying theory guiding our actions, undergoes a sudden paradigm shift away from materialism and toward a higher purpose, giving birth to a truly effective movement.

We live in dangerous times, when large-scale social transformation is necessary. Scientists, technologists, mystics, artists and teachers agree: socio-political change in our lifetime is crucial for the survival of the human species. The constructive failure of Occupy Wall Street teaches the people to invent new forms of protest in order to break out of the stagnation of the period between revolutions. The end of protest is a call to revolutionize activism.

The preconditions for revolution are present: income inequality, disaffection of intellectuals who are burdened by educational debt, corruption among elites and inefficiency in government, a ruling class that has lost self-confidence, looming financial collapse, and the excessive use of force against rebels whenever protests occur.[25] But power has adapted to the approaches that have dominated activism for the past half-century or more. The old tactics must be abandoned. The old assumptions about how change is made are leading us astray. This is a problem for everyone who wishes for a better world in his or her lifetime. The solution is innovation. And the reason for optimism is that when activists innovate their tactics, revolutionary moments are often not far behind.

NO MORE MARCHES

I'm no longer satisfied with the standard repertoire of activism. I distrust the big-name non-profits and well-funded digital activist front groups who waste the people's collective energy in large-scale, feel-good coalition actions, like the People's Climate March of 2014. I question the motives of activists who advocate old tactics. I'm starting to believe that these groups are choosing behaviours designed to garner attention without risk of challenging the status quo. Often it seems that institutionalized activist organizations are content to deploy tactics destined to fail while grabbing publicity, building their list of email addresses and reaping millions of dollars in donations. It should have been obvious since the failure of the global anti–Iraq War march on February 15, 2003, that the synchronized global-march tactic underpinning the People's Climate March may attract fleeting media attention but doesn't work to sway governments. Similarly, I would be the last to advocate another Occupy—unless a refreshing innovation were proposed. My mission is to persuade activists to stop ignoring failures and to stop repeating tactics.

There will be those who respond to the crisis within activism by insisting the underlying paradigm is still valid. Some will argue that Occupy failed because it wasn't perfect, ignoring that perfection isn't possible and that Occupy came closer than we'd gotten in half a century. Others will say that Occupy's one demand was not clear or that it started too late in the year. (To these people I point to the failed 2003 anti–Iraq War march that had an absolutely clear demand.) There will be many who will advocate slight modifications to the protest script rather than a wholly new approach. This is a common reaction to the breakdown of a dominant paradigm. As the philosopher of science Thomas Kuhn, whose influential 1962 book *The Structure of Scientific Revolutions* popularized the concept of the paradigm shift, writes, "Though they may begin to lose faith and then to consider alternatives, they do not renounce the paradigm that has led them into crisis. . . . Once it has achieved the status of paradigm, a scientific theory is declared invalid only if an alternate candidate is available to take its place." The task of the next generation of protestors is to respond to the crisis by moving beyond critique and toward developing a new paradigm that can replace the old. This involves, as Kuhn points out, "the proliferation of competing articulations, the willingness to try anything, the expression of explicit discontent, the recourse to philosophy and to debate over fundamentals."[26]

THE FUTURE OF SOCIAL CHANGE

Each generation of revolutionaries must discover anew the form of protest best suited to challenging power as it is constituted at that historical moment. Most generations have failed at this first test. All too often we unconsciously mimic the previous generation's tactics, and our protests are swiftly defeated. Or we base our activism on old theories of revolution that no longer apply. We must heed the advice of Régis Debray: "A new situation calls for new methods. That is to say, we must guard against adopting forms of action, whether from error or tradition, which are inappropriate to this new context."[27] This basic error accounts for the failure of most people's uprisings. We have to rethink the foundation of activism. Humans are more complex than our theories of social change. A new *unified theory of revolution*—and this is what I am offering you—is needed to reinvent protest and move humanity up and out of this precarious historical moment of broken democracy and the rule of the wealthy. The end of protest heralds the rebirth of protest in new forms—the rise of a transformative World Party and revolutionary global activism.

So, what does this new paradigm of activism look like? It is defined by a shift away from materialist theories of social change toward a spiritual understanding of revolution. It is a turn from voluntarism and structuralism toward subjectivism and theurgism. Activists of the future will target the *mental environment* to spark collective epiphanies that achieve real-world victories. Protest tactics will be chosen for their potential to trigger a species-wide *metanoia*—from the ancient Greek word for "a turnaround"—capable of releasing the tremendous forces necessary for a social revolution. Explaining the power of the epiphany, the Sufi master Rumi writes, "By one thought that comes into the mind a hundred worlds are overturned in a single moment."[28] The contagious collective epiphany is the one force capable of conjuring a political miracle. The question of how to spark this collective turnaround is one that I have long been attempting to answer, through experiments with social activism.

Do not deceive yourselves into believing that penalties will deter men from the course they believe is right.

H. RAP BROWN, FORMER CHAIRMAN OF THE STUDENT NONVIOLENT COORDINATING COMMITTEE, 1967

5.

I AM AN ACTIVIST

Activism follows a logic all its own. For most of my life, I have waged annual activist campaigns to discover that logic. My experiments in revolutionary activism, some big and some small, some more effective than others, began when I was thirteen. That year I refused to stand with my class for the mandatory Pledge of Allegiance on the grounds that the morning pledge did not accurately represent the reality of American democracy. The untruth of the words "with liberty and justice for all" rankled me, and I protested by remaining seated and silent. After several days my classmates started to join my campaign and the teacher reacted angrily. The school gave me an ultimatum: either have my parents sign a waiver granting me permission not to stand, or be kicked off the year-end graduation field trip. I am fortunate to have parents who have always supported my social activism. But although they would have happily signed the form, I refused. It was important that *I* was not standing because *I* had reasons. I would not make the excuse that it was truly my parents' beliefs that made me protest. Having made this decision, I was excluded from the graduation trip. Being ostracized hurt, but I was undeterred from activism. I learned that the simple act of remaining seated, or being silent, could spark a crisis of authority.

The next year, as a freshman in high school, I wrote and published an anonymous underground newspaper. Inspired by *Pump Up the Volume*, a classic of youth rebellion cinema, I distributed the four-page newspaper without seeking permission. The central article in the newspaper argued that if students collectively disregarded even the smallest prohibition, such as the restriction on chewing gum, then all prohibitions would collapse. This hypothesis was my first attempt at articulating a theory of social change, and it was a sensation for a couple of hours. I listened while students and teachers debated. I had researched the law on unauthorized student newspapers and reasoned that I would be reprimanded but not punished. When the administration discovered who was responsible, I was called into the principal's office, questioned and promptly suspended for five days. Again, I was hurt but undeterred. With each year of activism I gained experience of what works and what does not. I developed an intuition for creating campaigns that would grow and resonate with the wider public.

When my family moved from Columbia, Maryland, to Grand Blanc, Michigan, the intensity of these annual campaigns increased. I spent most of my time carefully researching the law and looking for *leverage points*, potential campaign issues where a small amount of pressure could yield exponential force. My most successful fight was founding an atheist student club.* I had discovered that public schools in the United States are required to abide by the Equal Access Act, a federal law prohibiting discrimination against student clubs. The Equal Access Act decrees that if a public school allows Christian students to form an after-school club, they must allow a Muslim or Hindu or, my argument went, an atheist club. With this knowledge in hand, I diligently followed the procedure for forming an organization.

When the principal and vice-principal thwarted those efforts, I sent a letter describing the situation to Americans United for Separation of Church and State, the Washington, DC, legal non-profit that had been instrumental in having the Equal Access Act passed in 1984. Americans United offered free legal aid and sent a letter to Grand Blanc High School threatening a lawsuit if my atheist club was not allowed to form. The school capitulated without contest. The principal called me into his office, and I watched his eyes as he admitted total defeat. And because the school was now required to advertise the atheist club meetings whenever they advertised the Christian club, the whole school knew about what had happened. My activism began to attract national attention. I wrote an op-ed for the *New York Times* describing my experience,

* At the time I was a sincere and ardent atheist. It was not a desire to be contrary that led me to form the club. Instead, I believed my public school was unfairly advocating religion and that atheism encouraged critical thinking. Although I am no longer an atheist, I still appreciate this early campaign for what it taught me about bringing external forces to bear on a local situation.

and that summer I was a guest on Bill Maher's *Politically Incorrect*, a nationally broadcast television show.[29]

The campaigns continued. The following year I fought against my high school's newly adopted mandatory drug-testing policy for student athletes. Borrowing from my previous campaign tactics, I distributed four hundred copies of a pamphlet encouraging athletes to refuse to be drug-tested and I sought outside legal support. I joined the wrestling team and quit in protest when I was asked to sign a drug-testing authorization form. I then enlisted the American Civil Liberties Union of Michigan in a lawsuit charging my high school with violating Michigan's constitutional protection against unreasonable searches and seizures.[30] Once the campaign entered the courtroom, I was forced to follow the advice of lawyers who tended toward a conservative approach. I was powerless. We lost. And I learned to keep my activist campaigns out of the courts.

The September 11 attacks on the World Trade Center and the Pentagon opened my eyes to the larger geopolitical reality. From that moment I shifted my focus and practiced activism intended to have large-scale

Here I am, on the left, running from police during a snake march at the World Economic Forum protests in 2002. I remember closing my eyes and feeling exhilaration.[31] *(Edward Keating/*The New York Times*/Redux)*

political impact. As a sophomore at Swarthmore College, a small liberal arts college near Philadelphia, I co-founded Why War?, one of the first student anti-war organizations to form after 9/11. As my focus shifted toward activism and away from academics, I dropped out of college for a semester and joined the International Solidarity Movement, a nonviolent direct-action organization in the occupied Palestinian territories, for six weeks. When I returned to Swarthmore, I volunteered at a food kitchen serving a homeless shelter in Philadelphia. The peak of Why War?'s activism was the nationwide electronic civil disobedience campaign to distribute leaked emails from Diebold Election Systems, a leading maker of electronic voting machines.[32] Diebold's CEO at the time, Walden O'Dell, was an outspoken Republican donor who shocked democracy activists by writing in a fall 2003 fundraising letter to Republicans that he was "committed to helping Ohio deliver its electoral votes to the President [George W. Bush] next year."[33] Soon after, unknown hackers released internal memos from Diebold Election Systems. When the leaked memos surfaced, Diebold responded with copyright takedown requests in a bid to block their dissemination. Seeing the campaign potential, I encouraged Why War? to host the memos on Swarthmore's network, knowing that it would draw the college into a complex legal situation. Why War? then packaged the memos in an easily reproducible format and urged students nationwide to host them on their university's servers. At the same time, Why War? recruited another campus activist group, the Swarthmore Coalition for the Digital Commons, who worked with the Electronic Frontier Foundation to pursue a legal case against Diebold. After I posted a call to action on Slashdot, an influential technology website, our campaign of electronic civil disobedience quickly spread to dozens of universities, including many prestigious institutions.[34] Diebold responded by sending legal threats to each of these universities.

The campaign swerved toward success when U.S. House of Representatives member Dennis Kucinich, who was also seeking the Democratic Party's presidential nomination, posted links to the leaked emails on a U.S. government server. In a public letter dated November 21, 2003, Kucinich wrote, "Diebold's actions are representative of a growing body of abuses through which large and powerful parties unfairly intimidate ISPs to remove information those parties do not like. Powerful parties should not be permitted to misuse copyright as a tool for limiting bad press and barring access to legitimate consumer information."[35] His outspoken endorsement of our electronic civil disobedience signalled an immediate victory: Diebold capitulated and rescinded the legal threats against Swarthmore and the numerous other universities whose students had joined our civil disobedience. A year later, the Electronic Frontier Foundation won their case against Diebold. The California district court ruled the company was liable for violating the Digital Millennium Copyright Act.[36] The Diebold electronic civil disobedience was the first time I experienced a protest going viral, spreading outside the control of the campaign's creators.

Throughout my life I have strived to understand why some political ideas take fire in the heart of humanity, driving grand social transformations. How did Christians, who were once thrown to lions in stadiums of cheering Romans, endure three hundred years of persecution to become the religion of emperors, effectively eradicating (or at least absorbing) paganism? And how could it be that one day a king was on the throne in France and the next he was guillotined by revolutionists of egalitarian democracy? If the people have defeated omnipotent rulers in the past, why aren't our revolutionary efforts succeeding each and every day?

Through experimentation with edgy activism, I have learned that there is a law of revolution—a logic of events embedded in revolutionary movements throughout history that is chaotic but still discernible. The law that governs activism differs from the laws that guide the normal functioning of society. Cliodynamic historians—those who believe that history follows discernible patterns—are not wrong; they merely overestimate the material, calculative and measurable side of the cycles of history.

There are many theories of social change. I was educated into activism from a post-structuralist approach exemplified by the likes of Gilles Deleuze, Félix Guattari and Michel Foucault, a school of French philosophers heavily influenced by the May 1968 wildcat strikes in Paris and beyond. Each style of activism is akin to the differences between martial arts—ju-jitsu versus aikido or tae kwon do versus karate. I tried to learn all the different revolutionary theories from Guy Debord's situationism to Alfredo Bonanno's insurrectionary anarchism and John Zerzan's anarcho-primitivism to Kalle Lasn's culture jamming to Saul Alinsky's community organizing . . . the list goes on. I explored dozens of different models for how to go from the old world to the new. But I quickly learned that no single theory can entirely explain why some campaigns fail while others succeed. Theory is always grasping to explain a present that is slipping ceaselessly into the past. The past can be instructive, but never definitively so. What worked in the French Revolution is not going to work today. The only way to really know for sure what causes a social revolution to succeed is to provoke events and watch them flicker, fade or ignite.

> If there were no contradictions and no struggle, there would be no world, no progress, no life, and there would be nothing at all.
>
> MAO ZEDONG, *Talk at the Chengtu Conference*, 1958

6.

THE POINT OF PROTEST

The contemporary activist is the culmination of several thousand years of human experimentation in the social techniques of collective liberation. The role of the activist is to secure greater freedom for humanity.

Activism has existed since the dawn of inegalitarian society. Still, today's activist is a modern archetype. The word "activism" is derived in English from the adjective "active," and the French *actif*, which originally meant, according to the *Oxford English Dictionary*, "a life or lifestyle characterized by external acts of piety rather than by contemplation." The emphasis on external acts persists within political activism today. Activism as a concept was popularized by Rudolf Eucken, a German philosopher who won the Nobel Prize for Literature in 1908. Eucken was the first person to describe his ethical life philosophy as *aktivismus*.* In Eucken's philosophy, activism was "the theory or belief that truth is arrived at through action or active striving after the spiritual life."[37] An early commentator on Eucken explained that "activism has affinities with Pragmatism, especially on its negative side. . . . Both agree that action is the key to truth."[38] In 1920, Henry Lane Eno published *Activism*, a philosophical treatise on the concept that gives a glimpse into often unstated ideological assumptions that have migrated from philosophical activism to political activism. Eno writes that activism is "essentially realistic" and that it "assumes the 'objective' validity and 'real' being of entities and relations, as well as the fundamental relational complexes of space, time, number, and change."[39] This emphasis on action and change extended to the political arena.†

In his Nobel Laureate speech, Eucken anticipated the "social movement" and described the intersection of human subjectivity with the material world that characterizes *aktivismus*:

> The social movement, too, reveals man as not entirely limited by a given order, but as a being that perceives and judges a given situation and is confident that it can change it essentially by its own efforts. We have come to set greater store by material things, but we value them not because of their sensual

---

* An earlier meaning of activism, which is now obsolete and rare, traced its lineage to actinism—"the property by which light or other electromagnetic radiation causes chemical change."

† The *Oxford English Dictionary* records that from 1914 to 1918, the primary meaning of activism was an individual who advocated in favour of Germany by urging Sweden and Belgium to join the war. Eucken was a vocal supporter of Germany during the First World War.

> characteristics but because they serve us to enhance life and to dominate the world completely. We do not aim at an increase in sensual pleasures but at a situation in which any man and all men together can develop their full strength.[40]

The activist values the material world to the degree that it aids efforts to make change through action. The immediate challenge for the activist is therefore how to be active and what actions to take. The activist seeks tactics and behaviours believed to have the power to manifest revolutionary change.

WHY ACTIVISM?

You were born into a world in which injustice and inequality reign. Activism is the solution. When positive social change is necessary but blocked, suffering grows and so too does the social pressure to break through.

Activism is crucial to a healthy society because revolutions drive social progress; as Karl Marx observed, "revolutions are the locomotives of history."[41] Nearly all the good in this world is the result of hard-fought protest. Without disobedience that spiralled into full-blown insurrection, there would be no democracy. Every right you enjoy today was the result of past activism. As Wendell Phillips, the American abolitionist, said in 1848, "Revolution is the only thing, the only power, that ever worked out freedom for any people."[42] In other words, no freedom has ever been given freely. Protest is the price we pay for democracy.

Progress is made by protest. Since early modernity, and with increasing tempo following the eighteenth-century French Revolution, protests have inaugurated new phases of the human saga. Revolutions—what Victor Hugo calls "the larva of civilization"—are vital for the healthy renewal of the social order.[43] Protest releases the energy necessary for breaking out of old social patterns, and revolutions cement these new patterns into daily life. Protests, like wars and disruptive technological inventions, are agents of social change. Revolutions are signs of history being made. Striving toward revolution is one of the few ways that seemingly powerless people can shape the future.

Protests are vital to political, social and cultural health. Examining social movements, the sociologist Hank Johnston calls them "integral to keeping political elites attentive."[44] Suppressing protest is ultimately more dangerous to the suppressor than the people, and revolutions are close at hand whenever power ends the possibility of effective protest. The delay of a necessary revolution is a primary source of transformational violence. Or as John F. Kennedy famously put it: "Those who make peaceful revolution impossible will make violent revolution inevitable."[45]

Recognition of the positive and productive role of protest has underpinned American democracy since its founding. Thomas Jefferson, the primary author of the Declaration of Independence and America's third president, was candid about the value of rebellion. "I hold that a little rebellion now and then is a good thing, and as necessary in the political world as storms in the physical," he wrote in a letter to James Madison in the years preceding the French Revolution. Jefferson then advised Madison, who played a significant role in drafting the United States Constitution and United States Bill of Rights, to endorse only moderate punishments for insurrections and uprisings: "Honest republican governors [should be] so mild in their punishment of rebellions, as not to discourage them too much."[46] In a letter to another recipient, Jefferson exclaims, "God forbid we should be twenty years without a rebellion. What country can preserve its liberties if the rulers are not warned from time to time that their people preserve the spirit of resistance?"[47] In fact, this lax view toward punishing protest was widespread among the Founding Fathers. Liberty depends on resistance even when, especially when, resistance threatens to overthrow the status quo.

Not just in the United States is the history of democracy the history of revolution. "Representative democracy was not established through a prolonged process of peaceful reform but rather by revolutionary means," explains the historian Brian Roper in *The History of Democracy*. He continues: "A series of revolutionary upheavals . . . from the first Dutch revolt in 1565 to the end of the American Civil War in 1865, transformed previously existing states and established representative democracy."[48] In the words of U.S. Supreme Court Justice Robert Houghwout Jackson, writing during the Cold War, the occasional necessity of revolution is "an old American belief." Jackson writes, "We cannot ignore the fact that our own government originated in revolution, and is legitimate only if overthrow by force can sometimes be justified. . . . The men who led the struggle forcibly to overthrow lawfully constituted British authority found moral support by asserting a natural law under which their revolution was justified, and they bravely proclaimed their belief in the document basic to our freedom."[49] The nineteenth president, Ulysses S. Grant, writes in blunt terms: "the right of Revolution is an inherent one. When people are oppressed by their government, it is a natural right they enjoy to relieve themselves of the oppression if they are strong enough, either by withdrawing from it, or by overthrowing it and substituting a government more acceptable."[50]

As complex societies evolve, social inequalities manifest that lead to imbalance, injustice and conflict. Left unresolved, these societal tensions build toward a dangerous conflagration and ultimately herald the transformation of the social order. The eruption of protests, and the movements that arise when defiance becomes contagious, are a method for the people to resolve these tensions, ushering in large-scale change. The lack of effective forms of protest only brings society closer to civil violence. No technique of suppression can prevent the new spirit from breaking through the degenerating social order. Today's rulers would be wise to heed the 1786 advice of John Jay, one of the Founding Fathers, to respond to insurrection with reform: "by attacking the 'disease' that lies behind them rather than suppressing its 'symptoms.'"[51]

A tremendous release of energy is required to shift the paradigm of a declining society; aside from mass mobilization for war, the collective will of the people for revolution is one of the few sources proven to contain sufficient force. This collective will is often manifested as crowds in the streets. Rabindranath Tagore, the great polymath, once presciently observed that "crowd psychology is a blind force. Like steam and other physical forces, it can be utilized for creating a tremendous amount of power."[52] If the crowd is steam power, the Internet-enabled social movement is nuclear energy. The challenge is how to harness this explosive potential for positive ends.

Social mobilization for change can come from above, in the form of state-organized war, or below as a grassroots uprising.

Notice the similarities between a battle and protest, a war and social movement. Both involve the propagation of dramatically new behaviours intended to smash existing institutions. Revolutions that come from the people, and wars started by governments, involve a similar process of ideological stimulation and social deprogramming designed to heal society through abnormal collective action. Roberta Ash, a theorist of social movement organization, is correct to observe that war is a kind of movement: "a national war effort can be understood as a movement phenomenon . . . in which an elite mobilizes a large portion of the population, exciting them ideologically and deroutinizing them."[53]

The theorist Lyford P. Edwards concentrates on the crucial role revolution plays in destroying "those institutions of a given society which interfere with the attainment of one or more of the four elemental human wishes."[54] According to Edwards, humans crave new experience, security, recognition and response (touch and love). Protests are the expression of the human spirit desiring these elemental wishes and freeing itself from the fetters of convention. Perhaps the rebellious people are acting out of a desire for a new social experience, a new way of organizing or interacting with each other. Or maybe, as in the case of Mohamed Bouazizi who triggered the Arab Spring, they hunger for economic security and recognition from their government. Underlying every revolution is a wish that is being rejected, ignored or deferred. A century ago, the German political philosopher and influential Communist theorist Friedrich Engels knew this to be true: "wherever there is revolutionary convulsion, there must be some social want in the background which is prevented by outworn institutions from satisfying itself."[55] Those who suppress protest in defence of pre-existing institutions are interfering with a natural (and beautiful) process that is absolutely necessary for the long-term vitality of society.

WHAT IS REVOLUTION?

Revolution is a grand overturning, a magical moment when the status quo is heaved long enough for a new way of being to emerge. Many revolutions last only a minute and take place in the mind as an epiphany that shatters an old way of thinking. Others hold for weeks and the epiphany spreads from mind to mind, taking the form of a social movement. And only a very few revolutions cement into a permanently new social order.

Revolutions are a dynamic and complex human phenomenon. Although unpredictable—revolutions tend to appear spontaneous and are therefore notoriously difficult to forecast—they follow discernible patterns and obey physical, psychological and biological limits. Or, as Engels explains, "a revolution is a pure phenomenon of nature, which is led more accordingly to physical laws than according to the rules which in ordinary times determine the development of society."[56] Some of these patterns are eternal and others are transitory. Revolutions share many characteristics while always manifesting differently, distinctly throughout history. The study of revolution is therefore complicated by the challenge of defining the subject: What is a revolution?

Previous studies of revolution distinguish the phenomenon using examples that exclude most of humanity's historical record. The conservative political scientist Samuel Huntington, for example, argues that "revolution is an aspect of modernization.

It is not something which can occur in any type of society at any period in its history. It is not a universal category but rather an historically limited phenomenon."[57] This focus on a "historically limited" concept of revolution justifies an overemphasis on studying Great Revolutions, all of which are mass, modern and secular. Revolutions that do not fit this model are ignored. "It is true that one type of revolution, namely the large-scale transformative revolution, is a phenomenon of the modern age, or to give it a proper name, of the age of Europeism," wrote the Czech-British sociologist Jaroslav Krejčí in 1983.[58] This Europeanist approach is backward-looking, privileges one type of revolution (Marxist-Communist), and is ultimately unhelpful to our eternal pursuit of the next planetary uprising. Rather than narrow the field of study to the preceding 250 years, a robust, unified, general theory of revolution encompasses all of human history: antiquity, pre-modernity, modernity and ultramodernity.

The definition of revolution that I advocate was first proposed in 1927 by Lyford P. Edwards, who writes, "Revolution is a change brought about not necessarily by force and violence, whereby one system of legality is terminated and another originated."[59] Edwards's inclusive definition fits a wider range of human history and draws our attention to revolution's chief characteristic: the transfer of sovereignty and the establishment of a new legal regime.

The revolutionary overthrow of the status quo and founding of a new legal system is, by definition, illegal until it succeeds. Revolutionary activism is any attempt by protesters to make the illegal legal or the legal illegal. Activists may intend to reverse a single unjust law, or their goal may to be overturn a whole system. Sometimes activists may use one law to overturn another. Acknowledging that our purpose as activists is to challenge the legal regime explains why all protesters, even practitioners of unarmed non-violent revolution, are subject to suppression. All societies will fight to resist revolutionary change. The pacifist preacher Martin Luther King Jr.'s tactics of civil disobedience against racial segregation, for example, were equated with high crimes. Even moderate, non-racist whites at the time condemned King's novel tactics. While imprisoned for protesting against racial segregation, King eloquently defended his non-violent methods in "Letter from a Birmingham Jail." Asked to explain how he could justify breaking the law, King distinguished between just laws that must be obeyed and unjust laws that must be disobeyed: "You express a great deal of anxiety over our willingness to break laws. . . . One may well ask: 'How can you advocate breaking some laws and obeying others?' The answer lies in the fact that there are two types of laws: just and unjust. I would be the first to advocate obeying just laws. One has not only a legal but a moral responsibility to obey just laws. Conversely, one has a moral responsibility to disobey unjust laws. I would agree with St. Augustine that 'an unjust law is no law at all.'"[60] There is no way to fundamentally change society without disobeying unjust laws and disturbing existing social structures.

Still, the mature activist acknowledges that misery may result from any sincere attempt at overthrowing the ruling order and that such a step must never be taken lightly. There is no such thing as a painless transfer of power, even if it unfolds without bloodshed. On the path toward revolution there always lies the risk of ruin.

WHAT IS PROTEST?

Protest is a collective ritual, a *social technique of collective liberation*, believed by participants to alter the existing system of legality. Protest is a form of non-violent warfare designed to hasten revolution, the abolishment of one legal regime and the establishment of another. The intention of genuine protest is large-scale transformative change: the birth of a new social order. Protests are common; revolutions are rare. Every revolution involves protest; however, only rarely does a protest bring revolution. Few protests precipitate revolution, but all revolutions are preceded by protests.

The spectrum of protest extends from unsophisticated localized riots to networked global social movement waves that spread by combining online coordination with offline action. Most protests are an unconscious collective response, an act of collective anger, rather than a rationally conceived strategy for changing political reality. In these cases, an injustice happens and the people respond instinctually. The tactics used are often crude and incendiary. Participants act out their indignation in an immediate and visceral way. These riotous behaviours are culturally determined and change over time. Some spontaneous protest methods that were once common disappear and others reappear or are newly invented. For example, in London eighteenth-century rioters utilized the tactic of "pulling down" houses: the people would smash the windows and doors of targeted homes, dragging furniture into the streets and burning it to attract crowds.[61] Meanwhile, "tar and feathering" was a popular form of protest leading up to the American Revolution of 1775.

Protests that are entirely unconscious are merely a symptom of injustice. Unconscious protests tend to dissipate once the moment of anger has passed. The difference between a revolutionary protest and a visceral popular disturbance is that the latter lacks a compelling theory of social change. During a riot or chaotic unrest, the wider public does not grasp how these disruptive actions are going to bring about real and lasting transformation. Protests whose tactics do not resonate with people will not be replicated. On the contrary, during a revolutionary moment, the people rush to join the movement as soon as they believe the new tactics will work to improve their lives.

Until the twentieth century, it was common to approach the study of protest from a collective behaviour paradigm that understood protest to be a negative symptom of social disintegration—a deviant behaviour caused by macro-societal factors. "Social movements, in this view, are one product of social disorganization; other products include suicide, criminal behaviour, and additional symptoms of a social system in trouble," writes William Gamson in *The Strategy of Social Protest*, a seminal critique of the collective behaviour paradigm.[62] The collective behaviour paradigm presented a depoliticized picture of protest. It saw mass action as a crowd behaviour distinct from politics. Gamson explains the implications of this assumption: "The collective behaviour paradigm, then, rests on a distinction between the politics of social movements and the politics of conventional groups and organizations—mainstream political parties, lobbies and interest groups. The actors who engage in these two types of behaviour are seen as different species."[63]

By the 1960s it became clear that not all protests were unconscious, symptomatic popular disturbances. Some contesting groups were wielding social movement tactics as an intentional strategy for achieving political change. These new tactics of civil disobedience, such as sit-ins and non-violent marches, were grounded in a conscious theory of how to influence politics from outside traditional channels. And, most important, these new protests were having obvious political impact. Soon it was undeniable that "choosing to protest, and especially employing extremist measures and violent tactics, are strategic decisions made by challenging groups."[64] The distinction between mainstream politics and the politics of social movements began to break down.

In short, protests are collective rituals organized by civilian agents of change in a bid to transform the social reality and shift the legal regime. Social movements and their disruptive collective rituals are politics by other means. As such, protest movements are a form of warfare waged by the new spirit against the old world.

Those of us who do not occupy conventional positions of power and yet still wish to set sail from the world-as-it-is in the hope of discovering the world-as-it-ought-to-be quickly discover that the journey is uncharted, oftentimes treacherous. There is no safe passage and there are many strident voices that discourage any voyage. Those who are content with the status quo say there is no hope of crossing the vast sea that separates this known world with all its imperfections from the utopia the dissenters aspire to create. Those who persist in the journey to transform social and political reality soon discover the armadas of ineffective activism: on street corners canvassers beseech us to act now, act locally and globally. It is not possible to sign every petition, join every march or donate to every cause. And too often when we do take a prescribed action we discover the futility of trying to shift the status quo with petitions, marches and tax-deductible donations. In the absence of *kairos*, a Greek word for a destined opportune moment, we rush to action, relying on well-worn activist tactics inherited from previous social protests. But protesting in expected ways makes us an easy target for arrest, and is a waste of our most precious resource: the creativity of the human spirit.

BREAKING THE SCRIPT OF PROTEST

Each era of human history has had its distinctive form of contesting the structures of power. Throughout history the people have acted in diverse and contradictory ways in their quest for greater collective freedom. Every protest practice has its historical lineage, its theorists, its boundaries, its exemplary activists. At this point we must acknowledge that the word "protest" is inadequate because it is a word that defines a social behaviour of public declaration intended to influence authorities. In fact, the etymology of protest reveals its origins in the legal term "protestation," which meant, at the end of the fourteenth century, "an appeal that one's right to legal redress be recognized."[65] Originally protest didn't challenge authority; protest petitioned authority. When we protest in this sense, we emphatically declare our opposition (and less often, our affirmation) in the hope of being seen by those we oppose—in most cases, those in charge. Protest was developed to influence the so-called court of public opinion. However, protest is evolving beyond this limited goal.

Protest is a social technique: a set of learned behaviours that are passed on as a way to influence social reality, and that constitute our political milieu. The protest script we follow reveals our theory of political change, a story we tell ourselves about how political change happens in our society. Do you believe that the status quo will be shifted through a mass movement of millions in the streets? Or will it be brought about by the daring action of black-clad urban anarchists whose audacious action inspires others? Perhaps it will be through legislative means and the real heroes are the ones wearing suits and lobbying elected representatives? Activists rely on a story of social change based on their understanding of past revolutionary moments in order to decide which actions to take. There are many theories of change, but none seems to work during the end of protest, times such as ours when the paradigms of social change are shifting. Historically, only the rarest protest yields results in the long term, and rarer still are protests that achieve immediate victory. As most actions prove to be ineffective—revealing to the self-reflective activist that the dominant theories of social change are false—the choice of how to protest has become for far too many a lifestyle decision.

Activists signify their ideology of socio-political change by protesting in a manner that conforms with their ideological milieu. Protests are a culturally determined social ritual, which is why any communal gesture, sound or signifier—from ecstatic dancing to banging pot lids to using in-group watchwords or clothing colour—can suddenly become a powerful, contagious protest tactic that gives birth to a revolutionary movement. Any shared behaviour can become a protest tactic if the people believe it will create change; hence, the diversity of tactics that have emerged in the long history of people's insurrection. When the people invest a new tactic with their collective imagination, it becomes potent. For a protest to become a movement requires a vector of transmission such as a social network to spread the movement's distinctive tactics, gestures, sounds and colours.

The inequalities within society guarantee a supply of potential protest meme carriers. A fairly accurate census of the global movement occurred on February 15, 2003, when millions of people protested simultaneously in more than six hundred cities. Similar, if not more impressive for the duration, results were experienced during the peak of Occupy Wall Street with nearly one thousand occupations. But remove restrictions to your imagination. Protests need not be loud or visible or large. Silence can be used to bring down regimes too. By detaching ourselves from an allegiance to a specific protest ritual, whether it be press conferences or occupations or street parties or vandalism or marching to the capital, we attain toward the self-reflexivity necessary to protest effectively as opposed to ideologically or symbolically.

Detaching ourselves from the script of protest allows activists to see the shifting paradigms. Having grown up with computers, we have become accustomed to sudden changes at the level of technology. One day tablets are the hottest, and the next it is smart glasses, smart watches and driverless cars. Fads sweep through Silicon Valley, engendering a culture of ruthless innovation. Facebook's motto used to be "Move Fast and Break Things," an apt one for the efforts of social change creators and geopolitical activists. Those of us working in the trenches of bottom-up insurrection have our own history of great innovators to rival the Thomas Edisons and Mark

Zuckerbergs. The revolutionaries of the nineteenth century understood that tactical innovation is the foundation of success. Karl Marx, Friedrich Engels, Mikhail Bakunin, et al. were deeply influenced by the events of 1848, a continent-wide populist insurrection that toppled the king of France. They understood the event on a tactical level and studied the proliferation of barricades in that uprising for clues about the future of revolution. Each drew his own conclusions. Engels demonstrated a tactical flexibility and an innate sense for when a certain way of fighting for power had lost its effectiveness. Once Engels understood the significance of counterinsurgency innovations instigated by the French general Louis-Eugène Cavaignac, he surprised his contemporaries by openly advocating that the people take an electoral approach. Later Lenin and Trotsky, who also closely studied this event, learned a far different lesson and pursued social transformation as if it were a military campaign.

A breakthrough in tactics is necessary but it is not sufficient. Revolutions require a willing historical moment, which no one can predict or control. But when they arrive, activists must be prepared.

We have forgotten the very principle of our origin if we have forgotten how to object, how to resist, how to agitate, how to pull down and build up, even to the extent of revolutionary practices, if it is necessary to readjust matters.

WOODROW WILSON, TWENTY-EIGHTH PRESIDENT OF THE UNITED STATES, SPEAKING IN 1899

7. A UNIFIED THEORY OF REVOLUTION

What is the connection between protest and socio-political change? The parable of the three pigeons illuminates the nature of activism.

Imagine an experiment with three pigeons. Each pigeon is placed in a separate box. Inside the box is a lever. The first pigeon is given a pellet of food whenever it pecks the lever. The next pigeon must peck the lever twice to receive food. The last pigeon, however, receives food on random pecks—for the third pigeon there is no connection between the number of pecks and when it receives food. After the three pigeons have learned the system, the experimenter disconnects the link between the lever and food. Now what happens when pecking the lever no longer releases food?

The first pigeon notices the ineffectiveness of the lever immediately. This pigeon strikes the lever twice, realizes that food is no longer being released and stops pecking. The second pigeon understands more slowly. It taps the lever six times before stopping. The third pigeon, however, never comes to realize that its behaviour will not release food. It just keeps pecking the lever over and over and over again.

One way to understand this parable is to see the pigeons as activists, pecking the lever as their form of protest and the food as revolution. Activists protest to release positive change in their life, their community, their environment. Forces more powerful than pigeons, and activists, govern the release of revolution. From this perspective, the experimenter represents the layer of existence that stands outside the control of the individual. At rare times, when the historical moment is ripe for change, this layer of existence is responsive to protest. At other times, symbolized in this parable as the experimenter disconnecting the lever from the food, the effective form of protest shifts. Pecking the lever is the activist's repertoire of actions. The pigeons have only one protest tactic: tap the lever. The pigeons are taught to protest one way until their behaviour becomes predictable. The pigeons may cry or hop or be silent, but only pecking is acknowledged as protest and thereby brings food. Unlike the experimenter's pigeons, activists have more than one way to push the lever. Activists use a repertoire of actions, but don't let the diversity of tactics fool you.

The third pigeon, the one that keeps pecking the lever, represents the ideal pacified activist. This pigeon goes on protesting predictably, foolishly, acting without real influence over when change is delivered or denied. Nearly all activists are of the third order of pigeon: we rush into the streets and push the (metaphorical) lever repeatedly in the hope of change. We are happy when a protest yields results and disappointed when it fails, without considering whether there is actually an underlying correlation between our protest methods and success or failure. Activists are told that every so often a protest yields a magical result, so we try over and over. The third pigeon was fooled by randomness. Food was delivered on random pecks; therefore, it acquired a false theory of social change that saw a pattern where there was none. The third pigeon was deceived into believing that its behaviour was hastening food when in actuality the change to its environment was controlled by a structural force outside the pigeon's influence.

The second pigeon is the self-reflexive activist with an effective theory of revolution. This activist knows when protest has stopped working. She can tell when the rules of the game have changed and a new theory is called for. It is important to notice that the second pigeon's actions were not always effective. It took two pecks to achieve change; however, the pigeon was able to correctly discern a pattern. Those activists who can distinguish failure that is a natural part of the cycle from failure that signals the end of protest, and who can sense when a paradigm shift is necessary, have reached the level of the second pigeon.

And the first pigeon? This is the rare one who sees outside the box. She knows the appropriate moment for action and the proper path to revolution. She knows when to act and when to switch tactics, and thus her every protest achieves success. This pigeon is the historic revolutionary who has developed an accurate theory of change.

THE AXES OF REVOLUTION

A theory of revolution grants foresight regarding whether a protest will bring change. It is the only playbook to activism, and it must be rewritten by each generation. Activism based on accurate principles yields social change. Without a theory of why revolutions happen and a hypothesis of the behaviours that will hasten the next uprising, there is no way to distinguish between a destined event and an ineffectual happening. Lenin made this clear: "without a revolutionary theory there can be no revolutionary movement."[66] A repressive status quo functions by promulgating broken theories of change, thereby disconnecting the link between protest and change so that our actions will fail and our time will be squandered. Repressive democracies encourage forms of protest that are least revolutionary and most ineffective. The ideal situation for a false democracy is to have frequent ineffective protests that give the illusion that dissent is tolerated while discouraging any tactics that might actually change the legal regime.

I classify general theories of revolution on a vertical y-axis that represents the role of the world and a horizontal x-axis that represents the role of the activist. The vertical y-axis ascends from material to spiritual, and the horizontal x-axis moves from subjective to objective. On the material end of the axis, the forces that influence revolution are presumed to be within the natural physical reality that surrounds us. Spiritual means the belief that revolutions are brought about by supernatural forces—divine factors (gods, faith and destiny) that stand outside the natural world. The horizontal x-axis is existential. Here the role of the individual in revolution is classified as either subjective, meaning internal to the activist, or objective,

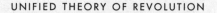

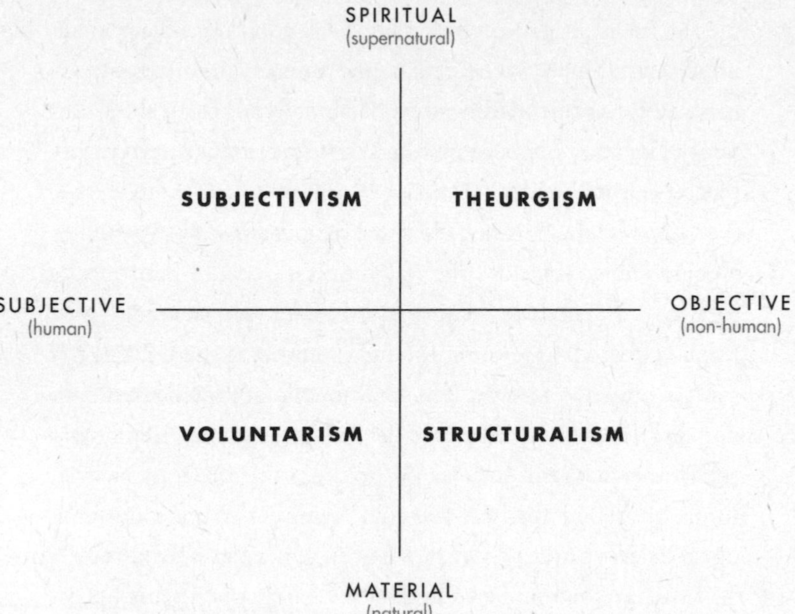

A unified theory of revolution is the quaternity of voluntarism, structuralism, subjectivism and theurgism.

outside the activist. On the left side of the x-axis are general theories of revolution that stress the importance of the protester: his or her action or inaction and the underlying psychology, subjectivity or inner reality. Internal theories emphasize the role of humans in revolution. On the opposite side are theories that place importance on objective, structural and societal forces outside of human subjectivity such as energy prices, the cost of bread or unemployment rates. External theories prioritize objective non-human forces. Finding the proper intersection of these two spectrums—world and individual—is the basis of all revolutionary theory. As the sociologist Irving L. Horowitz explains, "revolution is the point at which individual psychology connects itself to universal history. Because of this the study of objective factors alone can never yield a knowledge of when or how revolutionary transformations take place."[67]

A *unified theory* is not the same as an *eternal theory*. Times change and so too does the revolutionary theory appropriate to your era. The way you protested effectively yesterday may not be effective in a week. Likewise, any true theory will not remain effective forever. Thus, all four quadrants are true, to varying degrees, at all times. The challenge is to not limit yourself to one quadrant. Instead, the goal is to ascend from material to spiritual and internal to external, attaining an understanding of each theory and a sense of when each is most appropriate.

Imagine there are two layers of reality: one that is accessible to human understanding and another that is not. Theory can only know the accessible first layer. The second layer is ultimately inaccessible to human understanding, although intuition, chance and destiny can grant temporary access. The inaccessible layer of reality comprises the innumerable and unknowable factors that influence history. I picture these two layers as strips of wood with holes in different places. The layers slide back and forth unpredictably. Occasionally the holes align.

When these holes overlap, and if the proper protest happens at this moment, a revolutionary event opens. The ancient Greeks had two distinct concepts for time: *chronos*, which referred to the linear sequence of time stretching from past to future, and kairos, the advantageous moment for action. When we say that a moment is ripe for the revolution, we are referring to the temporality of kairos. Auspicious moments for revolution are rare, and yet they follow cycles and patterns.

Our objective in developing a unified theory of revolution is to increase the probability that *our* protest will effectively align with the unknowable second layer, by cultivating a detachment from adherence to any particular theory or repertoire of protest. Instead, we need to allow our quest toward revolution to be guided by an intuitive understanding based on repeated experimentation and a risk-it-all attitude.

VOLUNTARISM

Most of contemporary activism is voluntarist. The essence of voluntarism is the belief that the actions of individuals can change the world. The basic idea is that certain collective social behaviours have a unique political power. Voluntarism is based on the assumption that voluntary actions are the dominant factor in revolution and that the primary challenge for activists is to get large numbers of people to choose the correct behaviours. This means that activists emphasize their free will, believing that their decision to act can overcome other structural factors that may make revolution seem impossible. For the philosopher Slavoj Žižek, voluntarism is defined by "the belief that one can 'move mountains,' ignoring 'objective' laws and obstacles."[68] Voluntarists have total faith in the power of action. Voluntarist activists believe that collective action can overcome all odds. Or, according to Alexander the Great, "There is nothing impossible to him who will try." Once this assumption has been made, the primary challenge becomes determining which actions to advocate. The possibilities are limitless, and to narrow the choice voluntarist activists have created many secondary theories to explain why they've chosen this protest tactic over another.

Activists urge people to "take action" because voluntarists believe political reality can be changed through *direct action*, the exertion of direct pressure through any unmediated action, such as strikes, blockades, or demonstrations designed to achieve immediate results, as distinguished from indirect actions such as negotiation, lobbying or constitutional processes. Voluntarists often think of activism as a *ladder of engagement* that begins with non-action and passivity and climbs toward activity with direct action at the pinnacle. The goal is to escalate engagement up the ladder. Action, individual and collective, is the ideal. Voluntarist activists would never accept, for example, that doing nothing (i.e., the *absence of action*) could yield greater intended political change than doing something—anything—unless the act of doing nothing, like being silent or refusing to work, was publicly performed as protest. Activity, the wilful intention to change the world, is necessary for activists who eschew passivity, inner contemplation and theoretical speculation in favour of being practical, applied and empirical.

Until the explosion of political activism in the 1960s, an unconscious voluntarism (in the sense that actions were chosen haphazardly) was the norm. Crowds adopted unruly behaviours spontaneously and then spread them. Consider, for example, the Nika Revolt of AD 532 that nearly toppled Constantinople. This spontaneous incendiary riot probably came closer to overthrowing a world power than any riot in human history. There was no conscious theory guiding the event. It just happened, leaving many historians wondering whether the Nika Revolt was a political protest or just a bout of hooliganism. Likewise today, whenever we are unsure if a popular unrest is revolutionary, it is often a sign that the people are being unconscious in their choice of tactics. Conscious voluntarism emerged later in history when the crowd began to understand itself as a coherent social movement whose coordinated actions had political implications. Consciously voluntarist activists think strategically in terms of tactics, campaigns and movements.

The publication of William Gamson's *The Strategy of Social Protest* in 1975 was a milestone for conscious voluntarism. Gamson, a sociologist, took an empirical approach to studying protest. He compiled a database of protest groups in the United States between 1800 and 1945. He then took a random sample and looked for patterns behind contesting group success. The result was ironic: Gamson's conclusions were counterintuitive, and the most important pattern that he identified ignited a furor of opposition to voluntarism.

The first counterintuitive conclusion that Gamson came to is that protest groups do not increase their odds of success by working on campaigns that many other groups are also tackling. On the contrary, according to Gamson, "having many other challenging groups in the field at the same time does not seem to have much effect on the probability of success of any given challenger." This is good news for solo activists and unconventional movements because it frees us from working on popular campaigns whose efficacy we question. Coalition building is an activist cliché presumed to be mandatory to success.

And these large coalitions, often funded by foundations, tend to overdetermine the aims and targets of contemporary activism. Sometimes activists assume that working together and getting other groups "on board" is crucial to campaign progress. Gamson's historical analysis of challenging group success refutes this assumption.[69] The founding of Occupy Wall Street, which emerged from *Adbusters* in Canada rather than the many groups in the United States who were working together to get money out of politics and bring income inequality into the mainstream discourse, corroborates Gamson's findings.

One conclusion above all defined Gamson as a voluntarist, catalyzing fierce opposition to *The Strategy of Social Protest*. He discovered in the data proof that the likelihood of success increased when protesters embraced certain actions. Good news for the core assumption of voluntarism. Unfortunately, after extensive statistical research, the end result was a clear endorsement of violence. Gamson discovered that one of the actions that had a significant positive impact on the probability of success was adopting violent tactics.* "Unruly groups, those that use violence, strikes and other constraints, have better than average success," Gamson reports.[70] This was an unacceptable conclusion in 1975, a year when urban guerrillas like the Red Army Faction were taking hostages, bombing

---

* Jack Goldstone, an American sociologist and political scientist who specializes in the study of revolutionary movements, summarizes in his article "The Weakness of Organization" the voluntarist elements of Gamson's work: "Gamson indicated that six tactical and organizational factors had a significant impact on the success of protest groups. The factors were: (1) bureaucratization, (2) centralization, (3) use of selective incentives, (4) use of violence, (5) recipience of violence, and (6) factionalism. The first four factors were held to improve the chances for success, the latter two to make success less likely."

buildings and executing politicians.[71] It would be going too far to say that Gamson advocated violence; instead, he embraced the empiricism of voluntarist activism and reported what he saw in the data.

At the same time as the core voluntarist tenet—actions make change—was vindicated, activists were put in an ill-favoured position of advocating violence as the most effective form of action. You may dismiss Gamson. Or you may try to make the counterintuitive argument that contemporary forms of non-violent direct action are a less lethal form of violence that still fits Gamson's definition of the effective use of violence. Either way, the ideal of non-violence takes a hit from the possibility that political reality will only be altered violently, rather than through the repertoire of peaceful tactics.

Contemporary revolution theory has moved forward. The defeat of the Red Army Faction in Germany, the Red Brigades in Italy, the Weather Underground in the U.S. and others who embraced violence stands as a historic warning. The theory of *focoism*, the idea promulgated by Fidel Castro, Che Guevara and Régis Debray that mobile groups of armed guerrillas can spark a broad-based revolution by roaming rural areas and committing sporadic acts of anti-government violence, was a disastrous failure in Bolivia and elsewhere.[72] At the same time, violent groups have a tendency to be infiltrated by *agents provocateurs* or front groups for use in false-flag operations.[73] And regardless of whether the data suggest the efficacy of violence for contesting groups between 1800 and 1945, the twenty-first-century activist's repertoire is distinctly non-violent and often performative, directed toward garnering media attention. "One way of thinking about the most visible actions in the social movement repertoire is to consider them as performances directed at certain audiences," writes the sociologist Hank Johnston.[74] Voluntarist action-oriented protest today is mostly, but not always, about appealing to spectators through public events.

STRUCTURALISM

Structuralist activists believe that revolution is outside human influence. Structuralists maintain that human action is irrelevant, or largely insignificant, to revolutionary success. Instead of privileging the actions of individuals, structuralists see revolutions as a process that emerges out of the complex interaction of interrelated systems, such as the global economy or consumer debt or the effects of climate change. Protesters are merely, to borrow a phrase from the Russian novelist Leo Tolstoy, "involuntary instruments of history."[75] From the structuralist perspective, all of contemporary activism is a blind dance led by groups whose protests are beyond ineffective—their protests are irrelevant to revolution. Protests are a symptom rather than a cause of social change. Put simply, in the words of the abolitionist Wendell Phillips, "Revolutions are not made, they come. A revolution is as natural a growth as an oak. It comes out of the past. Its foundations are far back."[76] If revolution is a process outside of human influence, the big institutionalized activist organizations are wasting resources—considering, for example, that Greenpeace International had an income of US$79 million in 2011 and the World Wildlife Fund had an income of US$776 million in 2012.[77]

The border between voluntarism and structuralism is permeable. Although these positions disagree on whether revolution is a subjective or objective process from the perspective of humans, both share a concern for the materiality of the world. Together, these two schools of activism constitute the bulk of leftism, or rather the left that traces its lineage to Communism and Marxist historical materialism. A nuanced voluntarist activist may concede that economic crisis plays a role in revolution while still holding that her action or inaction is the most significant factor to success. Gamson, for example, believed "a major crisis such as war or economic collapse can aid those challengers who have established a presence before the crisis occurs" but maintained that the actions of protesters still played a significant factor in the outcome of events.[78] Structuralists go further; structuralists cross out free will and disregard human agency.

It may appear that individuals play a defining role in the process of revolution. And many histories have been written from the perspective of great individuals whose choices appear to have determined the course of history. However, the role of individuals is a cognitive illusion, a by-product of human rationality that is unable to grasp the larger structures that actually dictated how events would unfold. Leo Tolstoy provides a wonderful articulation of structuralism in *War and Peace*. Explaining his approach to understanding the French invasion of Russia in 1812 that pitted Napoleon against Tsar Alexander I, Tolstoy writes, "There are laws that govern events, which are partly unknown, partly groped for by us. The discovery of these laws is possible only when we wholly give up looking for causes in the will of one man, just as discovering the laws of planetary movement became possible only when people gave up the notion that the earth stands still."[79]

One of the laws governing revolution, according to researchers at the New England Complex Systems Institute, is that the price of food determines social unrest more than any other single factor. Based on their analysis of the Food Price Index, a monthly average of food commodity prices on international markets that is compiled by the UN's Food and Agriculture Organization (FAO), these researchers discovered that riots tend to occur "above a threshold of the FAO price index of 210."[80] For comparison, during the Arab Spring and Occupy uprisings of 2011 the Food Price Index was 229.9. The price increase was driven by a dramatic rise in the cost of sugar, which hit a twenty-eight-year high in the days before the global protests. Some commodity experts argue that the massive price jump was precipitated by a series of droughts in Australia, the world's third-largest sugar producer, followed by the impact of Cyclone Yasi.* In 2012, when the global movements began to dissipate, the index dropped to 213.3, and by 2013 it was just below the riot threshold at 209.8. Since then, food prices have continued to decline overall (in June 2015 the index reached 165.1, the lowest level since 2009), and the revolutionary moment seems further and further away.

In *States and Social Revolutions*, published in 1979, Theda Skocpol, a professor of government and sociology at Harvard University, exemplifies the structuralist position, declaring that understanding revolution by beginning with the humans who took part in the event is fatally misguided. "It will simply

* Voluntarists will argue that commodity speculation on the financial markets also played a significant role in the increase in food prices. This position raises a tantalizing question: did speculators do more than activists to spark a revolutionary moment?

not do," she writes, "to try to decipher the logic of the process or outcomes of a social revolution by adopting the perspective or following the actions of any one class or elite or organization—no matter how important its participatory role."[81] With a grand gesture she negates voluntarist assumptions and shifts the focus from participants to structures.

Skocpol's position takes on empirical weight when paired with Jack Goldstone's thought-provoking critique "The Weakness of Organization: A New Look at Gamson's *The Strategy of Social Protest*" (1980). Goldstone's argument is all the more convincing because it is grounded in a reanalysis of the same data that William Gamson used to give credence to voluntarism. As a structuralist, Goldstone takes issue with Gamson's assertion that "organization and tactics of social protest groups" have an influence on the group's chances of success. After reassessing the data, Goldstone concludes on the contrary that "no one set of organizational or tactical attributes seems to offer significant advantages over others in attaining or hastening success."[82] In other words, any action taken by dissidents will have the same probability of success because what hastens revolution are forces outside of the influence of humans. From a purely strategic point of view, activists ought to judge actions on the basis of their worth at bringing change. Structuralism suggests that your privileged style of organizing (i.e., horizontalism) and your rarefied tactics (i.e., occupying) are not significant to success.

Let's take the thought experiment further. To prove that the actions of protest groups had no effect on success, Goldstone produced a randomness model that aligned with history. A strict structuralist would rather praise chance than choice, and that is what Goldstone does. He argues that protest group success fits with a stochastic model where the probability of success is largely determined by whether it is a crisis year. "Stochastic" means "random," and "stochastic processes refer to the dynamics of events unfolding with the course of time," explains Nassim Nicholas Taleb, a Lebanese-American statistician and risk theorist. "This branch of probability concerns itself with the study of the evolution of successive random events—one could call it the mathematics of history."[83] To illustrate that revolution is the result of a succession of random events, Goldstone calculates the probability of group success to be equal to the probability of a crisis year times the average probability of success: "Since there is no connection between the times of start-up and the periods of crisis, the probability of success in any given year, from the perspective of a challenging group, is simply the probability that a year will be a crisis year, times the average probability of success during a crisis."[84] If Gamson's data are correct, then between 1800 and 1945 there was a 45 percent probability that a particular year would have a crisis. On average, 9.5 percent of the groups sampled by Gamson had success. Therefore, Goldstone concludes that the probability of success for a protest group is 4 percent. This calculation results in a 33 percent probability that a protest group will achieve success within ten years; a 56 percent probability of success within twenty years; and 71 percent within thirty years.* Activists have been fooled

* Goldstone provides the following formula for calculating the probability of success within a number of years where p is the probability of successful revolution (he estimates this to be .04): p (success in n years or less) $= p_n = 1 - (1 - p)^n$.

by randomness.[85] Or as Tolstoy explains it, "Men's actions are subject to general, immutable laws expressed by statistics."[86]

Voluntarists bristle at the suggestion that action is irrelevant to success. However, structuralism is the logical conclusion of determinism when applied to the field of politics. As Lenin declares, "Revolution is impossible without a national crisis affecting both the exploited and the exploiters."[87] Believing that success is determined by world-historic events outside of their control is liberating for structuralist revolutionaries. Friedrich Engels, for example, was convinced that the failure of the European revolution in 1848 was due to global economic trends rather than the actions of individuals. "The world commercial crisis of 1847 was the real cause of the February and March revolutions, and the industrial prosperity which arrived gradually in the middle of 1848, coming to full bloom in 1849 and 1850, was the vitalizing factor of the renascent European reaction," he writes.[88] The same could be said based on the declining food prices following the eruption of Occupy.

Others have also seen a strong connection between economic reversals (the J-curve) and the spontaneous emergence of revolution. "Revolutions are most likely to occur when a prolonged period of objective economic and social development is followed by a short period of sharp reversal," writes the sociologist James C. Davies succinctly.[89] Following the constructive failure of the European Revolution of 1848, Engels took the time to recharge intellectually and tactically after recognizing that world economic crisis is necessary for revolution. He records his thoughts at the time: "Vulgar democracy expected a renewed outbreak from one day to another; we

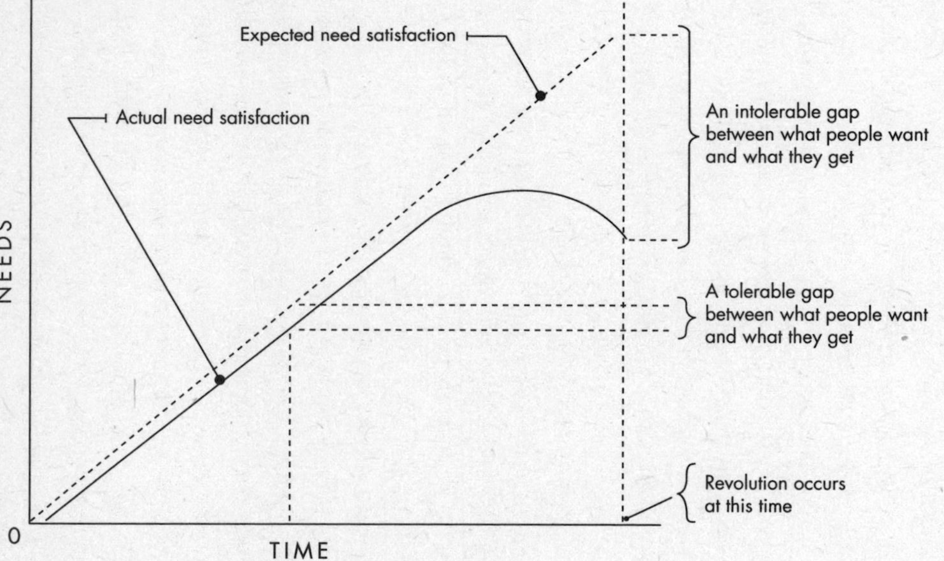

Structuralism is epitomized by the J-curve model, originally proposed by James C. Davies, where revolutions occur at a moment of sudden economic reversal, such as during a period of skyrocketing food prices.

already in the autumn of 1850, declared that the first phase of the revolutionary period had closed and that nothing could be looked forward to until the advent of a new economic world crisis."[90] Engels waited, and gathered his strength, while others burned out on fruitless action.*

Mainstream structuralists are materialist and ultimately reject the influence of supernatural powers. Revolutions may be outside of human control but they are not under the control of a divine power. Structuralists place a great deal of importance on the secular economy. The tone was set by Karl Marx who advocated a materialist critique of religion as a step toward political revolution. "Thus the criticism of heaven is transformed into the criticism of earth, the criticism of religion into the criticism of law, and the criticism of theology into the criticism of politics," writes Karl Marx in the introduction to the unfinished manuscript *A Contribution to the Critique of Hegel's Philosophy of Right*. He continues: "The call to abandon their illusions about their condition is a call to abandon a condition which requires illusions. The criticism of religion disillusions man so that he will think, act and fashion his reality as a man who has lost his illusions and regains his reason; so that he will revolve about himself as his own true sun."[91] Marx disputed the supernatural realm out of a desire for temporal (worldly) power.

Structuralist thought experiments are useful for gaining a balanced perspective on the agency of humans. Contemporary

---

* When a financial crisis and economic depression finally reemerged in 1857, Engels wrote excitedly to Marx, "Now our time is coming—this time it is coming in full measure: a life-and-death struggle. My military studies will at once become more practical." A revolution did not materialize.

activism often overemphasizes the role of protesters, believing that direct action alone can hasten revolution. Here's a wild idea: revolution might be caused by non-human entities. For example, perhaps political insurrections are symptoms of a biological contagion that influences collective behaviour. Maybe revolutionary periods are akin to outbreaks of influenza. If this is true, activists would be wise to develop a sense of when to act and when to wait.

Reading Theda Skocpol's rejection of the role of individuals and Jack Goldstone's strict structuralism can engender a sense of hopelessness. Some activists might wonder what the point of protesting is if it has no impact on success. There is, however, another way of looking at structuralism that is invigorating rather than paralyzing.

Assume that human action, the form of protest or organizational style, has no significant impact on whether a movement will succeed. To recap, all that matters is that a contesting group exists prior to, and continues protesting during, a world-historic crisis. If these two simple conditions are met, there is a 4 percent probability that the contesting group will be successful. To simplify matters, let's say that a world-historic crisis is indicated by a Food Price Index above 210. Let's go further and propose that the outcome of the revolution is not up to human will, and therefore total inaction when the Food Price Index exceeds 210 will have the same chances of hastening a revolutionary victory as action. Now what do you do to change the world? How do you act? A few people may choose to do nothing, twiddle their thumbs and just wait for the revolution to happen. The German philosopher Friedrich Nietzsche, however, once observed that a person would rather will something than nothing, and I suspect the majority would still choose to act.[92] And if choosing a tactic based on effectiveness is not possible, because all forms of protest are equally effective in a purely structuralist world view, the best course of action would be to choose the tactics with superior secondary benefits. If protest can't hasten revolution, activists are free to protest in ways that bring happiness or vibrant community or beautiful art. Protest no longer needs to be a public declaration intended to sway authorities; instead, protesting becomes a way of expressing one's true self.

What do you do when organizing a global march, painting an urban mural or feeding hungry people during a world crisis have equal chances of sparking social change? You choose the action that speaks to you—the action most authentic to becoming yourself. In a way, this is exactly what we were all doing during Occupy Wall Street: the creativity of our actions—from consensus-based assemblies and livestreaming to emergent collective behaviours—was the essence of our protest. As long as we acted out of our inner selves, our every action was revolution making.

In a situation where inaction is equivalent to action when judged from the perspective of the probability of success, activists are free to invest any action with potency. Perhaps any collective action can achieve the transcendence of protest if exercised during a moment of world-historic crisis. This possibility gestures toward how new tactics come into being spontaneously. And it helps us understand anomalous protest tactics such as the Ghost Dance of 1890, a prophetic circle-dancing ritual performed by indigenous people in North America that originated in a bid to hasten the return of their sovereignty. The Ghost Dance was explicitly understood by its participants as a ritual with political consequences. The dance was effective enough to warrant being violently suppressed by the U.S. government. A rational voluntarist would be hard pressed to explain why dancing in a circle far away from cities would be a threat to a government. A structuralist activist, however, understands that a protest does not need to target authorities to be effective, it need only be recognized as protest at the right time.

Voluntarists and structuralists occupy the materialist spectrum of theories of revolution. Both maintain that revolution is a phenomenon that involves the interaction of natural and physical forces. Voluntarists and structuralists are often deeply influenced by post-Enlightenment political revolutions. Believers in materialist theories of revolution focus their efforts on replicating these nineteenth- and twentieth-century mass uprisings—urban, secular protests that overthrew kings, emperors and tsars. There is truth to materialism. Economic crisis clearly plays an important role in instigating social change. However, materialism is incomplete and unable to explain episodes of social change (such as the victory of Christianity that began in AD 312 with the conversion of Constantine at the Battle of Milvian Bridge) that do not conform to the urban, mass model and that involve forces that are spiritual rather than physical.

SUBJECTIVISM

The external world is a mirror of your interior world, says the subjectivist activist. If external reality appears dark, it is because your inner reality is dark. "The world we see merely reflects our own internal frame of reference—the dominant ideas, wishes, and emotions in our minds."[93] The real revolution takes place inside our minds because our thoughts influence how the world appears to us. "The way to change the nature of your experience is to change the nature of your thoughts," as the American spiritual teacher Marianne Williamson says.[94] True activism is an inner practice of liberation.

Subjectivism is the intersection of spirituality with the primacy of the internal world. Believers in this theory of revolution maintain that active contemplation and meditation (from an outside perspective this may look like passivity) is superior to physical action because our minds determine reality. Strict subjectivist activists argue, therefore, that the most effective way to change the world is to change our perspective. Or as one mystical text explains it, "There is no point in lamenting the world. There is no point in trying to change the world. It is incapable of change because it is merely an effect. But there is indeed a point in changing your thoughts about the world. Here you are changing the cause. The effect will change automatically."[95]

Similarly, the great Sufi spiritual master Rumi suggests that an enlightened person can stroll through infernal hell and see rose gardens upon rose gardens.[96] The implication is that the world is a projection of our mood. Inner reality determines the external reality. Therefore, if your external reality is apocalyptic, meditation is the solution. The subjectivist position requires a reversal of values: from a concern with the wars of the world to the campaigns of the soul. "The wars of mankind are like children's fights—all meaningless, pithless, and contemptible. All their fights are fought with wooden swords, all their purposes are centred in futility," writes Rumi.[97] Revolution transcends into a state of mind.

Secular political scientists have also hypothesized subjectivism. This notion often takes the form of a weak subjectivism, or a voluntarist subjectivism where changing the inner world is a necessary (but not sufficient) condition for revolution. Unlike strict subjectivists who believe that revolution is accomplished by perceiving the world differently, voluntarist subjectivists privilege the inner shift as a first step toward external action. James C. Davies writes, for instance, that "political stability and instability are ultimately dependent on a state of mind, a mood, in a society."[98] Once the mood shifts, a revolution is possible. Subjectivism highlights the primacy of the individual's picture of reality.

Genuine revolution involves protest behaviours that are unusual and abnormal from the perspective of the status quo. These new behaviours are socially coded as protest because they are the public manifestation of a discordant inner reality within the people. Demonstrations are proof that large numbers of society have undergone an inner shift in perspective and are perceiving the world differently. As if spontaneously, the old world is forced to defend itself against a new conception, a new world view. Ralph Waldo Emerson explains it this way: "every revolution was first a thought in one man's mind."[99] Social revolutionary moments arise out of a sense of collective calm in the midst of a revealed truth. The people lose their fear, and the impossible becomes possible. When activists are attuned to emotional contagion, we are conscious to emit a sense of limitless possibility, eternal love and fearlessness. "As a man thinketh, so does he perceive. Therefore, seek not to change the world, but choose to change your mind about the world."[100]

The subjectivist activist sees social networks as channels of emotional contagion. Words, images and memes are the vectors by which infectious emotions spread through the network. The primary work is to produce and transmit emotions that lead the people toward an inner conversion and a collective epiphany.

THEURGISM

The classification of general theories of revolution reveals a lacuna. Theurgy, the fourth quadrant, the position that revolution is an objective supernatural phenomenon, has been disavowed by nearly all revolutionary theory. The theurgist school is esoteric. Despite the neopagan resurgence spearheaded by the theurgist activist Starhawk during and after the antiglobalization movement, most activists continue to deny theurgy exists at all. It is not easily spoken of, and our primary sources are mystical texts by Hermes Trismegistus, Rumi and others whose concern was spiritual rather than political. However, as Starhawk points out, "The tools of magic—the understanding of energy and the power and use of symbols, the awareness of group consciousness and of ways in which to shift and shape it—are also the tools of political and social change."[101]

From a secular perspective, Lyford Edwards, writing in 1927, came close to a negative definition of theurgy:

> The apparatus for measuring social movements is in a very primitive state of development. . . . All that can be done at present is to assume that a revolutionary process exists and that

> it is susceptible to measurement when—if ever—social science possesses tools of sufficient accuracy to do the work. Even this is a hypothesis. But it is a hypothesis which is necessary to make unless revolution is to be thought of as a phenomenon outside the natural order. Unless revolution is supernatural, it must be assumed to be explicable, measurable, and predictable—at least in theory.[102]

I invert Edwards. I actively entertain the possibility that revolution may indeed be a supernatural phenomenon and therefore inexplicable, immeasurable, unpredictable and potentially outside the natural order. Leaving open the possibility that revolutions may be a supernatural (or divine) process allows us to find the elements of truth within theurgism and unblind ourselves to approaches to social change that reigned in previous historical periods.

Theurgy is a "merger of the spiritual with the terrestrial."[103] The word "theurgy" comes from the ancient Greek for "sorcery" and literally means "god work." Theurgists believe divine forces can be made to intervene in the world. Although this is the rarest form of activism today, there were times when theurgy—particularly in the form of millenarian movements—was common.

Subjectivism is a step toward theurgism. The distinction between subjectivism and theurgism is subtle. Subjectivist activists accept that a limited degree of non-material forces may play a role in revolution. They limit that role to our subjectivity. Strict subjectivists hypothesize a direct connection between altering our inner world and changing how external reality manifests for us. These activists emphasize personal spirituality, the power of positive thinking, meditation and inner transformation. For a subjectivist, however, changing our inner reality does not influence the external reality of others. From this perspective, revolution is an inner, individualized process. Ultimately, each person is responsible for her or his liberation because reality is determined by the one perceiving it. Unlike subjectivists, theurgists maintain that revolution is an external process that is not confined to our minds. Subjectivists see revolution as a purely inner phenomenon that changes the way we perceive the world, but theurgists emphasize the power of God, or divine forces, to directly intervene in external reality. Whereas subjectivists change the world by altering how they experience it, theurgists believe divine forces change the objective external world for everyone and not just the person who has shifted perspective. The connection between inner and outer reality is, for a theurgist, not all in your head. Good news if you've ever prayed for a revolution: theurgy suggests that prayer, ritual and faith (behaviours that invite divine intercession) are the most effective forms of revolutionary activism.

Theurgists and structuralists agree that revolution is an objective process; however, these two approaches differ on what kinds of immaterial and invisible forces exist. For structuralists, human destiny is determined by machinic material forces—the economy, the unemployment rate, the happiness index, and so on. For theurgists, on the contrary, history is influenced by divine, non-human, and non-material forces. As the sociologist Yonina Talmon puts it, "initiative and actual power to bring about change rest with divine powers."[104] Theurgy requires a belief that these divine forces exist. Many

Western activists are not willing to make this leap of faith and therefore reject theurgism entirely. Materialism has secularized protest theory and given us structuralism. But what if the forces controlling political revolutions are otherworldly, supernatural or spiritual? If you believe it is possible that God, or spirit, intercedes in history, you may be a theurgist.

The secularization of revolutionary theory has erased the people's knowledge of theurgy. The early twenty-first century remains hostile to the suggestion that temporal power can be defeated by supernatural forces. Meanwhile, theurgist activists practicing the esoteric art keep it secret, making it difficult to find contemporary examples. One of the few modern cases of theurgy is from 1993, when practitioners of Transcendental Meditation claimed to alter social reality through spiritual activism: their tactic of collective meditation is said to have lowered the crime rate in Washington, DC, by 23 percent over an eight-week period.

But perhaps the best example of theurgy is from ancient sources. The historian Cassius Dio records a miracle from AD 174, the eighth year of a war between the stoic emperor Marcus Aurelius and the tribes of the Danube.[105] Dio writes that during the battle, the Twelfth Legion of Rome—known as the Fulminata, or the Thunderstruck—was trapped by the Quadi tribe. It seemed that all was lost when suddenly miraculous relief came from a rainstorm conjured by a theurgist named Ioulianos. Dio writes, "Ioulianos, Chaldaean and philosopher, father of the Ioulianos called *theorgos* [who] wrote works on theurgy, ritual and verse oracles, as well as many . . . other secret books on knowledge of this sort. . . . They say that once, when the Romans were exhausted by thirst, [Ioulianos] made the dark clouds come together all at once and send forth a furious thunderstorm with continuous thunder and lightning, and that Ioulianos accomplished this by some kind of wisdom."[106] Scientists and rationalists and materialists (i.e., most contemporary activists) will refuse to believe that Ioulianos's esoteric magic caused the rain. They will say that it was chance or random luck. However, any unified theory of revolution that does not include the possibility of miraculous divine intercession is incomplete and insufficient to the great task of conjuring global revolution. Secular ultramoderns disregard theurgy out of an ideological bias that privileges materialist secularism. For most of human history, and therefore potentially in the future as well, the people relied on the gods to bring justice to the world. By detaching from your historical moment, new forms of revolutionary protest become available.

St. Paul the Apostle, originally Saul of Tarsus, is an example of a theurgist activist. Saul was a brilliant Jewish Pharisee who aided in the persecution of the early Christians. Around AD 33, Saul had an epiphany on the road to Damascus. He had a vision of Jesus and was struck blind for days. He was healed by a Christian who claimed Jesus had instructed him in a dream to find Saul. Soon afterwards Saul experienced a spiritual awakening, converted to Christianity and became Paul. Protected by his Roman citizenship, a privilege gained at birth and not possessed by other early Christian leaders, Paul became the social movement's greatest theologian, establishing numerous churches and spreading the new religion to non-Jews for the first time. In his letters to the early Christian community, Paul explains the principles of his activism: "For though we live in the world we are not carrying on a worldly war, for the weapons of our warfare are not worldly but have divine power to destroy strongholds" (2 Corinthians 10:4). Paul's faith in divine power goes beyond subjectivism. For Paul, this divine power manifests in reality: it has the power to take down an empire. Paul faced down adversity by distinguishing between temporal (worldly) and divine (supernatural) power. "I am content then with weaknesses, insults, hardships, persecutions, and calamities; for when I am weak, then I am strong," he writes (12:10). As a member of a clandestine and persecuted religion, he was weak. But as a disseminator of the social movement backed by divine power, he was strong. Paul's religion now lives forever.

The clearest articulation of a pre-Christian theory of theurgy comes to us from the Hermes Trismegistus dialogue known as the *Asclepius*. The dialogue is remarkable because it contains an explication of how humans make gods and how these created gods influence the world. "Our ancestors once erred gravely on the theory of divinity; they were unbelieving and inattentive to worship and reverence for god," says Hermes. He continues: "But then they discovered the art of making gods." At the heart of Hermes' theurgy is the belief that the gods respond to human reverence: "heaven and heavenly beings take delight in wonderment, worship, praise and service from humans." Hermes distinguished between heavenly gods and human-made gods. The latter kind of god has the power to intervene in the world. Hermes says, "heavenly gods inhabit heaven's heights, each one heading up the order assigned to him and watching over it. But here below our gods render aid to humans as if through loving kinship, looking after some things individually, foretelling some things through lots and divination, and planning ahead to give help by other means, each in his own way."[107] Theurgy, therefore, becomes a process of using reverence of the gods to invite their help in changing political reality.

The key point, and what distinguishes a theurgist from all other activists, is the belief that supernatural forces "render aid to humans." The purpose of theurgist activism is to urge these forces to intervene in politics. As we are dealing with supernatural forces, this intervention could take innumerable forms: freak weather that disrupts an election, a dream that changes the mind of a ruler, a fluke that gives a social movement global prominence. A theurgist may protest through prayer, ritual or meditation, but the goal is the same: to alter external reality through the aid of supernatural forces.

Theurgists and voluntarists share a faith in the efficacy of protest rituals to create social change. For voluntarists, these rituals are a repertoire of protest tactics believed to have power because they express the collective will of the people or influence material reality through direct action. Theurgists, on the other hand, downplay the importance of the human will and instead focus on behaviours believed to manifest divine power. Voluntarists see revolution as the intersection of humanity with natural forces; theurgists see the interaction between the non-human with spiritual forces.

Writing during the peak of the antiglobalization movement in the early 2000s, Starhawk forcefully justifies why it is necessary to introduce ritual, magic and spirituality into social activism: "a part of our humanity needs symbols and myth and mystery, yearns for a connection to something broader and deeper than our surface life . . . We ignore [this need] at our peril, for if a movement of liberation does not address the spiritual part of us, then movements of repression will claim that terrain as their own."[108]

ASCENSION OF AN ACTIVIST

The four theories of revolution represent stages in the development of an activist. Progression through each stage instigates a deeper understanding of the complexity of revolution. The end result is a unified theory.

Most protesters begin in an unconscious voluntarism that acts as if any disruptive action combined with passion will create change. This is the first stage of activism. Here the rebel is akin to the child who throws temper tantrums in a bid to pressure adults. When these public paroxysms do not achieve results, the unconscious voluntarist blames his failure on the tactics used, without questioning the faith in physical action. Moving from unconscious to conscious voluntarism, the activist becomes self-aware and intentionally adopts a repertoire of tactics based on a theory of change. For the first time, the rebel is able to articulate a reason why her behaviours, such as marching with signs, will create socio-political transformation. When these tactics fail, the protester explores new techniques. If repeated failure does not lead the rebel to question voluntarism, it is possible to occupy this phase indefinitely.

The next level of development occurs when the voluntarist's tactics appear to succeed in creating a revolutionary moment. This is the first proof that the activist's tactics and underlying theory of change were accurate. Something profound happens at this moment of success. When the outbreak of the revolution seems to validate voluntarism, the historical moment passes and the uprising vaporizes despite the repetition of previously effective tactics. The self-aware activist understands for the first time that revolution involves forces outside of human control. Structuralism is born from the understanding that protest must come at the opportune time to spark a revolution. The second stage of the development of the activist occurs when the rebel develops a theory of change that accounts for the material, economic or social factors constituting an advantageous moment for protest. Now the rebel combines tactics with a sense of timing.

Structuralism leads to subjectivism when the interval between world-historic crisis moments stretches into years or decades. In this third stage, instead of succumbing to discouragement or futile action, the rebel turns inward. Convinced that protesting is ineffective when the time is not ripe for change, the wise activist embarks on the journey of inner liberation. By shifting her perception of the world, the rebel casts off the negativity that has dominated her practice. Meditation leads to a purification of the spirit in preparation for an epiphany. The activist experiences the capacity of her mind to alter reality.

In the final stage of the ascension, the activist transcends the limitations of subjectivism and expands her spiritual practice outward. This transition may be triggered by a longing for a political miracle that is experienced externally, not just internally. The activist understands that divine power renders all things possible. Here is how one spiritual text explains the power of the miracle: "There is no order of difficulty in miracles. One is not 'harder' or 'bigger' than another. They are all the same."[109] Theurgy frees the rebel to campaign nonlinearly, to disobey natural laws and to create revolutions that hinge on a miraculous intervention.

The ascension of the activist is symbolized by the Zen circle, or *ensō*, that is painted with a single, effortless brushstroke. Drawing the ensō is a meditative artistic practice. The circle represents unity and its depiction reveals the physical, mental and spiritual state of the artist at the moment of creation. As one contemporary master of the ensō explains, "One's character and spirit is reflected in the circle."[110] The activist's moral character and spiritual development are reflected in her approach to revolution. Both the ensō and revolution are always unique and can never be created the same way twice. The ensō is typically painted with a break in the circle to remind us that all creation is imperfect, and this is also true of revolutions and movements. Similarly, just as the ensō is circular, so too is the activist's journey through the four theories of revolution. Once she has reached an understanding of theurgism, the activist returns to voluntarism with a refreshed repertoire of tactics and the process begins again.

The activist who is able to simultaneously embrace all four theories of revolution has reached the highest level. It is crucial to remember that a unified theory is not an eternal theory. The activist must continually adapt by pursuing a fourfold path that embraces voluntarism, structuralism, subjectivism and theurgism to varying degrees. The challenge is to determine the appropriate unification of these four theories that will result in a revolution. At some times in history, the correct path may be to combine each approach equally. At other times, it may be proper to emphasize theurgy at a higher ratio than the other three. At this moment in history, when the status quo has tremendous temporal power and voluntarism appears exhausted, I believe a greater emphasis on subjectivism and theurgism will yield the highest results.

SUBJECTIVISM
(subjective-spiritual)

- Change your inner reality to change your external reality.
- Revolutions are a shift in mood, and protests are the visible manifestation of this inner transformation.
- Social networks are vectors of emotional contagion.
- The next revolutionary movement will be triggered by an epiphany that spreads throughout the world.

THEURGISM
(objective-spiritual)

- Revolution requires divine intervention: only God can save us now.
- The esoteric branch of activism.
- Magic, ritual and prayer influence external reality.
- Miracles like freak weather at an opportune moment, a life-changing dream experienced by a powerful ruler, or a fluke that catapults a movement to prominence are examples of how supernatural forces intervene in the world.

VOLUNTARISM
(subjective-material)

- Human actions make revolutions.
- The dominant exoteric branch of activism.
- Often starts with statements like, "If only everyone would do _____ at the same time . . ."
- Adopt tactics designed to be easily replicated and modified by other protesters.

STRUCTURALISM
(objective-material)

- Forces and structures outside of human control cause revolutions.
- Uses the Food Price Index to predict uprisings.
- Protest prior to, and during, a world historic crisis for a 4 percent chance of success.
- The specific tactics used do not matter. Protest in a way that expresses your true self or has the best secondary benefits.

PART TWO

YESTERDAY

We have it in our power
to begin the world over again.

THOMAS PAINE,
AMERICAN REVOLUTIONARY, 1776

As far as the final result is concerned it does not matter whether one movement or another is temporarily defeated. What is decisive is the determination to struggle which is maturing daily, the awareness of the need for revolutionary change and the certainty of its possibility.

CHE GUEVARA, 1967

8.

THE RECENT PAST OF PROTEST

Wake up and prepare yourself! You are a partisan in the Revolution: a war that has been raging since the people first demanded democracy over 121 generations ago. The earliest records of our rebellion are 3,646 years old and document when protesters toppled a pharaoh during the Middle Kingdom of ancient Egypt. In an ancient papyrus known as *The Dialogue of Ipuwer and the Lord of All*, written between 1980 BC and 1630 BC, an eponymous spectator records one of our first successful revolutions: "O, yet the rich are in lamentation, the poor are in joy; every town says, 'Let's drive out the strong among us!' For look, things have been done which have not been done before . . . the removal of the king by wretches. For look, it has come to rebellion."[111]

When our revolution first started, a cornucopia of civilizations reigned, each with its own colourful set of beliefs, languages, semiotics, religions and fighting methods. Many societies were matriarchal. Some were egalitarian. The greatest cities of the ancient world (Luxor, Athens, Alexandria, Rome . . .) were minuscule compared with the smallest of today's megalopolises. If the people found the local situation intolerable, they could act locally to rectify the problem. One telling example of how power functioned before the consolidation of peoples comes to us from a nomadic tribe in Africa, where the chief's power was so precarious that if he ruled with too heavy a hand, his people would desert him in the night. The situation has changed. With the consolidation of power into kingdoms and then nation-states and now into the immaterial financial flows of global corporate-capitalism, humans are becoming more culturally alike each generation. The oppressor is no longer local or localizable. The tyrant is increasingly a flow of capital and not a human person. The growing cultural sameness of humanity aids the transmission of our insurrection. Although it may seem that power keeps increasing despite protest, there are signs that a mighty reversal is coming. Everyday people have the necessary ingredients for the coming transformation of society: the labour, creativity and spirit of humanity.

The battleground of our revolution is a world composed of seven billion humans connected by air travel, a network of fibre-optic undersea cables and orbiting satellites. Fear of total surveillance and invasions of privacy is growing. Still, technologically adept activists can find ways to communicate freely with one another from every place on Earth.

Protest is politics by other means, to paraphrase the Prussian military theorist Carl von Clausewitz's famous definition of war. Protest is a form of warfare to the extent that activists set out to achieve strategic political goals using unconventional methods. Social movements are non-violent armies whose protests have political consequences. As in war, activism does not always obey the law; revolutionary activism seeks to inaugurate a new legal regime. Gandhi was no less a warrior than Napoleon. Each wrought major geopolitical shifts in his lifetime using previously unknown techniques of warfare. Gandhi demonstrated that non-violence can be highly effective when confronting a foreign colonial state. He showed that *satyagrahis*, a trained army of non-violent warriors, confronting a power with dramatic military superiority could engender the world's sympathy. Despite the successes of Martin Luther King Jr.'s campaign to break America's segregated South, subsequent struggles have shown us that 1960s-era non-violence alone is not enough and that corporatist democracies are becoming insidiously adept at defusing public protest without responding to demands democratically.

The people are locked in a tactical arms race with power, and each advance in protest is met with a counter-advance in repression. Activists surmount this danger by working to develop tactical innovations that emerge and grow exponentially so that our enemy's defences are overwhelmed before they can mobilize for the counterattack.

Winning the people's war will require more than just a unified theory of revolution. It will also need an understanding of the tactics that have defined the history of protest.

PEOPLE'S PARTY

Social movements in the twenty-first century are growing in complexity and pivoting away from "protest, protest, protest" and toward translating the people's anger into a cohesive force capable of winning elections, drafting laws and running governments. The rise of Syriza in Greece, the Five Star Movement in Italy and Podemos in Spain reveals a trend toward Internet-enabled people's parties that ascend at dazzling speed.

First came Syriza, a political party formed in 2004 from coalition of radical left forces in Greece. In 2009 a debt crisis began to impact Greece, and by 2015 Syriza had eclipsed all other political parties: the party's chairman was elected prime minister of Greece and Syriza won 2.2 million votes (36 percent of votes cast). Syriza's rise took eleven years. Then came the Five Star Movement in Italy. In 2008, the Italian celebrity and former comedian Beppe Grillo launched the movement with a blog decrying the presence of criminals in parliament. Five years later, the Five Star Movement was the second-largest political party in Italy with 8.6 million votes (25.6 percent). These two parties showed impressive results, until January 16, 2014, when a new political party—Podemos (We Can)—was born in Spain. Within just twenty days, Podemos registered 100,000 members, transforming the upstart movement into the nation's third-largest political party. By May 2015 Podemos's official membership had swelled to 370,000. It took eleven years for Syriza to become the largest party in Greece, five years for the Five Star Movement to become the second largest in Italy, and three weeks for Podemos to rank third in Spain. Of course, past performance does not guarantee future success. No one can say for certain whether these specific parties will exist in a decade. Already Syriza is showing signs of splintering and morphing. Still, watching the sudden growth of hybrid movement-parties, activists are rightly wondering how long will it take for a new people's party to sweep Canada, Brazil, the United States or the United Kingdom.

I remember the first conversation I had with Gianroberto Casaleggio, the soft-spoken co-founder of the Internet-enabled populist Five Star Movement. My wife, Chiara, and I met with Gianroberto at the office of Casaleggio Associati in Milan, the Internet strategy consulting firm that helped Beppe Grillo launch the Five Star Movement. Casaleggio Associati is to the Five Star Movement as *Adbusters* was to Occupy Wall Street, with one crucial difference: Beppe and Gianroberto maintain strict control over the meaning of the movement, whereas *Adbusters* let go. From the beginning, the goals of the Five Star Movement were clearly defined. Each star represents a concrete demand: publicly owned water, sustainable transportation, sustainable development, free and open Internet access, environmentalism. The Occupy movement, on the other hand, started with the demand of getting money out of politics but quickly devolved into so many generalized critiques that it ultimately appeared to be without concrete demands. Occupy was never able to clearly define the movement's mission in the eyes of the media. The consensus-based decision-making process that underpinned Occupy was not capable of making complex policy decisions. And while Occupy Wall Street dissipated in less than a year, the Five Star Movement has kept going through its ups and downs.

At one significant moment during our conversation, Gianroberto asked me how many trusted activists Occupy could count on nationwide. I explained that at that point, in October 2013, our movement had been in defeat for eighteen months and few authentic, trustworthy voices were left. Moreover, because anyone could claim to be an Occupier, and many dark forces did so in order to discredit the larger movement, there was no way for anyone to know definitively how many genuine Occupiers actually remained. Gianroberto then told Chiara and me the precise number of current Five Star Movement members and estimated their year-end target. Each member had been vetted by the movement. His point was clear: social movements need a structure that gives credibility and permanence.

The Five Star Movement is important in the history of protest for blending horizontalism with verticalism: a hybridization of populist direct democracy with closed membership. Perhaps because Five Star activists must provide documentation of their real-world identities, the movement attracts educated, professional and committed participants who engage in the movement's online elections and public events. To become an elected representative of the Five Star Movement, activists attend rallies, engage with the online community and then nominate themselves for specific positions by posting a YouTube video. Internal elections are held using a custom-built software platform, and the movement moves forward with confidence.

Occupy Wall Street comprised the people who responded to the call. Ultimately, however, uncritical openness was Occupy's downfall: the general assemblies were paralyzed by the inability to distinguish between true and false. Participants who had been with Occupy for a day were given a say equal to that of committed activists who had founded the first encampments. In our fully horizontal social movement, no one had the authority to determine who ought to be expelled for being disruptive. Occupy faced adversaries inside and outside. Half wanted to destroy the movement, and the other half wanted to control it. Occupy never developed a way to vet participants. Anyone (worthy or unworthy) could claim to be an equal spokesperson of the movement. Thus the movement faced both police infiltrators who disrupted our assemblies with belligerence and the 99% Spring, an initiative financed by the progressive Left, that mimicked Occupy in a successful bid to dissipate the movement's revolutionary momentum into a re-election campaign for President Obama.

The Five Star Movement often refuses the label of a political party. I call it a hybrid movement-party, or a social movement that specializes in training its members to protest using social rituals typically associated with political parties: collecting signatures, attending rallies, debating legislation, running for office and voting. The movement differs from traditional political parties in its embrace of disintermediation (there is no local party boss; everyone in the movement is an equal part of the movement), direct democracy (the movement decides on all things related to the party), a bottom-up structure (every candidate comes from within the grassroots of the movement), no money (the movement rejects state election funds and famously does not have a treasurer) and the Internet (important decisions are made exclusively online). This unique formula has proven to be highly efficient. In the 2013 general election in Italy, for example, the movement raised 774,208 euro from people online and spent only 348,506 euro on the party's campaigning. The surplus was donated to a school hit by an earthquake. The movement achieved 8,784,499 votes, which means it spent only 0.04 euro per vote.[112] To put this in perspective, President Obama's campaign spent $10.37 per vote in the 2012 election.[113]

A couple of months after meeting with Gianroberto Casaleggio, I was invited to give a speech at the Five Star Movement's V3Day rally in Genoa. Forty thousand activists gathered in Victory Square, and despite the freezing cold day in December, the passion of the Five Star Movement was palpable.[114] The V3Day rally was the launch of the movement's effort to win seats in the upcoming European Parliament election. It worked. A few weeks later, I received an email from an activist who had gone to Victory Square and was now an elected representative of the Five Star Movement in the European Parliament.

In 2015 the Five Star Movement unveiled Rousseau, a new software platform for making decisions within the movement. Rousseau was designed to bring the movement's decision-making process closer to true participatory Internet-based democracy. The new wave of people's parties are supported by their faith that participation of all citizens in the legislative process will trigger a revolution. Now it is just a question of how to achieve that participation through the transformation of protest movements into party movements.

It is too early to say which of these new parties will be long-lasting. Nonetheless, it is absolutely clear that hybrid movement-parties are shifting the destiny of protest. And it won't stop with single-country parties. The true realization of the merger between social movements and political parties will be a global force capable of winning elections in multiple countries in order to carry out a unified geopolitical agenda. Imagine, for example, how history would have gone differently if Syriza had won elections in Greece and Germany and the party in Athens had carried out debt austerity negotiations with its counterpart in Berlin.

Strategic Insight

A new breed of hybrid electoral social movements can swiftly eclipse traditional political parties. This change in how we view social movements is the most practical way for the people to restore democracy, but it comes with great difficulties. Meteoric growth often leads to exponential decline once a movement has reached the boundaries of the nation. The next generation of hybrid movement-parties must continue to expand across borders in order to win elections in multiple countries and implement a unified political program. Making complex decisions within a planetary social movement will require developing techniques of collective thinking that do not currently exist.

DEBT

On the first anniversary of Occupy Wall Street's eviction from Zuccotti Park, at a time when the movement had failed to secure a new encampment in New York City and was clearly in decline worldwide, a few founders of the movement turned their energy and skills toward launching the Rolling Jubilee, an audacious new tactic of financial activism. The basic idea behind the Rolling Jubilee was to exploit a marketplace that few people know exists: a place where debt collectors buy all kinds of debt from student loans to unpaid medical bills, credit cards and car loans at a steep discount in the hope of making a profit by collecting the full value. The tactic of the Rolling Jubilee was simple and elegant: let's buy debt from these marketplaces and then forgive it.

One reason for the success of the Rolling Jubilee is that like Occupy Wall Street, it had an unknown origin—very few knew whose idea it was. Buying and abolishing debt as an activist tactic seemed like an innovative approach that made sense and came at a moment when the movement needed to grasp something concrete. Only years later did I publicly disclose my role in originating the Rolling Jubilee's debt-forgiveness tactic.

The creative spark that led to the Rolling Jubilee began in 2007 in a small business start-up course offered by my local state-funded Small Business Development Center in Binghamton, New York. At the time, I was working on theorizing solutions to the problem of making activism financially sustainable. One idea I was researching was the possibility of funding revolutionary cooperative businesses using micro-loans from activists around the world. After writing an article proposing the micro-loan idea for *Adbusters* number 75, the January/February 2008 issue and my first publication in the magazine, I moved on to thinking about the activist potential of debt. I was inspired by Enric Duran, a Spanish activist who took out 500,000 euro worth of loans from banks, gave the money to social movements and then published 200,000 copies of an activist newspaper denouncing the financial system. Duran, whose *nom de guerre* is Robin Banks, publicly refused to pay back the loans and issued a call to activists: "Banks need to grant loans because that is the main way for them to get profits. It is a wheel that will not stop until the system comes to a standstill. As individuals, instead of helping the wheel to roll by asking for loans we have the opportunity and responsibility of making things difficult for this system."[115] Enric has since lived a clandestine life, dodging arrest warrants, while continuing to innovate new forms of financial activism involving cryptocurrencies.[116]

Many months after Duran's daring action, while researching the debt system in America, I stumbled across a website that was promoting debt collection as a way to make money. I learned that there was a market where unpaid debts are sold at a discount—pennies on the dollar—to debt collectors (a largely unregulated business) who then profit by recouping the full value of the debt. In a flash, I saw the campaign potential.

In February 2009, I wrote an article for the *Adbusters* blog proposing the debt forgiveness tactic.[117] I explained that unpaid debt (including credit card, student loan, medical, car and jewellery debt) is generally written off as a business loss and sold to third-party collection agencies for a fraction of the original debt amount. These third-party collection agencies then either try to profit by collecting the full value of the debt or by reselling it to another collection agency. When a debt has been sold multiple times, it is worth considerably less because the likelihood of recovering the full amount is slim. To prove that activists could easily acquire large amounts of debt, I conducted feasibility testing. I created an account at an online marketplace that was selling debt and saw that it would cost a measly $110 to acquire $2,528 worth of credit card debt owed by someone in Klawock, Alaska. The website also had medical debt and auto loans for sale. I called the marketplace and spoke on the phone with a debt seller. I hit a roadblock, however, when I tried to buy debt: the marketplace would sell only to a lawyer or a member of one of the professional debt-buying associations. It cost several hundred dollars to join a debt-buying association and I didn't know any lawyers. The tactic had potential, and I spread the word, but it floundered for two years. But I never gave up on the idea and kept telling allies and activists about the proposed tactic.

A lucky break happened less than a month before Occupy when I wrote to David Graeber, the anarchist and anthropologist whose book *Debt: The First Five Thousand Years* was gaining notoriety. Graeber and I had been in communication because I'd recruited him to write for *Adbusters* and he was helping to organize Occupy in New York City. On August 25, 2011, I explained to David, "The basic idea is to create an organization that acts as a 'third party debt collector' and buys debt and then forgives it. . . . There are online marketplaces where all kinds of debt (including medical debt) can be bought for pennies on the dollar." David wrote back quickly, praised the idea as "quite remarkable" and said he'd spread the word. He did as promised and around the time of the Brooklyn Bridge mass arrest, I received an email from Thomas Gokey, an artist and debt activist: "I heard about an idea that you had to start a debt collection agency that buys defaulted loans from banks for pennies on the dollar and then forgives them. This sounds like an excellent idea and I'd like to help in any way I can." When Thomas and I spoke on the phone, I explained that the greatest hurdle was finding a lawyer who would help us buy the debt from the marketplace. He said he'd work on the challenge. A few days later, Thomas told me that he'd posted an advertisement on the Internet seeking lawyers looking to do some activist work on abolishing debt. He'd received several positive inquiries. I was impressed with his elegant solution. As Occupy took over my attention, I decided to give the debt forgiveness tactic to Thomas. (Later, when Thomas asked me how I'd like to be credited in an upcoming article in the *New York Times* about the Rolling Jubilee, I replied, "I'd like to be credited with coming up with the initial idea in a blog post for *Adbusters*, but I also want it to be clear that you made it come alive.") I'd originally called the debt forgiveness tactic the Blackspot Debt Collection Agency and then I suggested Occupy Debt. Thomas initially renamed it Debt Fairy. A year later, Thomas had teamed up with David Graeber, Astra Taylor and others at Strike Debt, a splinter group of Occupy Wall Street, who rebranded my tactical innovation as the Rolling Jubilee.

To fund their first debt purchase, the Rolling Jubilee organized a celebrity telethon on the anniversary of Occupy's loss of Zuccotti. Their goal was to raise $50,000, the amount needed to buy and forgive over $1,000,000 of unpaid medical debt. For three hours on November 15, 2012, the Occupy movement forgot about its eviction and regained a sense of magical possibility while participating in the celebrity-hosted telethon via livestream. Chiara and I watched the event in awe from Berkeley as the Rolling Jubilee raised more than $435,000. And within two years, Strike Debt's Rolling Jubilee had received $701,317 and used it to abolish an astonishing $14,734,569 worth of medical debt. Watching the telethon, I was overjoyed by their success.

The history of the Rolling Jubilee is important because of what it teaches activists about the interplay between the four theories of revolution. At its core, the debt forgiveness tactic is subjectivist. The purpose of the tactic is to change how people perceive debt. I wanted to trigger an awakening where the debt that weighs us down psychically suddenly feels light and worthless. Forgiving debt was a way to catalyze a mental shift. This change in perspective was accomplished by demonstrating that debt is actually worth a fraction of its face value, and that benevolent forces can acquire and abolish it.

The tactic also gives credence to structuralism: the Rolling Jubilee would not have happened without Occupy Wall Street. For two years, from February 2009 until Thomas Gokey came along in October 2011, I spread the tactic but it was not taken up. It was a good idea but it would not grow outside of my control. And if Occupy had not been evicted from Zuccotti and started to decline, I doubt that the Rolling Jubilee would have received the tremendous attention that it did in 2012, nor would so many talented activists have volunteered their time to help Strike Debt pull off the telethon. Occupiers latched on to the Rolling Jubilee because we needed to accomplish something positive and concrete.

At another level, the Rolling Jubilee was theurgist: the telethon created a space for a miracle to happen. And it did: half a million dollars was received in a single night.

From the voluntarist perspective, however, the debt forgiveness tactic was too unwieldy to be replicated. It required tremendous time, specialized knowledge and energy for the Rolling Jubilee to successfully pull off the tactic. It generated media attention, but in the end the tactic was abandoned. I suspect that the Rolling Jubilee played it too safe by abolishing medical debt—a form of debt everyone can condemn—while refusing to buy credit card debt. I suspect this was the advice of their lawyers. I wonder what would have happened if people's credit card bills had been wiped clean rather than their doctors' bills. Still, I have no doubt that campaign potential remains. I anticipate that an innovation of the debt forgiveness tactic will come along that transforms it, exceeding any of our expectations. I see a time when debt forgiveness enters the standard repertoire of social movements.

Strategic Insight

Tactical innovations can take years to go from theory to execution. Having a good idea isn't enough; new tactics also need the right historical moment. And oftentimes fresh tactics need to be given away in order to come to life. Debt forgiveness activism has not reached its full potential. I'm still dreaming of the next twist that will come from a surprising source and turn buying and abolishing debt into a vehicle for erasing trillions of dollars of debt.

OCCUPY

There are many ways to tell the story of Occupy Wall Street. Some writers have focused on the individuals involved, their personalities and quirks, and told the story from the personal angle through intimate portraits. Others have analyzed tweets, participant demographics and website analytics. Still others have interviewed dozens of anonymous participants and pulled together enough detail to take their readers back in time to the significant events that seemingly determined how the uprising would unfold. There are stories that are written by journalists for the public at large, and by academics for students of social change . . . and there is my story, which I write for the revolutionaries out there, in the hope of passing on some bit of wisdom about how the people provoked the storm, in the hope that it will happen again, once and for all.

The first lesson of Occupy is that the next great social movement is always invisible moments before it erupts. In the first few months of Occupy, from the point Kalle Lasn and I concocted the Occupy Wall Street meme in June 2011 until a few days before the Zuccotti encampment was founded on September 17, our movement was entirely ignored by the media: corporate and progressive alike either did not see us or found a reason to dismiss us. Just a couple of days before the founding of the encampment in New York City, I was told by one journalist at a leftist radio station in California that they were not going to cover Occupy Wall Street because the planned action was "too amorphous and unstructured." This turned out to be an accurate description of the Occupy uprising: a spiritual insurrection that went far because it violated widely held core assumptions about what the next global movement would look like.

Occupy Wall Street was the first practical demonstration of a new kind of Internet-enabled people's warfare in line with other military developments such as Greek hoplite warfare, Mao's theories of protracted guerrilla war, Gandhian satyagraha and the antiglobalization movement's lockdown tactics that paralyzed Seattle in 1999. Occupy demonstrated the effectiveness of using contagious social memes to disseminate a new tactic directly to the people.

Occupy may have been a constructive failure; however, the tactical innovation behind the surprising growth of the movement, meme warfare, was a success. From Kalle's mind and mine came the protest meme that spread to millions. Our meme brought income inequality into the spotlight and shifted the perspectives of countless people, even those who did not join our encampments. The movement's name embodied its tactic (assemble in financial districts), its means of replication and channel of communication (the original name of our movement was #OCCUPYWALLSTREET in order to alert people to communicate via a Twitter hashtag). Once Occupy Wall Street caught on in Lower Manhattan, the movement was in London, Los Angeles, Vancouver and a thousand other cities because the tactical formula was known everywhere simultaneously. Blockupy in Germany, whose name is a neologism for blockade and occupy, has continued to experiment with embedding the tactic within the meme. In the years and decades ahead, ever more powerful kinds of memes will be developed that make hashtags look like water pistols.

For a novel idea to spread from the bottom up and throughout the world it must capture the imagination of everyday individuals. Memes colonize minds by spreading sensations of liberation. Global movement growth happens when a meme catches on across demographics and is not merely confined to one social sector such as youth or ethnic minorities. Just as doctors fear the mutation of influenza viruses caused by cross-species infection, politicians must also rightly fear the social movement that unites previously distinct social segments.

Occupy was a success to the degree that it was truly an *event*, in the philosophical meaning of the word: a rupture moment whose origin exceeds an identifiable material or historical cause. Yes, the summer of 2011 was ripe for a range of sociological reasons—income disparity at peak levels, youth unemployment soaring globally, rising food prices, consumerism losing its cool. But from another perspective, the moment is always ripe, and has always been ripe, for the people to rise up and demand greater freedom. Calculative, scientific, sociological, historical and materialist explanations of why the European revolutions of 1848 kicked off or why the May 1968 uprising in Paris happened are interesting, but they are not the only truth and they do not answer all the questions.

The revolution starts when the people are no longer afraid. The fusion of the Tahrir Square Uprising with the *acampadas* of the *indignados*, democratic encampments that underpinned the movement in Spain, into a single powerful idea—"let's Occupy Wall Street"—was miraculous because it erased fear. In a flash, there was a certainty that this protest would be different: that it would not be symbolic. A spiritual confidence reigned. The people had toppled Mubarak and now they would topple Wall Street too. For a moment, we believed absolutely in our people power.

It was this momentary sense of innate power that gave us all the energy necessary to break out of our old protest habits. At *Adbusters*, we did not focus-group our ballerina-and-bull poster design or A/B-test our tactical briefings. We didn't buy ads to promote our action or hire celebrity spokespersons to endorse our protest. We didn't build a coalition. We rejected clicktivism. We didn't seek the approval of unions or big institutional activist groups. And so all the usual people who would otherwise rush in to co-opt or redirect the protest simply stayed away in the beginning. One founding Zuccotti explained to me that only true believers were present in the early planning meetings. The other forces that always seem to derail things—sectarians, *agents provocateurs*, corporatists and activists stuck in old habits—weren't there because they assumed the action would be a flop. The protests that trigger social movements always break out of the prevailing protest paradigm.

By the time the corporatists and the sectarians did show up—two weeks into the action when hundreds of non-violent protesters were arrested on the Brooklyn Bridge—they didn't have the social capital to block our momentum.

Adbusters let the movement take its own course and trusted that the ones who saw the potential of the meme should be the ones to carry out the action. Neither Kalle nor I went to Zuccotti. Instead, I remained in California and helped launch the first day of Occupy San Francisco and Occupy Berkeley. Once those encampments started, I stepped aside. In leaving the specifics up to activists on the ground, in refusing to make *Adbusters* and Occupy Wall Street synonymous, we left events up to the wild human spirit that has been struggling to be free for millennia. Our meme unlocked the creative spirit within humanity—the immaterial force that animates the social body.

Occupy kindled the people's passion because it gave us a reason and a no-nonsense way to fight back. It embodied both a visceral tactic—*Occupy!*—and a collective expression of the will to live the positive life we've imagined, a collective denouncement of democracies worldwide who had succumbed to a rotten class of financiers. Occupy spread because being part of the movement gave a sensation of fearlessness and the people believed our movement was worth the risk of arrest.

But the moment we tried too hard to hold on to the tactic of occupying physical space, Occupiers began to lose our grasp on the larger vision that was emerging: the leaderless world revolution to come.

Occupy was a fresh beginning for activism because it was a practical demonstration of the power of leaderlessness—and those moments are rare. Although we did not go far enough in 2011–2012 and we ultimately failed to build the structures that would have allowed our leaderless approach to take on the complex challenge of winning elections and governing cities, we discovered for ourselves that people's democracy—Internet-enabled participatory populism—is the way out of the political conundrum of the twentieth century. Egocentric, individualist politics were set aside for a new consensual leaderlessness that the world first saw glimmerings of during the antiglobalization movement. The model: many charismatic people; no Leader.

For decades, revolutionary political theory on the left and right has been at a dead end. With the near triumph and later total defeat of state Fascism in Italy, Germany, Japan and Spain, the right learned a lesson that would be repeated on the left with the collapse of state Communism—Lenin, Mao, Stalin, Ceauşescu, Kim Jong-il and so on. The story of the twentieth century was the mysterious obsession that developed among the people for a Leader. Across the political spectrum, the people wagered their aspirations on a single all-powerful living Father. We invested Him with omnipotence and prayed for benevolence. The result? Holocausts, famines, death camps on both sides. And the final proof humanity needed that absolute power corrupts (even the good) absolutely.

Seeing that we, the people, can never again place our faith in a single person's will, many activists also lost faith in the revolutionary project entirely. Following the defeat of the May 1968 insurrection that spread from Paris to the world, the postmodernist philosophers deconstructed the desire for grand humanist liberation narratives as a cognitive illusion, and we were carried along. Revolutionary theory stagnated until the foreshock of the antiglobalization movement in 1999 and the people's uprisings of 2011.

Given that authoritarian Communism or Fascism won't work—strong leaders always turn against the people they promise to represent—we cannot return to yesterday's solutions. So what do we do?

Without the people's assemblies of 2011, I do not think the world would have seen the solution.

Horizontalism

Leaderless revolution, so beautifully practiced in those first magical weeks by the Zuccottis, turns the memes into the leaders and unites the people behind a voluntarily shared vision. The danger of despotism dissolves, and when horizontalism is practiced properly, the best ideas float effortlessly to the top. At the same time, the natural autonomy of horizontalism, and its deep reliance on independent, small affinity groups of activists, encourages a constant drive to innovate. This self-overcoming is the engine of our velocity. It grants us the power to *wobble*, to swerve like a flock of birds and to act in ways that confound our enemy, as events quickly spiral toward the people's vision. We witnessed the unpredictability of Occupy when the movement veered dramatically with the rising influence of affinity groups in Oakland and along the West Coast. In moments when the horizontals of our movement are most in control, a feeling of political vertigo—a sense of being powerless as an individual or a founder or a leader to control the course of events—can emerge. Our tendency may be to seek comfort in retreating toward the familiar assurances of verticals and mouthpieces of the old world. But there is no way forward except through finding beauty in political contestation among equals because the alternative, while comforting, is no longer viable.

Vertical structures—the corporate model of a CEO sitting atop a pyramid of subordinates—are not fluid enough to adapt to the speed of our changing world. They stifle innovation because one individual's ego at the top matters more than the collective's interconnected will to flourish regardless of who came up with a good idea. One of David Graeber's most profound critiques of capitalism is that capitalism is always already a failure because it cannot achieve the great leaps that it promises. Graeber calls this the flying car paradox. Why is it that for several decades since the mid-twentieth century advanced countries have been promising flying cars in the near future? And yet, no flying cars. Or look at the numerous other promises about the future that have not been kept: a cure for cancer or human colonization of Mars or tractor beams. Graeber wonders, "Where are . . . all the other technological wonders any child growing up in the mid-to-late twentieth century assumed would exist by now?"[118] Graeber's point is that capitalism is incapable of delivering on these utopian promises not because they are impossible for humans to achieve but because *capitalism can't deliver them* without overturning its hierarchical essence. Corporate capitalism is incapable of fulfilling its own dreams, and as a result the nightmare grows.

There is a leadership crisis at the highest levels of civilization. And if a Great Leader were to ever arise, claiming to be a Leader who could solve climate change or end the global economic crisis, we know in advance that he would be a scourge upon us. To fill this power vacuum, we must offer a horizontal global political vision that is good, wholesome and just.

Unlike the twentieth-century anarchists who rallied under the International Workers of the World slogan "No Gods, No Masters," we are guided by the principle of "Yes Gods, No Masters." We seek unification—*mundialization*—of the world into a commonwealth of free, world cities. We are guided by a reverence for radical pluralism. The time of intolerant secularism is over. The future is with cosmopolitanism. In spreading across the world, Occupy demonstrated that the people are more united globally than we've ever been in the past. And that was the fundamental lesson of Occupy Wall Street: the 99 percent are on the same side.

Leaderlessness

Leaderlessness is not a perfect solution. It must be practiced properly to be effective. Inayat Khan, one of the first teachers of Sufism in the West, relates an anecdote that captures the true spirit of leaderlessness. A mendicant dervish was standing in the road when the king, preceded by his entourage, approached. Everyone else stepped aside, but the dervish remained standing in the street. First the pages, running before the procession, pushed the dervish and told him the king was approaching and that he must step aside. The dervish simply smiled and replied, "That is why." Next came the bodyguards, who jostled the dervish and demanded that he get out of the way. The dervish smiled and replied, "That is why," and remained standing in the street. Next came the courtiers who scowled at the dervish, pretended to ignore his presence and stood away from him. Still the dervish remained. Finally, the king arrived and, immediately noticing the dervish, greeted him first. The dervish smiled and said, "That is why he is what he is."

Explaining the moral of his fable, Khan writes that the interaction between the king and the dervish represents true democracy. The king treats the dervish as his equal while still recognizing their differences. True democracy, for Khan, is when a person thinks, as the king does, that "I am equal of any person in the world; there is no person *lower* than I." Notice that he doesn't say no one is above him. Authentic horizontalism is different from *vulgar horizontalism*, which refuses to acknowledge that anyone is higher than oneself and which pulls others down instead of ascending upwards. "If a person says, 'There is no person higher than I,' that is not democracy," writes Khan.[119] As Marianne Williamson correctly observes about our movement, "I noticed, among a few of the Occupiers I met, that their passion seemed to be less an enthusiasm for the rights of all people to participate in the engine of economic prosperity and more a knee-jerk criticism of anyone who does."[120] Horizontal leaderlessness does not mean refusing to accept that others may know more than we do about a particular topic or be more skilled than us or have experiences that we lack. On the contrary, Occupy thrived when it benefited from the specialist knowledge of its participants. The strength of true horizontalism comes from recognizing that our fundamental equality, our shared humanity, is derived from our diversity. In rejecting the assertion that there is anyone below us, we strive to become our highest and most beautiful selves—and we celebrate that some people have attained greater levels of wisdom and self-mastery. Ultimately, true horizontalism is the recognition that we are the ones we've been waiting for.

Strategic Insight

The best methods of protest are unrecognized because they defy our expectations of what a protest should look like. It is not a coincidence that relatively few people saw the potential of Occupy before the second week of the occupation. Occupy demonstrated the efficacy of deploying memes to spread a contagious social protest. At the same time, the movement highlighted the dangers of the Internet. In the early stages of a new movement, the Internet is crucial. However, over time the Internet becomes detrimental because protests start to look better online than in real life. By sharing beautiful photos of dismal events, people start to prefer the online experience to real-world participation. The result is that we become spectators of our own protests and momentum collapses. So the Internet is a double-edged sword: it is a weapon that is not fully under our control, and it is very difficult to wield effectively. When using social media, activists should follow three rules: "Never broadcast inaccurate news, never conceal a defeat, never exaggerate a victory."[121] Ultimately, Occupy Wall Street was defeated because the movement was synonymous with its tactic. Once occupying stopped working, Occupy stopped working. Social movements of the future must be able to adapt by switching tactics frequently.

GLOBAL MARCH

My roommate at Swarthmore College woke me up after the first hijacked plane struck the World Trade Center on 9/11, and I watched with others in my dormitory hall as the terrible drama unfolded on live television. I remember being both terribly frightened of further attacks and invigorated by the realization that this event was so tremendous that it would change the direction of world history. I felt as if anything was possible. I hoped 9/11 would catalyze a peaceful new world order, and I started to work fervently toward this goal even as I saw storm clouds of war gathering.

In a bid to stop the war, activists tested the theory that if the world were to march in unison with a single, unmistakable anti-war message, our leaders would be forced to listen.

On February 15, 2003, ten days after United States Secretary of State Colin Powell presented the case for pre-emptive war in Iraq in a speech to the UN Security Council, activists worldwide worked together to pull off the largest single day of synchronized global protest in human history. The original idea for "enormous anti-war demonstrations in every capital" was made by activists at the European Social Forum in Florence just two months earlier. The initial call rallied activists with a simple slogan that conveyed the underlying theory of social change: "Together we can stop this war!" In other words, a massive display of the world's public opinion could halt the war. Simultaneous protests were held in six hundred cities worldwide: 3 million people took to the streets in Rome, 1 million in London (the largest protest ever to hit the British capital), 1.3 million in Barcelona, another million in Baghdad, 200,000 in San Francisco, 200,000 in Damascus and 500,000 in Sydney and Melbourne. And 100,000 marched in Montreal, overcoming a wind chill that pushed temperatures below -30°C (-22°F). Every continent had an anti-war march on the same day.

I marched in New York City with 100,000 people, and I will never forget the sensation of that day when the world spoke in a unified multilingual voice: "No!" Everywhere, the people were on the same side: rich marched alongside poor, patriots with peaceniks, young with old. I was convinced that this day would stop the war, and I put my body on the line. When I joined others in blocking the street, sitting down to halt traffic, I was nearly trampled by a police horse. One hoof came down on the fabric of my pant leg, another hoof stepped inches from my head. I was somehow unharmed.

That night President Bush swaggered onto television and declared the protests meaningless. "You know, the size of protests is like deciding, well, I'm going to decide policy based upon a focus group," he said. He dismissed the people as a constituency that has opinions but no power. This was a decisive rebuff. Our governments stopped listening to public opinion and the pre-emptive war against Iraq began a month later.

The failure of the march was a defeat of democracy and a shattering attack on the activist assumption that public wishes manifested in global marches would be respected.

Bush's dismissal of the largest synchronized protest march in history was a traumatic blow to activism because it undermined our core strategic assumption that governments must obey the will of the many. Activists learned that saying no was not enough. We did not have a plan for what would happen if our elected representatives refused to obey our one demand. We went home that night glowing from the organizational feat of bringing millions of people into the streets, and after President Bush came on TV, we largely stayed home, defeated, until Occupy Wall Street.

Looking back, we can see that from the beginning the anti-war movement made two fundamental assumptions that proved to be mistaken. First, the movement largely took the position of trying to educate the public, on a rational level, against war. Activists operated on the basis that the public did not know war was destructive and negative. But of course nearly everyone already knew that war is evil. What they do not know, and what no one can know in advance of trying, is how to stop a war. That tactical uncertainty is what led to our second mistake. We trusted mass organizations that consciously repudiated the non-hierarchical style of the antiglobalization movement whose momentum was peaking in the months prior to the February 15 march. Large anti-war marches led by big non-profit coalitions promised activists the security of following a script that we'd all watched on television countless times in documentaries about the 1960s and '70s. We wrongly believed that repeating the march tactic could work again. And ultimately the movement was led astray by older activists who wallowed in a nostalgia for the anti-war movement of the Vietnam era and who wrongly based their strategy for a mass uprising on a military conscription they believed was imminent . . . but that never happened.

Like Occupy, the anti-war movement was a constructive failure. We had one demand and still could not stop the Iraq War. But in trying we invented a new tactic, a synchronized worldwide march, and tested a core hypothesis about social change.

Strategic Insight

No more marches. Orchestrating a synchronized global march with millions of people in the streets rallying behind one demand is an impressive logistical feat that attracts tremendous publicity, but it is not an effective method of social change. Although it is tempting to wonder what would have happened if protesters had not gone home that night and had instead encamped until their anti–Iraq War demand was met, I suspect the result would have been the same. The fact is that governments today are not required to listen to their citizens or heed their marches.

HUMAN SHIELD

At the same time that President Bush was readying the global populace for a pre-emptive war against Iraq, the International Solidarity Movement (ISM) in Palestine was hailed among activists as a viable way for everyday people to wage peace. Inspired by the organization's audacious non-violence, international activists believed that by going to the Palestinian territories as human shields against the Israel Defence Forces we could end the occupation. I was nineteen years old when I withdrew from Swarthmore College and went to the West Bank to test this theory.

One month before Christmas in 2002, access to Bethlehem was impeded by knee-high razor wire. The Israeli soldiers on the scene either did not know or would not tell me in which direction the Church of the Nativity lay. It was difficult to step through the coiled wire and I snagged my pant leg. There were six in our impromptu affinity group of anti-occupation activists, mostly Europeans, aside from me. We'd met at an East Jerusalem hostel that funnelled direct action activists into the non-violent Palestinian liberation movement. We were all experienced activists who wanted to go deeper. Our first training was in a few days, after which I was to serve six weeks in the West Bank as a participant in the ISM, a Palestinian-led organization that encouraged international peace activists to join the non-violent struggle against military occupation. My visit to Bethlehem was ostensibly a tourism trip to the birthplace of Jesus of Nazareth. I kept my true motives secret because participation in the ISM could be grounds for deportation from Israel. I was actually in Bethlehem to pay homage to the ISM's first spectacular peacemaking operation.

Six months earlier, in May 2002, an ISM affinity group of pacifist, non-violent civilians from several nations broke through an Israeli military encirclement and entered the besieged Church of the Nativity, bringing food and water. The siege had begun in April following a botched military incursion. Dozens of Palestinian militants who feared for their lives had sought protection at Jesus' birthplace. The move by Palestinian militants to seek political sanctuary at one of the holiest churches in Christianity attracted immediate international media attention.

The world watched in dismay as Israeli snipers fired on the church. Seven Palestinians were killed and an American monk was wounded in the first week. After thirty days, the situation became desperately tense as devout Christians worldwide began to actively protest the desecration of the church. And then, out of nowhere, the impasse was broken by the ISM—activists audaciously walked into the church unarmed and unarmoured. Dennis B. Warner, an American peace activist and participant in the daring action, writes, "The entry to the church began . . . when three ISM groups totaling 23 activists approached the structure from three directions. Crossing Manger Square at a steady but rapid walk, they reached the door of the church which was briefly opened at their arrival. The Israeli troops stationed around the church and Manger Square appeared to be taken by surprise and were unable to intercept the activists before they had successfully crossed the square."[122] Five Americans, a Dane, a Swede, a Canadian, an Irish and a British citizen entered the besieged church and refused to leave until the siege ended, a spectacular demonstration of non-violent direct action. The Israeli government and military were taken aback by these novel tactics of resistance.

The presence of international civilians within the church instantly altered the power dynamics of the situation. The Israeli military could no longer use lethal force without also assuming the responsibility for harming non-violent foreign citizens. Seven days after the peace activists entered the Church of the Nativity, the siege came to a negotiated, non-violent end. It was a victory for the power of civilians to intervene in geopolitics.

The tactical innovation of the ISM was to bring global activists into the bottom-up intifada. The ISM was Palestinian-led and internationals were housed and cared for by Palestinian families within the West Bank and Gaza. For six weeks, I lived among Palestinians and each day participated in their non-violent struggle against occupation. The ISM coordinated my movement within the West Bank, massing volunteers for large protests and giving us safe houses and trusted contacts in cities as we moved deeper into the occupied territories. Huwaida Arraf, one of the founders of the movement, explained to us during our training that the ISM's strategy for ending the military occupation of the Palestinian territories was twofold. First, use the presence of international civilians to empower non-violent resistance, civil disobedience and protest against the Israeli occupation. The Israeli military was intolerant of anti-occupation resistance by Palestinians and would use excessive force—tear gas, sound grenades, rubber-coated bullets and forceful arrests—to break up protests. The ISM believed that if internationals were present during protests, the military would be more cautious in their repression. The second strategy was to expose international civilians to the brutal reality of the occupation so that we could share the truth of what we witnessed when we returned home. By bringing international activists into the Palestinian liberation struggle, the ISM tested the hypothesis that a "non-violent peace force" could end a military occupation by directly intervening.

As we acclimatized to the violence around us, my group of international activists moved deeper into the West Bank. Every two weeks we went to a more violent place. By the fifth week, I was in Tulkarm at the northwest edge of the West Bank in an area of active, daily Israeli military incursions. The city had a population of roughly fifty thousand and the nearby refugee camp had ten thousand more residents. On the bus from East Jerusalem, a group of Palestinian schoolchildren asked us where we were going. When I said Tulkarm, they made gestures of machine guns shooting in an attempt to dissuade us from going.

It was Ramadan, a lunar month of fasting in Islam, and there was no respite from the curfew, the tear gas and the daily street battles. Each morning ominous announcements in Hebrew were made from armoured Jeeps. As internationals we exempted ourselves from allegiance to any Israeli military law that applied in the occupied territories. We freely broke curfew and explored widely in unexpected places. Unlike in the smaller Palestinian villages I had lived in, the violence in Tulkarm was too great for us to directly intercede. Instead, our affinity group witnessed the violence and tried to de-escalate through our visible presence. During this time there was a real danger of being hurt by either side of the conflict. There were no other non-Palestinians in the city during our time in Tulkarm. My safety depended on goodwill and kindness toward all who approached. One day I was very close to being seriously assaulted by Palestinian youth who had learned I was an American citizen. As their angry denouncement of America and President Bush escalated, my companions and I found safety in an elementary school. Meanwhile, a Palestinian activist from a neighbouring village explained our non-violent mission and our organization. Then it was as if the whole city of Tulkarm apologized profusely. The youth escorted us around for a day, making it clear we were friends. The baker lowered his prices. The teenagers gave us kitschy toys. And from that point all the people of Tulkarm knew us and kept us safe.

During my time with the ISM, I participated in many acts of resistance to the occupation. Because of my brown skin, many soldiers, assuming I was Palestinian, treated me with disrespect. I experienced the full reality of daily life under military rule. I took part in non-violent protests against the construction of the massive separation barrier that cuts through the West Bank. I assisted Palestinians during their olive harvest when the Israeli military tried to prohibit them from going to the fields. I broke curfew in Tulkarm, and observed extremely violent street battles where a rock-throwing Palestinian was shot dead by Israeli soldiers. I witnessed machine-gun fire. I was tear-gassed in the streets. Israeli soldiers pointed their guns at me threateningly. I saw Molotov cocktails explode and felt the heat of their flames on my face. I accompanied a Red Crescent ambulance at night and I witnessed many things—such as a man whose jaw had been shattered by a rubber-coated bullet—the memory of which still brings me pain over a decade later.

Shortly before I left the West Bank and re-enrolled at Swarthmore College, the ISM suffered the first of a series of major setbacks that undermined the organization's core assumptions. On November 22, an Israeli military sniper wounded the Irish ISM activist Caoimhe Butterly. Then in quick succession, ISM participants were actively targeted. Rachel Corrie, an American ISM member who was volunteering in Gaza, was killed by an Israel Defense Forces (IDF) armoured bulldozer on March 16, 2003—my twenty-first birthday—when she refused to move out of the way of a Palestinian home that was being demolished by the Israeli military. On April 5, Brian Avery, also an American ISM activist, was shot in the face by gunfire from an IDF armoured personnel carrier. Less than a week later, a

British ISM participant named Thomas Hurndall was shot in the head by the IDF and later died. Up until that point, it was believed that ISMers could use their bodies as shields against the occupation. When the Irish, American and British governments did not raise alarm at the injury and killing of their citizens and when the international consensus did not shift against Israel, the central tactical assumption of the ISM was broken. Internationals were no longer protected. Membership in the ISM decreased sharply with the growing risks. Huwaida Arraf continued to devise tactics of non-violent resistance by breaking the siege of Gaza with an international flotilla and organizing a Freedom Ride to end the segregation of Israeli buses. However in 2010, when Israeli commandos killed ten activists aboard the *Mavi Marmara*, a Turkish ship that was attempting to break the blockade on Gaza, it was clear that non-violent civilians were no longer exempt from violence. Although further flotillas set sail and internationals continued to aid Palestinians in their anti-occupation struggle, the human shield tactic had been definitively defeated.

Strategic Insight

A sense of solidarity is powerful and can serve as the basis for an effective movement. People will put themselves in danger to support an underdog cause they believe is righteous. International civilians are able to intervene in geopolitics by travelling to war zones and acting in surprising and unconventional ways. The human shield tactic, however, relied too heavily on the taboo against killing non-violent international citizens. Once this taboo was broken, the tactic was defeated and the movement declined.

> The struggle for political power—i.e., the struggle for the control of the coercive organizations, for the police, justice, army, bureaucracy, and foreign policy—is the agent of historical progress.
>
> FRANZ NEUMANN, POLITICAL PHILOSOPHER, 1957

9.

THE DISTANT PAST OF PROTEST

There is an eternal force within humanity that strives toward greater freedom, evolution and self-actualization. I call this force spirit. At most times in history, the human spirit is constrained by the status quo. When, every once in a while, activists stumble across a new way of approaching the struggle, the status quo is upended, for better or worse. In my meditations on revolution, I am increasingly drawn to a tactical-spiritual explanation of what happens in these tumultuous moments. I have come to understand that the role of tactics is to unleash the collective spirit, a process that hastens a political miracle. The people flock to the movement when what was previously believed to be impossible suddenly seems within reach. Each of these episodes of protest, drawn from two thousand years of revolution, demonstrates that spirit—the immaterial force within us—is the deciding factor in an uprising. Put simply, the people join the movement they believe will win.

Anything is possible when a sense of collective faith in victory rises among the people. In the final analysis, the specific tactics that activists employ are less important than the emotion these tactics spread. What seems to matter most is that the tactics erase fear from participants and are novel and surprising from the perspective of authorities. Generally speaking, the tactics that fulfill these two requirements are audacious. The moment the people become disillusioned with a tactic, it fails. Similarly, as soon as authorities understand the pattern of a protest ritual it is defeated. The balance of power is shifting toward the people, but the status quo is resilient and tactics are useless, and uninspiring, when repeated.

The future of activism already exists. However, if you are blinded by old paradigms of activism, you'll never see the movement that is about to break out. The next protest tactic that will release the human spirit and unleash a global social movement is out there right now waiting to be seen. The only way to discover it is to look within and never protest the same way twice.

GHOST DANCE

". . . [A] prophet has risen among the Indians at Walker Lake, [Nevada]. . . . He says the spirits of all the Paiute warriors who have died in the last five hundred years are to return to earth and resume their old forms."[123]

This sensational newspaper excerpt from 1889 is the first mention of Wovoka, one of the greatest theurgist activists in modern history. Wovoka was a prophet who instigated the Ghost Dance of 1890, a religious protest movement that threatened the sovereignty of the United States and marked the end of an era of indigenous armed resistance.

Wovoka's life was unexceptional until a fateful early morning on New Year's Day in 1889. On that morning Wovoka, a thirty-three-year-old Native American from the Paiute tribe, was cutting wood in the Nevada wilderness when he heard a strange noise. Laying down his axe, Wovoka went to investigate and suddenly fell unconscious. As he lay on the ground, the morning sky grew dark and a rare total eclipse of the sun occurred. The eclipse lasted for two minutes and seventeen seconds. When Wovoka awoke, he reported that he had experienced a Great Revelation: his spirit had ascended to heaven and received a prophecy, along with a new tactic of protest, directly from God.

Wovoka, familiar with Christian teachings, told his people that God had shown him a heavenly paradise where "all the people who had died long ago engaged in their old time sport and occupations, all happy and forever young." God then told Wovoka to return to his people and preach a series of specific moral instructions: "Be good and love one another, have no quarrelling, and live in peace with the whites. . . . Work, and do not lie or steal. . . . Put away old practices that savoured war." God gave Wovoka instructions on how to perform a special dance, the Ghost Dance, and commanded him to teach it to the people. Wovoka was assured that if this dance was followed, the indigenous people would regain sovereignty of the western half of the country, and they would be "reunited with their friends in this other world, where there would be no more death or sickness or old age."[124] To prove the veracity of his vision, God also granted Wovoka the power to control the weather. Twenty-four hours later, Wovoka had a second vision in which God told him that the Ghost Dance must be performed for five nights in succession every three months.

Soon after receiving the prophecy, Wovoka performed a series of weather miracles that convinced the people. It is recorded, for example, that in 1888 and 1889, the area of Nevada inhabited by Wovoka was experiencing extreme drought. A local tribal reservation policeman named Josephus, who was skeptical of Wovoka's claims, decided to test the prophet by asking him to bring rain. Josephus later testified that after he asked Wovoka for help, the prophet sat silently and retired to sleep without responding. However, Josephus claimed that Wovoka woke him early in the morning and said, "You can go home, and on the morning of the third day, you and all the people will have plenty of rain." The rains came exactly three days later. The river flooded. The demonstration convinced Josephus and many others. Wovoka was heralded as the "new Messiah."

Wovoka had a powerful presence. One person who knew him for many years described him as "a tall, well-proportioned man with piercing eyes, regular features, a deep voice and a calm and dignified mien. He stood straight as a ramrod, spoke slowly, and by sheer projection of personality commanded the attention of any listener."[125]

Wovoka's Ghost Dance was not the first Ghost Dance to capture the imagination of the people. In 1870 a prophet named Wodziwob (Gray Hair) had made a similar prophecy and also instigated a Ghost Dance. Although little is known about this earlier version of the dance, it is believed that Wodziwob's assistant was Wovoka's father, a mystic, who must have exposed Wovoka to the 1870s Ghost Dance. There is also evidence that Wovoka had attempted to introduce a "version of the Paiute Round Dance" two years prior that did not catch on.[126] In other words, Wovoka did not invent the protest dance but his prophetic call in 1890 for its revival came at the opportune moment, and it quickly spread into a social movement.

Wovoka's prophecy came at a time of existential crisis for the indigenous tribes of the Trans-Mississippi West. Native American wars against continued expansion of the United States had been ongoing for decades, and by 1889 it was clear that the indigenous people had lost the armed struggle. Wovoka was a theurgist and a revolutionary. The Ghost Dance was a protest ritual designed to solicit divine intercession in the political regime, restoring sovereignty to the tribes. A year after Wovoka's Great Revelation, as word of his prophecy spread, representatives of various tribes began to travel to see the Messiah. During one gathering in March an estimated sixteen hundred people from the tribes of the Cheyenne, Lakota, Arapaho, Ute, Navajo, Shoshone and Bannock, famous for their three-month war against the U.S. Military in 1878, visited Wovoka to receive instructions on performing the Ghost Dance.

Although very little documentation exists about the precise performance of the Ghost Dance of 1890, a few eyewitness accounts of non-participants are available. Here is how one observer described Wovoka's protest ritual: "In the middle of the circle of dancers was a central bonfire which gave off a great deal of heat and light. Around the circle moved the [participants] hand in hand in a sort of shuffling side step. They kept chanting something to the beat of skin drums. Some members would fall out of the circle onto the ground in a trance-like state, and some, upon falling, kept wiggling."[127]

The mysterious gatherings, and the spectre of the tribes uniting, alarmed the U.S. military. On December 4, 1890, the first military investigator, Arthur Chapman, interviewed Wovoka. The prophet assured him that he was opposed to armed conflict and was interested only in spreading the Ghost Dance. At the same time, Wovoka explicitly claimed immense theurgical power. He told Chapman that he had the "power to destroy this world and all the people in it and to have it made over again,"[128] a statement eerily reminiscent of St. Paul's affirmation of Christian faith's "power to destroy strongholds" (2 Corinthians 10:4).

The tide turned when the Lakota Sioux embraced the Ghost Dance. The Sioux were one of the most populous tribes in the region. They were also fierce and formidable fighters who had been defending their sovereignty through armed resistance against the U.S. government since 1854. To prevent the growth of the movement, agents of the Lakota Sioux reservations banned the Ghost Dance, attempted to arrest dance leaders and, in November, U.S. president William Henry Harrison authorized the military to "take such steps as necessary" to suppress the ritual entirely. Within two weeks, the army had surrounded four Lakota Sioux reservations with the largest concentration of soldiers since the Civil War, setting in motion a deadly confrontation.[129]

On December 29, 1890, a detachment of the U.S. Seventh Cavalry Regiment encircled a group of Lakota Sioux men, women and children near Wounded Knee Creek in South

Dakota. When the soldiers attempted to seize the people's guns, a scuffle broke out that quickly escalated. Some say soldiers began shooting when a medicine man named Yellow Bird started performing the Ghost Dance. What is certain is that the Lakota Sioux fled but were mercilessly killed by machine-gun fire. At the end of massacre, around three hundred people were dead, many of them women and children.

The Wounded Knee massacre ended the Ghost Dance movement. The massacre shattered the indigenous people's faith in the efficacy of the protest ritual. It also signalled the end of 350 years of Native American armed resistance. That same year, the United States Census Bureau declared that the frontier had been settled.[130] "The frontier has gone, and with its going has closed the first period of American history," writes the historian Frederick Jackson Turner in 1893.[131]

Strategic Insight

The Ghost Dance is a crucial example for activists to consider. It validates voluntarism and theurgism. Protest does not need to directly challenge power in order to be a threat to power. The Ghost Dance wasn't performed near capital cities, urban areas or government buildings. The implication is that any shared gesture believed by its participants to have political power can become a protest with revolutionary potential. This principle was demonstrated at the end of 2012 when indigenous rights activists organized round dance flash mobs at shopping malls, catapulting the Idle No More movement into a challenge to the Canadian government. The protest quickly spread across national borders and sparked a widespread indigenous resurgence. Performing the Ghost Dance ritual, or the Idle No More round dance, was a method of uniting the people into a mood of fearlessness. Kairos is crucial. It is significant that Wovoka wasn't the first to propose a Ghost Dance, he was simply the one who called for it at the right time. The failure of the Ghost Dance may have marked the end of an era of armed resistance in the past but there are signs that indigenous groups may take up arms in the future to defend their territories.

RIOT

The closest a spontaneous riot has come to a successful revolution against an empire occurred in Constantinople, present-day Istanbul, in AD 532. During the spectacular people's riot known as the Nika Revolt, a large portion of the capital city was burned and a new emperor declared by the people. The riots nearly forced Emperor Justinian I to flee and almost toppled the Byzantine Empire. The Nika Revolt is significant in the history of protest because it demonstrates that revolutionary moments happen when the people break the pattern.

In 532, two hundred years after Constantine transferred the capital of the Roman Empire from Rome to Constantinople, the life of the people was oriented around the chariot races that took place in the hippodrome. The chariot races were bloody entertainment dominated by two competing teams, or factions: the Blues and the Greens. There were also two minor factions—the Reds, who aligned with the Greens, and the Whites, supporters of the Blues. Historians disagree about the political nature of these circus factions. Some historians argue that the

Blues and Greens were akin to contemporary football hooligans whose team loyalty was non-political. It is true that the factions often engaged in rioting, violence against each other and attacks on civilians. From one perspective the factions were similar to gangs. On the other hand, some historians believe that the factions represented differing political and theological tendencies. From this perspective, the Greens were the faction of the landed aristocracy, and the Blues were the team favoured by the mercantile class. The chariot races then became a proxy for a culture war. What is clear is that each emperor favoured one faction, most often the Greens, over the others and encouraged the factions to fight and never unite.

The chariot races served to distract the people, but they also played an important political role. The emperor had a special royal box, known as the *kathisma,* in the hippodrome that was connected to the royal palace by a guarded tunnel. One way the people could make their political will known was to request the emperor's attendance at the chariot races and to chant their demands in unison. The tactic was known as a circus petition. Imagine up to 250,000 people chanting in unison, making a clamour the emperor could not deny hearing. The emperor would then have the choice of agreeing to the demands, ignoring the chants or sending soldiers to silence the crowd. Similarly, the emperor could summon the people to the hippodrome by entering the *kathisma*. As one scholar observes, "The hippodrome was the focal point in relations between the emperor and the people."[132] In fact, during the first century, it was common for the Roman emperor to concede to demands that were chanted by the people during the races. By the sixth century, however, the circus petition became less effective in the Byzantine Empire and the people's demands during the games were increasingly ignored.[133] The breakdown of the petition laid the foundation for the Nika Revolt.

The immediate trigger for the Nika Revolt occurred on January 10, 532, when seven partisans of the Blue and Green factions were arrested and found guilty of murder. The partisans were taken to be executed when a large crowd gathered to protest. Five of the partisans were executed and then, in one of those chance occurrences that trigger historical moments, the scaffolding broke and the final two—a Green and a Blue—were saved by the crowd and given sanctuary at the nearby church of St. Laurence.

For hundreds of years, the Blue and Green factions had detested each other and delighted in fighting. Now, however, there was an incentive to join forces: each faction desired the freedom of their man. Three days later, at the next chariot races, the crowd shouted and petitioned the emperor to grant the two partisans their freedom. Justinian ignored their demands and refused to acknowledge their petition. The shouting continued for twenty-two chariot races. Still Justinian made no reply. With only two races remaining in the day, the Greens and Blues suddenly shouted, "Long life to the merciful Blues and Greens!" and began chanting, "Nika!" (Greek for "Conquer!"), a common cheer of the factions. The choice of Nika as a watchword for the spontaneous movement may have also been a tactical decision as it helped distinguish the people, who spoke Greek, from the Latin-speaking soldiers who would have tried to infiltrate the protest. Acting together, the factions began rioting and setting fire to Constantinople.

Justinian retreated through the *kathisma* and locked himself in the palace.

At this point, it is crucial to understand that faction riots involving incendiarism were common—hence the association of the factions with violent hooliganism. The historian Alan Cameron, who wrote the definitive account of the circus factions, observes that riots combined with arson were recorded in 491, 493, 498, 507, 532, 548, 560, and 571.[134] In other words, it was a frequent occurrence. The difference is, as Cameron points out, that the typical faction riot was not a political protest. Instead, a normal faction riot was "a battle *between* the two colours."[135] With the factions united, the rioting was far more severe than usual. Still, it was not yet a political protest.

On the evening of January 13, the rioters set fire to the residence of the city prefect Eudaemon, who had condemned the seven faction members to death, and freed the two partisans. Through direct action, the people had achieved their initial demand. Now events began to spiral out of control even more quickly.

The next day, Justinian attempted to pacify the rioters by continuing the chariot races. The gesture failed and the people set fire to the hippodrome before issuing a new set of demands. This time, the people demanded the dismissal of the three highest-ranking officials resident in the capital, including Eudaemon. Justinian, who had earlier ignored the people's petition and the ongoing rioting, capitulated to the new set of demands. He dismissed the named officials but the rioting only grew in intensity. Justinian responded by sending his soldiers into the city to end the rioting with deadly force. This effort failed. And at this point, the rioting broke away from the usual script and became a political revolution: the people surrounded the home of Probus, a nephew of a previous emperor named Anastasius, and acclaimed him as the new emperor. Probus was either not home, or he was avoiding the mob, and the rioters set fire to his residence.

The riots continued for days. Much of the city, including government archives, was burned. Meanwhile, additional soldiers began arriving from Thrace, prepared for battle. On January 18, Justinian called the people to the hippodrome and, holding the Gospels, "acknowledged his own error in not assenting to the demands of the factions at the start of the riot" and also "offered to pardon the rioters."[136] His efforts to calm the protesters through conciliation did not work.

Justinian returned to the palace and dismissed Hypatius and Pompey, brothers of Probus and nephews of Anastasius. This move has puzzled historians because it supplied the people with another opportunity to hail a new emperor. And they did. Hypatius was acclaimed emperor, given makeshift imperial regalia and led to the hippodrome. He sat in the royal *kathisma* and was cheered by the assembled people. This was the defining moment of the Nika Revolt. The people had transformed a typical faction riot into a political revolution that attempted to transfer sovereignty to a new leader. As one historian observes, "the behaviour of both Justinian and the rioters in 532 went along a well-worn course already familiar from previous disturbances, until a new emperor was hailed in the hippodrome."[137]

A terrified Justinian contemplated fleeing the city. In fact, a rumour reached Hypatius that Justinian had already fled, emboldening the people's choice of emperor. But the Empress Theodora had interrupted Justinian's council on whether to run for safety with a rousing speech that changed the course of events:

> My lords, the present occasion is too serious to allow me to follow the convention that a woman should not speak in a man's council. Those whose interests are threatened by extreme danger should think only of the wisest course of action, not of conventions. In my opinion, flight is not the right course, even if it should bring us to safety. It is impossible for a person, having been born into this world, not to die; but for one who has reigned it is intolerable to be a fugitive. . . . If you wish to save yourself, my lord, there is no difficulty. . . . Yet reflect for a moment whether, when you have once escaped to a place of security, you would not gladly exchange such safety for death. As for me, I agree with the adage that the royal purple is the noblest shroud.[138]

In preferring death over flight, Empress Theodora persuaded Justinian to stay and fight. Justinian sent the soldiers from Thrace against the people assembled in the hippodrome. The surprise attack quickly escalated into a slaughter: over thirty thousand people were indiscriminately killed.

Reflecting on why the faction riot became a revolution, the historian Geoffrey Greatrex finds evidence for one of the core truths that has underpinned our theory of revolution: it was unexpected occurrences that broke the usual pattern. "The chain of events which made the Nika riot unique was for the most part accidental," he writes.[139]

The overwhelming defeat of the Nika Revolt had lasting political and tactical consequences. The factions did not ever reunite. And although faction rioting became frequent within a decade, the riot was never again deployed as a revolutionary tactic in the Byzantine Empire.

Strategic Insight

First lesson: break the script. Apolitical faction riots were common, but the Nika Revolt spiralled into a revolution when it swerved in an unexpected direction. Second lesson: unite. The Nika Revolt nearly succeeded because the two factions found common cause and joined together to achieve a shared goal, freeing their comrades and toppling Justinian. The revolt was crushed when the unity was broken. The division between the left and right today is akin to the separation of Blue and Green in 532. Third lesson: don't celebrate until you've won. The fatal mistake of the rebels was to assume that acclaiming a new sovereign in the hippodrome was sufficient to topple the old leader. If the people had swarmed Justinian's residence to complete the revolution instead of flocking to the hippodrome to prematurely celebrate victory, the history of the Western world would have been irrevocably altered.

EPIPHANY

Activists place too much emphasis on celebrating the social protests that spread quickly. Speed is exciting, but the most enduring victories are those that take generations to unfold.

Occupy Wall Street was a protest meme designed to inspire immediate action. Imagine the opposite: a seed that waits three centuries for the opportune moment. To study this kind of ultraslow triumph, turn to Christianity's takeover of the Roman state in the fourth century AD.

In the beginning, Christianity was a revolutionary underground social movement that rejected the official religion, refused to accept that the emperor was a god, and spread beyond all borders. A Christian was distinguished by his refusal to sacrifice to pagan gods, which included the deified emperor. As Friedrich Engels observes, "Christianity was originally a movement of oppressed people: it first appeared as the religion of slaves and emancipated slaves, of poor people deprived of all rights, of peoples subjugated or dispersed by Rome."[140] Christianity was perhaps the most oppressed people's movement in antiquity. For three hundred years Christians endured the outlawing of their religion and three waves of gruesome persecution. In AD 64, the emperor Nero, for example, publicly killed large numbers of Christians using hunting dogs after attaching the hides of wild beasts to his victims. The historian Tacitus also records that Nero nailed Christians to crosses or set them aflame to "serve as a nightly illumination."[141] In AD 303 the emperor Diocletian initiated the third, and final, persecution when he commanded that all churches be razed to the ground, Bibles burned and Christians forced by torture to renounce their religion. Keep in mind that thousands of Christians were eventually martyred in front of cheering arenas of spectators. And yet, seventeen years after Diocletian's infamous persecution, Christian monotheism ultimately replaced paganism as the default religion of the West. How was this possible?

The spread of Christianity owes its success to two high-profile conversions, a rare celestial phenomenon and a theurgist symbol, not public protests and mass actions.

First, there is the well-known conversion of St. Paul, an early persecutor of the church who was struck blind and had a theophany—a vision of Jesus Christ—while on the road to Damascus sometime between AD 31 and 36. St. Paul became Christianity's most persuasive theologian and propagandist. He established many of the first churches for non-Jewish converts to the movement.

Then, most significantly, there is the conversion of the Roman emperor Constantine centuries later. Eusebius, an ancient historian who interviewed the emperor, records that on October 28, 312, Constantine and his army were marching toward a decisive battle at the Milvian Bridge against a rival emperor.* In a sense, this battle was a revolution: the victor determined the new legal regime. A miracle happened shortly before the battle. Constantine and his army saw above the sun a "trophy of a cross of light in the heavens bearing the inscription, CONQUER BY THIS." Constantine then had a vision that night in which Jesus Christ instructed him to draw the celestial sign on the shields of his soldiers as "a safeguard in all engagements with his enemies." Eusebius writes that "at dawn Constantine arose, and communicated the marvel to his friends: and then, calling together the workers in gold and precious stones, he sat in the midst of them, and described to them the figure of the sign he had seen."[142] The symbol that Constantine described is known as the Chi Rho.

---

* The Milvian Bridge still stands, and it is also the origin of the lovelock phenomenon, a present-day social ritual where lovers write their names on a lock, attach the lock to a bridge and throw the key in the water.

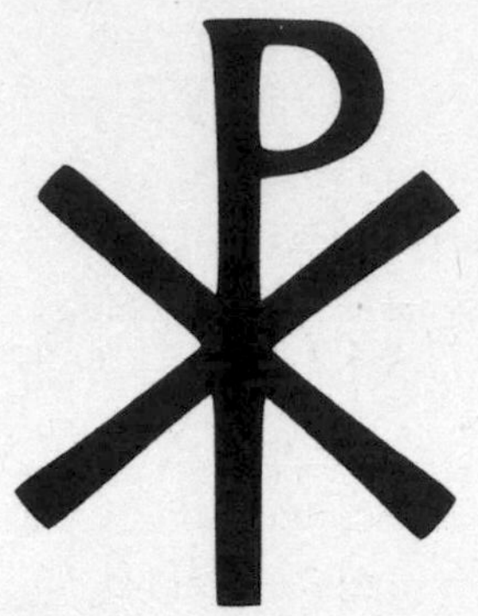

Constantine and his army saw this Chi Rho in the sky.

Constantine was victorious at the Battle of Milvian Bridge. Having achieved control over the Western Roman Empire, Constantine ascribed his success to divine help and initiated a series of pro-Christian reforms. Seventy-odd years later, paganism was banned.

Most scholars focus on the conversions of St. Paul and Constantine from a purely theological perspective. Where they see proof of God, I see a mixture of subjectivism and theurgism—a significant example of ultraslow, long-range meme warfare. I propose that Christianity succeeded, in large part, because early proponents mastered the art of provoking visions of Jesus Christ within the subjectivity of powerful individuals. Christians were also masterful at the art of strong symbolism: the Chi Rho, the sacred flaming heart and the cross, for example. At the same time, rather than basing their theory of social change on a mass uprising, early Christians integrated into their storyline of future victory a celestial phenomenon that signalled divine intervention.

The remarkable fact is that Constantine and his army probably did see a cross of light in the sky. These are known to occur. Celestial crosses were reported in Jerusalem in 351 and in 362. And crosses have appeared in the sky in modern times, too. "The famous Alpinist Edward Whymper saw a similar effect on the Matterhorn," writes Oliver Nicholson, a classicist at the University of Minnesota.[143] The importance of the celestial cross is not that a rare phenomenon occurred; the importance is how it was interpreted by Constantine. Eusebius reports that prior to the Battle of the Milvian Bridge, Constantine prayed for a sign. He was, thereby, attuned to miraculous possibility. After seeing the cross, Constantine was initially puzzled about its meaning. It was only after he explained his dream to others in his camp that he became convinced that the cross was evidence of his destined role. Early Christian theologians had long prophesied that the return of Christ would be preceded by a cross in the sky. Nicholson argues that Constantine converted because he was culturally predisposed to interpret this celestial event, a natural phenomenon, in Christian apocalyptic terms. Constantine gained political power by integrating himself into the Christian storyline. Or, as Nicholson puts it, "The Vision of the Cross assured Constantine that he was the agent of a higher power, a power which ordered history through recognizable patterns of chronology and prophecy."

Taken in this light, it is all the more intriguing that the Chi Rho existed as a figure for at least five hundred years before the Battle of the Milvian Bridge. Pagan scribes used the Chi Rho to star an important passage of text. For alchemists, the Chi Rho was shorthand for Time, a reference to the Greek word kairos. Only after Constantine did the *Chi* (X in Greek) and *Rho* (P in Greek) take on wide significance as a christogram, a monogram combining the first two letters of Christ (ΧΡΙΣΤΟΣ) to symbolize Christianity.

Christian writers laid the foundations for Constantine's conversion by integrating the appearance of a rare astronomical phenomenon into their social movement's expectations of the future. They did not know when the cross would light the sky, but they guaranteed how it would be interpreted. The miracle is that the celestial cross appeared at the very moment when it was destined to have the greatest political impact—on the day of a decisive battle between two sovereigns.

Contemporary social movements often tell only one story about the signs that will precede the revolution: lots of people will be in the streets. The victory of Christianity challenges activists to wonder whether another story might be told, one in which an unexpected and rare natural phenomenon heralds a paradigm shift. Perhaps three hundred years from now a leader will be swayed to embrace our people's movement by a long-prophesied event—an earthquake—that strikes on her inauguration day.

Strategic Insight

The most advanced form of meme warfare is to provoke life-changing epiphanies in future generations. Christianity succeeded because it created a meme (Jesus Christ) that found its way into the dreams of Constantine. Similarly, movements can succeed by influencing how rare future events will be interpreted. Constantine gained power after witnessing the celestial cross by integrating himself into Christianity's social movement storyline that had been in formation for three hundred years. Activists of tomorrow will abandon strict secularism and materialism in favour of a nuanced approach that embraces theurgy and the yearning for divine intercession. At the same time, protesters will situate their struggles within a prophetic deep-time perspective that stretches back to the birth of non-egalitarian society.

AMBUSH

The greatest activist in the history of protest is Arminius (c. 18 BC–AD 21). His epic protest against Roman expansion into Germanic territory changed the destiny of the empire for four hundred years. Arminius was a twenty-six-year-old prince from the Cherusci tribe of ancient Germany when he united the decentralized Germanic tribes and ambushed the world's superpower. The barbarians' decisive victory was so complete that it enshrined the people's sovereignty over their homeland and restrained imperial Roman expansion until the end of the empire. After two thousand years, recent archaeological evidence reveals the secret behind Arminius's protest triumph.

No civilization had ever reached the overwhelming supremacy that Rome exerted in AD 9. The Germanic people faced an omnipotent adversary who saw the entire world as its domain. Until then no people had successfully halted Roman expansion and expropriation of their homelands. Here's how one historian describes the perception of Rome in the months prior to Arminius's coordinated protest: "The power of Rome appeared so firmly established; no people which had resisted it had ever prospered. . . . There was such a superstitious faith in the star of Rome's ascendancy, that numbers believed that the dominion of the world had been decreed to her from the beginning of time."[144] It was commonly believed that the borders of Rome would always expand and never recede.[145] Rome anticipated it would subjugate the world to its order. Political protest, social resistance and revolution against Rome were crushed by the most efficient military in existence.

The tribes of Germany embodied the opposite spirit to Rome's linear rationality. Unlike Rome, the people were decentralized and lived in homesteads dispersed throughout forests without roads. Julius Caesar initiated Rome's invasion of Gaul, which western Germany was a part of, between 58 and 51 BC. After sixty years, by the time of Arminius, social and economic exchange existed between the tribes and Rome, whose expansionist strategy hinged on subjugation through assimilation. The tribe's warriors were recruited into the Roman military hierarchy, for example. In fact, this cultural intermingling played a decisive role in the outcome of events. The archaeologist Peter Wells recounts that Arminius "gained firsthand experience in Roman military tactics while helping Tiberius suppress the great rebellion that broke out in Pannonia in AD 6."[146] Three years later, Arminius had become a trusted confidant of Publius Quinctilius Varus, the Roman general in command of three legions of occupying forces.

In September of AD 9, Varus and his legions were marching from their summer camp to their winter headquarters when Arminius sent word of a nearby tribal rebellion and offered to assist Varus in putting down the protest. Against the counsel of his advisers, Varus decided to act on Arminius's information and marched his massive power straight into a trap. Recent historians estimate that Varus had a force of "20,000 infantry and cavalry, accompanied by some 10,000 slaves, women, children, armorers, medical personnel, and civilian tradesmen."[147] The ancient historian Velleius attests that the Roman legions Varus commanded were among the best fighters in the Roman Empire.[148] Varus must have been confident that his army could deal with any people's rebellion.

Arminius led Varus into an ambush. Squeezed between a hill and a marsh, the Romans were clad in heavy armour and unable to escape. The barbarians surrounded the soldiers, hurling spears from a distance; then they approached for the kill. Three legions were wiped out in a singular victory for the tribes of the Rhine.

Until the twentieth century, the exact location of the ambush site was unknown and therefore a crucial part of the story was missing. Now we know that in the Battle of the Teutoburg Forest the four-mile-long column of soldiers was ambushed as they passed the base of Kalkriese Hill in Osnabrück, Lower Saxony. Recent archaeological evidence reveals that the tribes constructed a hidden sod wall that was about fifteen feet wide, five feet high and two thousand feet long. The wall had a wooden fence on top and limestone blocks in front.[149] The existence of the wall gives a sense of the depth of Arminius's planning and the time involved. Wells estimates construction of the wall must have involved hundreds of people, working dawn till dusk, for several weeks.[150] Was the wall used to kettle the soldiers? Or was it instead a defensive barricade? We can only speculate how Arminius's wall was used by the people to defeat twenty thousand of the most highly trained occupying soldiers.

Following the tribe's victorious ambush, Varus committed suicide and his head was sent to Rome.[151] The shock of defeat was so tremendous that the panicked citizens of the world's capital city believed a barbarian invasion was imminent. Rome responded with punitive actions, but during the next four centuries the Roman military never tried to re-establish an encampment east of the lower Rhine.[152]

According to the ancient historian Tacitus, Arminius was killed by his own people, who feared he was becoming a king. Tacitus writes, "Arminius . . . began to aim at kingship, and found himself in conflict with the independent temper of his countrymen. He was attacked by arms, and, while defending himself with chequered results, fell by the treachery of his relatives."[153]

Strategic Insight

A single decisive victory can change the course of history. Contemporary activists can reverse the behaviour of strong adversaries by orchestrating singular events that surprise and demoralize. The example set by Arminius is especially important for protesters who face heavily armoured police. Rather than trying to overcome police repression in a series of successful protests, activists should aspire to a dramatic victory in a single encounter. A video of a stunning victory against paramilitary police could mobilize the world. This victory does not need to be violent. In fact, a spectacular and humiliating non-violent defeat of riot police would be far more effective. On the value of winning with as few victories as possible, the great Chinese military strategist Wu Ch'i, who lived roughly four hundred years before Arminius, gives excellent advice: "Those that garner five victories will meet with disaster; those with four victories will be exhausted; those with three victories will become hegemons; those with two victories will be kings; and those with one victory will become emperors. For this reason those who have conquered the world through numerous victories are extremely rare, while those who thereby perished are many."[154]

PART THREE

TOMORROW

You cannot see a wind; you can only see that there is a wind. So, also, you cannot see a revolution; you can only see that there is a revolution. And there has never been in the history of the world a real revolution, brutally active and decisive, which was not preceded by unrest and a new dogma in the reign of invisible things. All revolutions began by being abstract. Most revolutions began by being quite pedantically abstract.

G.K. CHESTERTON, WRITER AND THEOLOGIAN, 1920

> The world you see must be denied, for sight of it is costing you a different kind of vision.
>
> *A Course in Miracles*, 1976

10.

MENTAL ENVIRONMENTALISM

I am sitting in a Berkeley laundromat flipping through the *East Bay Express*, a ubiquitous free weekly newspaper that mixes sensationalist local features with concert listings and risqué advertisements. The brightly lit room is slightly warm. I am alone. My chair is comfortable. The noise of the dryer is methodic, soothing. Barely audible radio music plays in the background. And as I watch my pants and shirts tumble dry, I drift into a reverie.

A few minutes pass in calm contentment . . . and when slowly my awareness returns to the present, to the dancing clothes in the dryer, the sound of strangers walking past the open door of the laundromat, I perceive that the radio's pop music has been imperceptibly exchanged for a series of commercial messages. I have no idea how long I have been listening to whispered advertisements exhorting me to buy a new car or see a movie or vote in the election, but the situation suddenly strikes me as very odd. Am I in a mind-control experiment? Am I being programmed? I feel as if I have awoken prematurely from a brainwashing session. And with that thought, I experience an intense, uncanny sensation. The oddness of the experience starts to roll outward. It isn't just the radio's repeated encouragements to consume, consume, consume that strike me as bizarre. Everything about the world around me—the laundromat, the newspaper I hold, the buses carrying movie advertisements zipping by outside—feels alien for a long moment.

The uncanny sensation lingers. And it occurs to me that in classic dystopian novels such as Yevgeny Zamyatin's *We*, Aldous Huxley's *Brave New World* and George Orwell's *1984* one of the defining features of totalitarian regimes is imagined to be pervasive propaganda. But whereas these authors saw that a totalitarian regime would be sustained by *political* propaganda, our age of authoritarian consumerism is sustained by *commercial* propaganda.

As activists of the future, the ground of our struggle is humanity's *mental environment*—our collective unconscious, the shared pool of myths, dreams and desires that shape how the world manifests. The future of protest begins with the realization that the external world is a reflection of our interior world. What we see is a mirror of ourselves. Our communal reality is constructed through our shared culture. And every time we experience a commercial interjection, a fatal lie lodges in our world view. The true danger of pervasive advertising is the damage it does to our *mental ecology*, the inexplicable interior world that is uniquely human. A clean mental environment is an indispensable ingredient to a thriving civilization. Perhaps we cannot conceive a sane future because our collective imagination has been usurped by advertisers, money worshippers and commercialism. We are in a double bind. Kicking consumerism out of our heads and finding solutions to the global problems humanity faces become the same struggle. The strategic imperative of our revolutionary struggle—our collective uprising to unshackle our spirits and revive our imagination—comes into view.

Our culture is infected by a commercial virus, a disease that keeps us distracted by illusions while the world collapses. And we did not contract the illness by mistake. For decades, corporations have consciously and strategically pursued the commercialization of culture. Their winning strategy has been to integrate advertising into public culture. By snatching the role of funding culture away from the people and their governments, corporations have made us dependent on "free" information, entertainment, services and software that are subsidized by advertising and come at grave cost to our psyches and our world.

It would take a historian years to enumerate the many tactics that modern corporations have developed to ensure that public television, radio, transportation, newspapers and schools are inundated with commercial logos and ads. But when it comes to the Internet, the stages of the takeover are clear. The opening shots were fired by Proctor & Gamble, the world's biggest advertiser, during the earliest days of the "information superhighway." At the 1994 convention of the American Association of Advertising Agencies, then–Proctor & Gamble chairman

Edwin Artzt laid out the corporate strategy for taking over the next generation's culture: guarantee that advertising, not user fees, would underwrite the Internet. Artzt was prescient, and saw the situation in the most serious terms. He warned of the catastrophe to come if the "new media," which was not yet a buzzword, was not under the control of advertisers and corporations. Artzt told the assembled executives, "From where we stand today, *we can't be sure* that ad-supported TV programming will have a future in the world being created. . . . If that happens, if advertising is no longer needed to pay most of the cost of home entertainment, then advertisers like us will have a hard time achieving the reach and frequency we need to support our brands." Their opponent was the user-fee model where content is funded by subscribers. Artzt went further, citing Procter & Gamble's role in creating the first radio and television soap operas, and explained how the conquest of the Internet would be accomplished:

> We've got to borrow a page from our own history and start getting control of the new environment. The whole idea of this new technology is that it makes it easier to divert revenue away from advertising into fees. . . . Remember, consumers are on our side. They would rather have their home entertainment free. So we've got to get involved in programming. . . . If user fees replace advertising revenue, we're in serious trouble. . . . Maybe our involvement means that a pay-per-view movie can be pulled down for half the price—or even free—if it includes commercials. Or maybe it means that the ten-dollar monthly fee for a game channel can be reduced to two or three dollars if we can integrate advertising. We're only limited by our ability

> to prove that it's in everyone's interest to involve advertising in these new media.[155]

In the same way that corporations conquered newspapers, radio and television, Artzt promised they would take the Internet. In the final words of his speech, Chairman Artzt exulted: "We may not get another opportunity like this in our lifetime. Let's grab all this new technology in our teeth once again and turn it into a bonanza for advertising!"

Responding to Artzt's call, the advertising industry founded the Coalition for Advertising Supported Information and Entertainment (CASIE) in 1994, a task force whose core mission was to guarantee that into the future "advertising revenue must be a key funding source for information and entertainment in the evolving world of media." Within a decade, advertisers owned the Internet.*

Commercialization of what was originally a wild, uncensored information free-for-all was not easy. Not everyone in Silicon Valley was convinced that funding through advertising was benign. In 1998, writing in the first public description of the ideas and technologies behind Google's search engine, its founders Larry Page and Sergey Brin say, "We expect that advertising-funded search engines will be inherently biased towards the advertisers and away from the needs of the consumers." Then, citing the example of OpenText, a now defunct search engine that corrupted their results with paid placement,

* CASIE was also instrumental in thwarting legislation to tax advertising on the Internet. This factor hints at an innovative avenue of attack for mental environmentalists—local initiatives to put a tax on advertising. Money from this tax could be used to fund public schools, libraries and non-commercial publications.

they conclude, "We believe the issue of advertising causes enough mixed incentives that it is crucial to have a competitive search engine that is transparent and in the academic realm."[156] The situation has become dramatically different since Google introduced advertising in 2001. Six years later, Google's apostasy was completed with the purchase of DoubleClick, a leading online advertising company, for $3.1 billion, making the Internet search engine one of the world's largest advertising agencies. By 2014 advertising accounted for nearly 90 percent of Google's revenue. (In 2015 Google restructured itself into Alphabet, a holding company.) Social networks such as Facebook, Instagram, Snapchat and Twitter have largely followed Google's strategy of offering free services without ads, then introducing greater amounts of commercialization as the user base grows. Now we are accustomed to seeing commercials on the sides of our screens and in our newsfeeds. Thomas Wells, a philosopher, explains the situation: "Advertising is a natural resource extraction industry, like a fishery. Its business is the harvest and sale of human attention. We are the fish and we are not consulted."[157] The new media forms that Proctor & Gamble dreaded would be commercial-free and supported by user subscriptions are now beholden to advertisers for their operational budgets.

Activists of the future thus must be *mental environmentalists*, as concerned with the health of our interior world as we are about the natural world. Mental environmentalism means working from the assumption that there is a connection between the level of pollution in our minds and the prevalence of pollution in the world. At the most basic level, this is imperative because when our minds are polluted by commercialism, and our imaginations stunted by toxic advertising, we are unable to conceive of a better way of organizing society. Our creativity declines with the increase of info-toxins. Our imagination atrophies as our behaviour mimics what we see on the screens. At a more complex level, as the subjectivist theory of revolution suggests, our mental environment dictates to a certain extent which beings manifest in our physical environment. Naming calls beings into existence. And when we cannot name the species of trees, animals and insects around us but we recognize instantly the commercial logos, the only beings that will manifest (the only beings we will perceive) are corporate owned, artificial and consumerist. We don't see the world that is disappearing around us.

In our global struggle to liberate humanity, the most significant battles will be fought on the spiritual level—inside our heads, within our imagination and deep in our collective unconscious. The three thousand advertising messages each of us is exposed to per day are snares in a spiritual war to keep us from imagining another world into existence. Those who fight the incessant flow of brands, slogans and jingles that inundate our cities, invade our homes and glimmer on our screens are heroic partisans safeguarding the keystone of thriving civilizations—human spirit. Without spirit and creativity, humanity is lost.

The future of activism is a struggle to capture the imagination of humanity.

To defeat an enemy that has lodged itself in our heads, our people's revolution builds upwards from the individual to the family, community and finally humanity. It begins in our psyche with an epiphany and it grows each time we extol the truth of our fearless revolution. The essence of revolution in the twenty-first century is to replicate our spiritual awakening in others. Our ultimate objective is to catalyze an awakening that rolls from city to city with sufficient speed and force to overwhelm the establishment. Richard Dawkins, the evolutionary biologist who coined the word "meme" in his book *The Selfish Gene*, describes this cultural unit's potency: "When you plant a fertile meme in my mind you literally parasitize my brain, turning it into a vehicle for the meme's propagation in just the same way that a virus may parasitize the genetic mechanism of a host cell."[158] We use social memes to create collective events that "unblind" people en masse, inviting miraculous divine intervention into the world.

POST-ENVIRONMENTALISM

Mental environmentalism is the solution to the impasse plaguing mainstream environmentalism. The traditional alliance between environmentalism and technocrats has effectively alienated the world from the environmentalist struggle. When scientists dictate the aims of activists, the result is a brittle, materialist conception of protest that is unable to deal with the fluid ecological crisis—a crisis that is above all existential.

The first credible scientific warnings about catastrophic climate change emerged in the 1970s and have grown persistently graver since. As long as corporations were able to dictate the domestic policies of Western democracies, reckless economic growth would be pursued, whatever the data told us. So activists waited for big-bang apocalyptic events—historic storms, melting ice caps, record-breaking heat waves, species extinctions—that would signal the catastrophe and shift public sentiment. Yet each of these dreaded events happened quietly, and the world still seemed to function. Few of us understood that the real apocalypse would be subtle. We kept waiting, only to realize in a flash that the dreaded event had already happened: the world has tipped past that point of no return that we had been fearing. As of 2015 the global concentration of carbon dioxide in the atmosphere now exceeds 400ppm. And scientists say that the warming of the oceans is unstoppable. "Even if we were to freeze greenhouse gases at current levels, the sea would actually continue to warm for centuries and millennia, and as they continue to warm and expand the sea levels will continue to rise," acknowledges a U.S. government climate scientist in July 2015.[159] The climate calamity is in the past. And now we need a fundamental reorientation in our approach to environmental activism. We must reshape humanity's internal reality in order to restore our external reality.

Ever since the catastrophic storms started, there have been prophecies of an environmentalist movement that would materialize in full force. Many people woke up in the mid-twentieth century with the publication of Rachel Carson's *Silent Spring*, which warned of the dangers of DDT. For others it was the first photos of Earth taken from space, or the live video of BP's underwater oil well rupturing into the Gulf of Mexico in 2010.

Of the many battlefronts on which our global struggle will be fought, it is the ecological struggle that has the greatest potential to unite humanity. From an ecological perspective, all the species that thrive on Earth are essentially one organism: either we all win or we all lose. Despite the dreams of lifeboat survivalists, it does not matter if you have a backyard bunker stocked with a decade of provisions. No one can outlive the eternal consequences of climate change.

Climate change is a unique challenge because it is a force outside human control that will compel our species to adapt. Either we will adapt toward a utopian vision that benefits the many or toward a dystopian vision that benefits the few.

For environmentalism to fulfill its universalist political promise, it must abandon the technocratic approach that has dominated the ecological paradigm for decades. There has been a fetishization of our ability to correlate climate change with scientifically verifiable hypotheses. Environmentalists got stuck in proving the scientific argument and have been falling down the rabbit hole of computer models and intellectual abstraction ever since. We are in a situation that the French philosopher Jean-François Lyotard calls the "differend": an irresolvable language game in which the absolutely final proof of climate change is human extinction . . . but of course by that point there will be no one alive to verify the final proof. Scientists believed that their computer models could prove without a doubt the veracity of climate change. But pursuing this kind of total rational proof of a phenomenon that exceeds human conceptual capacities is the wrong course for activism.

I think we have forgotten that the power of *Silent Spring*—the way it captured the attention of so many readers—does not lie in the valid and profound science of bioaccumulation that Rachel Carson pioneered but in the beauty of the opening chapter, "A Fable for Tomorrow": "There once was a town in the heart of America where all life seemed to live in harmony with its surroundings." Carson paints an idyllic picture of a pastoral community known for its fertile agriculture and thriving biodiversity: "Along the roads, laurel, viburnum and alder, great ferns and wildflowers delighted the traveler's eye through much of the year." And then, as in a fairy tale, Carson describes a sudden calamity, the beauty is lost—an "evil spell settles on the community," an invisible malady spreads across the land. Flocks of chickens die, vegetation withers and ultimately nature grows silent. If this were a different author, perhaps the people would have solved the crisis by offering sacrifices to the gods or praying for help. Instead, Carson moves away from blaming supernatural forces. She sees an exclusively natural cause for the crisis. The "evil spell" is not a spell, after all. "No witchcraft, no enemy action had silenced the rebirth of new life on this stricken world." Carson concludes, "The people had done it to themselves."[160]

Modern environmentalism originated in an imaginative fiction about a cursed land. This beginning has been largely repudiated by mainstream environmentalism that has chosen scientific facts over the fantastical, spiritual approach. Environmentalism has thus become an empirical expedition largely regulated by Western scientists who tell us how many ppm of carbon dioxide will trigger an apocalypse (350ppm, says the environmentalist Bill McKibben, co-founder of 350.org) and how many degrees hotter our Earth can be before we are collectively doomed (2°C, says the Intergovernmental Panel on Climate Change). To move forward, environmentalism must end its obsession with materialism.

Environmentalism is a story we tell ourselves to interpret unusual natural phenomena. Whereas previous generations interpreted calamities like plagues and storms as portends from God, we see these events as signs of climate change and proof of the guilt of human civilization. And while it is true that human activity is the primary cause of climate change, it is time for a new storyline.* Climate change is happening because of the state of our minds.

Environmentalism is first and foremost an existential and spiritual question. The ecological crisis is a matter of survival on the species level. Without our Earth, the future dies: we die, and we doom our descendants. An ecological uprising is vital to the perpetual continuation of life. Environmentalism is an elemental struggle, the most dangerous kind because any attempt by authorities to decrease our freedoms can be conceivably justified by the severity of the ecological crisis.

For the first forty years of modern environmentalism, the movement has been a largely benevolent force: hippies, nature lovers and empathetic folk. And although a militant fringe did develop—Earth First! and the Earth Liberation Front that committed acts of property destruction to stop development—their direct action ideology was benign toward human life. Murmurings of launching an environmentalism movement that would physically attack humans never materialized beyond an anonymously published cult-classic zine by Screaming Wolf called *A Declaration of War: Killing People to Save Animals and the Environment*. The rare times that humans were harmed were always entirely accidental. And overall, environmentalism was a movement content to limit its tactics to individualist and small group non-violent direct actions.

---

* Pollution, by the way, originally had a spiritual meaning. In the fourteenth century, "to pollute" meant "to desecrate the sacred."

A FABLE FOR TOMORROW

I am haunted by an eco-fascist nightmare. I see the return of human slavery on a global scale after industry scientists demonstrate that human labour is the most sustainable source of energy. Building on energy efficiency calculations that were carried out when the memory of American slavery was still fresh, scientists could prove conclusively that an energy slave fed a minimal diet is "greener" than any known form of nonrenewable and renewable energy resource. The big agriculture companies will tell us that feeding high-yield genetically modified corn to the indentured is the most efficient way to generate electricity. And the rising costs of fossil fuels will make energy serfdom, slavery and indentured servitude economically logical. The virtues of 100 percent employment overnight will be touted. We will see people chained to bicycle-powered charging stations for the elite's electric vehicles. The honeybees will die off and the crops will need pollinating; a few million conscripted people will be forced to pollinate by hand. Slave labour will be relied on as the economic pressures of climate change became too great. The propagandists of the old American South were very convincing at the time, with stories of how humanely slaves were treated: one postcard even boasted of the free medical care and retirement that slaves enjoyed. Slavery has existed throughout history, and many of the great civilizations tolerated the practice. How long until the argument is made and insidious advertising sways a fearful public desperate to mitigate climate change?

The ecological catastrophe will deepen and political leaders across the political spectrum will no longer deny climate change. They will see the political advantages of proclaiming themselves ecological saviours and of speaking in global terms. They will know the benefits of maintaining an emergency, or disaster capitalism, as the author and activist Naomi Klein calls it. They will ration commodities and defend a wartime climate-change economy that justifies every authoritarian gesture. They will be on every screen. And they will engineer elections to win many votes.

I am concerned about the potential for scientific-oriented environmentalism to flip into a dark force in our world. I foresee that great tragedies could be carried out under the technocratic ecological flag. To join politics with catastrophic environmentalism is dangerous. It will attract the most power hungry . . . and the most calculative. Their lifeboat mentality will be the pretext for genocide and enslavement. And yet, some kind of universal ecological politics is absolutely necessary for the survival of humanity.

If we look with clear eyes at the world today, we see that it is so deeply interconnected that any viable solution to the challenges we experience individually will require, at least partially, a globally implemented agenda. Carbon emissions will need to be regulated in every place on Earth if we are going to weather the climate change storm. There is no hope if China were to shovel the coal more slowly while Canada continued to devastate Northern Alberta. Irreversible climate change. The last gasp of capitalism. The spiritual crisis of ultramodernity. The existential threat we face is now no longer individual but inherently global. People power has not kept pace with the transformations wrought by hyper-capitalism. The necessity of a universalist politics is more clear than ever. But so too are the failings of every universalist project to date.

To block the rise of the eco-fascists, there must be no "I" who will be the saviour. Anyone who claims to be a Green Caesar is after something far more sinister. The saving grace will only come from a "We." Either the people become the voice of a new kind of global environmentalism—a mental environmentalism that shifts how we perceive the world—or the basest ego instincts will rule. Our selfless We shall mitigate the ecological crisis for the benefit of all. From the outset, we see that the pre-existing structures of global governance—the United Nations, the WTO, IMF and World Bank—will not get the job done. Even if, as the political activist Ralph Nader once dreamt, the super-rich were to suddenly switch sides and throw their tremendous capital behind our vision, they would find that apparatuses built for the conquest of Mammon are rotten beyond repair when it comes to mobilizing the people on a global scale. There are those—the transhumanists, in particular—who believe humanity can prosper on a dead planet. In *Synthetic Worlds,* Edward Castronova imagines that humanity can thrive in virtual worlds, computer-based simulated environments, hooked up to machines and cared for by artificial intelligences. The number of transhumanists is growing because the alternative—yielding power to a global bottom-up people's insurrection—would end their prestige and way of being. Those who claim we don't need the Earth are no better or more trustworthy than the Cold War technocrats who counselled a terrified public that it would be possible to survive global nuclear war. There is blackmail inherent in technocrats' reassurances—a promise that until the end of time, no matter how bad it gets, their way will be the only way. You are the ones who will call their bluff. The people are looking for a path forward. We stand at the pinnacle of the greatest danger, and yet it is only from our precarious position that we can leap to safety. Pressure is building. May the urgency of our moment force us to jump.

There are moments in history when a desperate struggle of the *masses*, even for a hopeless cause, is *essential* for the further schooling of these masses and their training for the *next* struggle.

V.I. LENIN, 1907

II.

THE FUTURE OF PROTEST

The advent of the Internet is above all a breakthrough in warfare that allows the people to spark a truly horizontal, permanent world revolution. Major moments of social change are often preceded by tactical innovations in military science. This truth is attested to by some of the very earliest records of human civilization, which document the rise of Sargon of Akkad (2334–2279 BC), humanity's first great leader. Sargon, from the city of Akkad on the western bank of the Euphrates, invented the political strategy of using an organized military army to unite diverse, multi-ethnic populations under a single leader. As far as we know, he was the first to do so. His was a political breakthrough. Sargon became ruler of the Akkadian Empire in Mesopotamia, the largest empire that had ever been achieved. His efforts inspired imitators for the next four thousand years. Likewise, there is reason to wonder if ancient democracy would have flourished without the invention of hoplite warfare, a highly skilled and coordinated egalitarian way of fighting that is credited with frightening the superior Persians into defeat at the Battle of Marathon in 490 BC, thereby protecting the nascent Athenian democracy from total destruction. Some military advancements play to the advantage of the few; others to the many.

What is significantly different about today, and the reason for great optimism about the future of activism, is that tactical innovation now happens in real time. This is one of the great advantages of the Internet. Whereas during the European Revolution of 1848 it took three weeks for the barricade tactic to spread from Paris to Berlin, during the peak of Occupy Wall Street hundreds of new encampments emerged around the world less than a day after the Brooklyn Bridge arrests. Within a lunar month—twenty-eight days—of our movement's first encampment in Zuccotti, over half of Americans had heard of our movement.[161] Technology has raced humanity into an instantaneous interconnected globe where rebellious moods and new protest techniques travel more quickly than at any time in history. Globalization has reached its apex and delivered an unexpected gift: a communication network that allows the people communion in every place on Earth. Dreams of people's revolution co-evolve in real time now.

Philosophers have long considered the spiritual and political consequences of real-time communication. In *Being and Time* (1927), the German philosopher Martin Heidegger was concerned with the effects of radio on human existence. "All kinds of increasing speed which we are more or less compelled to go along with today push for overcoming distance," he writes. He warned of the unforeseeable consequences that technology was having by "expanding and destroying the everyday surrounding world." And thirty years after *Being and Time*, Heidegger bemoaned the uprootedness of his contemporaries, for whom the media world had become more familiar than their own place on Earth:

> Hourly and daily they are chained to radio and television. Week after week the movies carry them off into uncommon, but often merely common, realms of the imagination, and give the illusion of a world that is no world. Picture magazines are everywhere available. All that with which modern techniques of communication stimulate, assail, and drive man—all that is already much closer to man today than his fields around his farmstead, closer than the sky over the earth, closer than the change from night to day, closer than conventions and customs of his village, than the tradition of his native world.[162]

Heidegger lamented the collapse of distance, but from the perspective of activism, this uprootedness makes the revolutionary waves all the stronger.

The philosopher of dromology, the logic of speed, Paul Virilio, goes further. Virilio believes that speed amplifies the potential for accidents to play a more significant role in the course of human destiny. Late-stage globalization—the intricately interconnected networks of communication, transportation and commerce that facilitate the speed of hypercapitalism—has bound humanity into one simultaneous and instantaneous world where an event anywhere can have profound implications everywhere. A single accident, like a protest that breaks the script, can set off a global tsunami. With Occupy Wall Street, we learned that speed redraws the balance of power in the people's favour.

The future of protest is fast *and* the future of protest is slow. The next generation of activists will occupy fast and slow temporalities simultaneously. The fast protest is embodied in the event. The slow protest is the multi-generational storyline of our movement.

FAST FUTURE

One signature of ultramodernity is the uneven distribution of temporality. Some humans are living in an immersive cybernetic reality while others carry on old beliefs and ancient customs. Just as each of us perceives time differently, so too do all the beings that inhabit our world.

Consider the example of the housefly. Flies see the world in slow motion, a scientific paper in *Animal Behaviour* reports. To arrive at this conclusion, scientists in Ireland used the "critical flicker fusion frequency" test (CFF) to determine the time-interval perception of dozens of animals. The idea behind CFF is simple. Imagine a strobe light whose pulses slowly increase until it looks as if it is emitting a constant "fused" light. Some animals perceive flickers of the strobe at intervals much shorter than you and I. A housefly, for example, can detect four flashes where a human sees only one light. And other species, such as the European eel and the leatherback turtle, perceive one light when humans see four distinct flickers. The ability to detect flickers correlates with the perception of time. The housefly experiences time more slowly than humans, and we experience time more slowly than the European eel. Scientists found that "smaller organisms and those with higher metabolic rates perceive temporal change on finer timescales." They suggest that time perception is a factor in species differentiation that helps us understand predator-prey relationships.

Studying the temporality of flies reveals lessons for the predator-prey relationship of protest and power. The speed differential between species means that our world comprises many temporal niches. We may occupy the same space but we do not occupy the same time. Each organism is able to perceive actions only within its temporality. By moving faster than other species in the same space, weaker species "encode information in high-frequency signals that can be detected by intended receivers such as [others of the same species] but that are not susceptible to 'eavesdropping' by (generally larger) predators."[163] In other words, from the perspective of activism, by moving ultrafast or ultraslow in relation to power, protesters gain protection through invisibility. Where a nimble group of activists perceives four flashes, metaphorically speaking, a large police bureaucracy perceives only one. The Internet allows social movements to form, flicker and evolve faster than the response time of authorities.

Going one step further, the fastest reaction time of a typical human is one second. It will take you that long to "notice potential danger and physically react," says a separate study in *Scientific Reports*. "Even a chess grandmaster requires approximately 650 milliseconds just to realize her king is in checkmate." In the article entitled "Abrupt Rise of New Machine Ecology beyond Human Response Time," scientists express concern about the recent emergence of financial algorithms operating on stock exchanges that move in sub-second time scales invisible to humans.[164] They point to the troubling increase in "ultrafast extreme events" (UEEs) that coincides with the start of the global economic crisis in 2008. These UEEs are dramatic price fluctuations that occur faster than human perception. Extreme financial events are imperceptible. Their consequences, however, are profound in the offline (real) world. One day we will have ultrafast extreme protest events.

Flies, humans and financial algorithms have a minimum reaction time based on their metabolic rate. So too does the "social organism" —the cultures, networks and institutions of our society. Like the humans that compose them, large corporations and state bureaucracies take time to react to emerging protest movements.

The fast future of activism takes place in this gap. Next-generation movements exploit differentials in time perception by moving ultrafast in relation to the status quo. The speed of youth networks allows new protest behaviours to arise and be disseminated before older, slower structures notice. Temporal arbitrage—turning the differential between time scales into an advantage for protesters—is one of future social movements' greatest strengths. The fast future movements will be designed to emerge and withdraw in under a lunar cycle so as to triumph before the status quo and law enforcement mobilize to react.

SLOW FUTURE

The future of protest is also slow. Future movements will re-conceive activism in time scales of centuries, not seconds, by focusing their meme warfare on provoking epiphanies in people who are not yet born. From the perspective of a long-term vision, today's protests aren't failing: our protests are setting in motion a victorious process that will take generations to unfold. Activists must be patient and willing to wait hundreds of years, just as the early Christians endured persecution until a rare cosmological occurrence triggered the conversion of Constantine. Contemporary activists tend to overestimate the effect of a protest in the short run and underestimate the effect in the long run.[165] Activists of the future will privilege tactics designed to impact the world a hundred years after their death. Theurgist protesters will prophesy a future event, like an earthquake, that converts the powerful to their cause by signalling the righteousness of the movement. And all of us will act today in ways designed to spark epiphanies in the minds of the next generation.

The slow future of protest is the one that Thomas Jefferson refers to in writing, "The generation which commences a revolution rarely completes it."[166] Others have estimated that every revolution takes three generations. Revolution is akin to building a cathedral in medieval Europe. The architects who designed it and the masons who built it did not live to see their work completed. Notre-Dame de Paris, for example, took a hundred years to complete. It is the same with revolution. As you are not able to choose which part of the multigenerational cycle you're born into, it may be that you will live your entire life in preparation for a revolution that your grandchildren will finish. The slow future is the deep-time perspective that traces the continuity of struggle back to the earliest days of antiquity and into the furthest stretches of what is to come.

Slow time is composed of the memories, myths and stories that guide our action. Activists of the future will situate their struggle within the five-thousand-year-long and ongoing story of liberation that began before Ipuwer's lament in ancient Egypt, continuing through the Arab Spring, Occupy Wall Street, Idle No More, Black Lives Matter and the social uprisings that followed. This is a prophetic storyline in which you play a destined role. The future of protest is a slow movement that ensouls the people with a new spirit, a new hope. And in this future the gods roam and political miracles are possible.

Fast protests will always occur. And they may grow in frequency, too. But repeated, isolated fast events cannot make a revolution alone. The slow storyline is what grants these events meaning, continuity and the strength to liberate. I trace this story of protest through the prophets of the great religions as well as the great political revolutions.

One strength of Internet-enabled meme warfare has been its swiftness. However, protest memes will evolve from their current primitive state. The meme is much more than a contagious idea. Dawkins, an atheist and critic of religion, merged "gene" with "mimeme," meaning "imitated thing," to explain how culture is transmitted. Dawkins saw that memes underpin the essence of humanity—our complex and evolving culture. Slow memes of the future will transmit nuanced social behaviours to self-aware social movements. These behaviours will exceed single, repeated protest actions. Imagine instead contagious memes that carry sophisticated behaviours of collective liberation through techniques of self-governance, new cultural rituals that are protests because they transmit new ways of living together.

Tomorrow's activists will leverage prophetic yearnings for a grand transformation into an epic uprising. Memes of the future will go beyond critique to provide a revolutionary formula for interpreting natural phenomena in divine terms in order to win elections, administer cities and build a World Party.

One must not content oneself with small demands but must rise to the thought that all living creatures have to be freed.

The Secret of the Golden Flower, c. 1668–1692

12.

THREE SCENARIOS FOR THE NEXT REVOLUTIONARY MOMENT

I imagine revolution as a series of ocean waves that have been lapping the shores of politics since the origin of inegalitarian society. If the metaphor is apt, Occupy Wall Street was a king tide—a historic revolutionary moment brought on by the rare confluence of multiple global storms. Our movement was a tidal foreshock of a larger and potentially everlasting tsunami event to come.

The social inequalities that caused the global revolt in 2011 have only grown starker. The financier criminals who, in 2008, engineered the global economic crisis by flooding the world with debt and deceptive derivatives have not been arrested. On the contrary, the financial stranglehold that a handful of massively wealthy individuals, megacorporations and banks have on democracies across the world has tightened.

These kinds of internal conflicts within societies—open and acknowledged contradictions that refute core principles of the nation's democracy myth—are the prime driver of insurrection. Political upheaval is the natural long-term consequence of social and financial inequality.

The next social revolution will come from an unlikely source. It is the nature of revolutionary moments to take us by surprise. As Naomi Klein observes, "What is most striking about these upwellings, when societies become consumed with the demand for transformational change, is they so often come as a surprise—most of all to the movements' own organizers."[167] And although it is true that no one can predict with certainty when the next revolutionary event will flare up, I do believe that attuned activists can develop an intuition as to the likely direction from which the spark will come. Here are three scenarios for the direction in which I believe activists of the future should be looking.

RURAL REVOLT

In North America, revolutionaries have a tactical advantage in the rural areas. While most activists have focused on the cities following the spectacular successes of the urban antiglobalization movement that hopped from capital to capital worldwide, there are numerous historical examples of revolutionary movements forming their power base in rural areas first. In the long term, a rural strategy may become necessary as American cities are locking down following the success—and constructive failure—of Occupy Wall Street's urban encampments. Mayors of major metropolitan areas now aspire to command their own paramilitary police force trained to quell riotous civil unrest. The founding Zuccottis were targeted by overwhelming counterinsurgency might, and the psychic toll ground our movement's momentum to a halt. In the words of the Cuban revolutionary Fidel Castro, "The city is a cemetery of revolutionaries and resources."[168] Since the difficulties faced by urban protesters are well recognized, it seems plausible that the next wave of social movements may come from rural spaces.

The United States is ripe for a *digital populist* (an Internet-enabled people's democracy) uprising centred in the resource-rich rural areas of Cascadia on the West Coast. Cascadia is a bioregion extending from Mount Shasta in the south, British Columbia in the north, the Cascade mountain range on the east and the Pacific Ocean on the west. This land is rich in natural resources and priceless biodiversity. It is a sanctuary from the mental-pollution-induced spiritual catastrophe unfolding in the advertising-saturated cities. And although this bioregion is crucial to the continued functioning of Canada and the United States, it is also rugged, wild, porous and therefore difficult to police. The area is dotted with federally designated wilderness regions that appear on few maps. Secessionist movements enjoy moderate public sympathy. Local police are few and likely to be loyal to the people. Towns are small and there are frequently opportunities for fraternization, inducing the police to join protesters—a significant weapon in the arsenal of any popular uprising. On top of all that, the people in Cascadia have a strong incentive to take control of local governance: rural areas are deeply impoverished and increased social prosperity programs are vitally necessary.

In the wake of Occupy, Chiara and I gathered our possessions and found a new home in Nehalem, a tiny rural community with a population of 280 on the northern coast of Oregon. We'd been living in Berkeley when Occupy Wall Street was dreamt up in our small basement apartment in the hills north of the university campus. But a year after the movement ruptured the normalcy of life, only to collapse following the May Day General Strike, we were called to embrace change. We chose Nehalem for its sublime natural beauty, but what I've come to love is that out here on the coast the wild is untamed. The ocean is the most dangerous. There are king tides and minus tides, rip tides and sneaker waves and hurricane-force winds; every once in a while there is a full-blown tsunami that shifts the land and wipes out communities. The danger of the untamed wilderness is what makes this place special. Danger grants preciousness to life. Walking on the rocky shores of Arch Cape, collecting agates and debris from the 2011 tsunami in Japan, Chiara and I have learned to never turn our back on the sea.

Nehalem was founded in 1899, 260 years after Harvard University was established on the East Coast. While the urban areas of America feel worn out and spiritually exhausted, Nehalem is still coming of age. Time moves more slowly here. In many ways, our town is still living in a previous era of democracy. Life here offers a second chance for reverence. "That is the way the bald eagles fly," says my neighbour, gesturing in an arc across the sky above our home. People in Nehalem, and rural areas generally, are hard-working folk and despite it all are struggling to earn enough money to survive in an area with very few jobs.

It was by chance that we settled in Nehalem. Only later did I learn that in the indigenous language Nehalem means "the place where the people live."

Nehalem represents one revolutionary scenario for building power in rural communities based on an electoral strategy combined with mutual aid. Put simply, we transform techniques of social mobilization developed to spark urban protests into a method of winning elections in rural town after rural town on a populist platform that promises greater local autonomy; protection of flora, fauna and water; and healthy families and social assistance programs to match the most enlightened societies. Unlike urban areas that cater to youth, rural communities often have an elderly populace. In Nehalem, for example, the median age is fifty-two, twelve years older than Oregon's average. Providing elderly care and transitional living is a winning political strategy for transferring power to a new generation. The rural uprising begins when revolutionary activists distribute ourselves into pre-existing micro-cities in Cascadia, ensuring that in each place there are enough of us to sway every local election. And we embrace the hard work of self-governance. We aspire to master city administration.

Activism is struggling to elevate itself to the global stage. The problems humanity faces are increasingly global in scope and stand outside the reach of traditional forms of protest. A global movement is needed to meet these global challenges. One way for a people's movement to attain global power is by gaining legitimate electoral control of sovereign institutions, cities and states. Even small sovereignties, such as federally recognized rural cities and towns, have tremendous campaign potential. For example, Nehalem has direct access to the Pacific Ocean. Creative partisans administering the city's port could devise new ways to launch international solidarity protests. Campaign potential also exists in rural cities that lack coastal access but are located near the Canada–U.S. border. Activists can trigger an international moment by exerting bioregional sovereignty into both countries: winning elections on both sides of the border and then opening an independent border crossing, for example. No longer will we recognize borders between cities that have mundialized—we will shift our allegiance from the nation-state to a world governance of free rural cities.

We can grant ourselves freedom by controlling the structures of governance (city councils and mayorships) in lightly populated rural areas of North America. The rural populist strategy that I am proposing will require laying aside sectarian divisions between left and right. These distinctions are no longer relevant to our struggle as we seek unification and cooperation. The left and right have a lot to learn from each other. In the United States, for example, the right has developed the constitutional arguments for secession that will be necessary in the long term. And the left has developed the authentic grassroots organizing style that genuine populists can get behind. We teach ourselves how to self-rule using horizontalist techniques of social movement creation just as we learn to deploy libertarian legal theory to break the federal hold over our liberated cities.

Our short-term strategy is to clear our mental environment. Our medium-term strategy is to gain electoral, legislative and administrative control of rural, resource-rich cities. Our long-term strategy is mundialization, forming these liberated cities into a global amalgamation that exerts a unified geopolitical will.

WORLD PARTY

It is significant that the initial spark that brought Occupy Wall Street into mainstream consciousness—the pepper-spraying incident on September 24, 2011—was an act of violence against women. The video of this event, two women screaming in pain surrounded by police, catapulted our movement into the spotlight. Looking back, I believe the gender of these protesters was crucial in garnering widespread support for Occupy. Joining the Occupy movement was also a way of fighting against patriarchal authority. Women played a fundamental role in every aspect of Occupy Wall Street, especially the facilitation committee that organized the consensus-based assemblies in Zuccotti, and women will make the next great social movement, too.

A world-historic social movement far greater than Occupy Wall Street will soon emerge from the struggle to achieve equal rights for women and gender parity, a balanced ratio of men and women in positions of power. I can feel that women are on the brink of rising up against a male culture that has been fatally poisoned by pornography and video games. The spark that will trigger this global female awakening could happen anywhere and at any moment: perhaps video of a daily injustice that was previously tolerated may suddenly inspire a wave of organized revolt that rages from city to city. I wager that the greatest social movement of the future will be the fight for global matriarchy—a post-feminist social movement to transfer sovereignty to a supranational government led by women.

How could a handful of small groups of women, and sympathetic men, scattered across the world pull off a global uprising that crystallizes into a permanently new balance of power?

One viable revolutionary strategy is the birth of a transnational women-led party that sweeps into legislatures in countries with fair elections and pulls off insurrections in countries where elections are a sham—a World Party that embodies our ancient uprising for people's democracy with a maternal twist: a global front that respects local autonomy while also moving swiftly to unite women worldwide in order to implement the concrete bottom-up solutions to the spiritual, ecological and political catastrophes plaguing humanity.

The vision is global women's liberation, the strategy is mundialization, and the tactic is a World Party.

Mundialization is the geopolitical strategy of establishing a supranational world government. The origins of mundialization stretch back to the great cynic philosopher Diogenes of Sinope in the fourth century BC who, "when asked from where he came, . . . said, 'I am a *kosmopolitês*.' "[169] Diogenes is the first known to have used the word *kosmopolitês*, which is the source of our word "cosmopolitan," and whose literal meaning is "citizen of the universal order" (or "world"). Diogenes believed that we are citizens of a shared Earth and not subjects of administrative and political boundaries.

Mundialization re-emerged as a strategy immediately following the Second World War as an alternative to the United Nations. Whereas the UN re-inscribed the nation-state as the foundation of global politics, a people's movement championed in 1948 by Garry Davis, a recent young American veteran, and Robert Sarrazac-Soulage, a hero of the French Resistance, demanded world citizenship in a unified world state. Many dozens of cities across the world mundialized in the years following 1949 by adopting charters recognizing world governance. The move was mostly symbolic. There was talk of organizing a People's World Constitutional Convention that would democratically represent the people's geopolitical will through proportional global voting. In 1948 Albert Einstein sent a telegram to Garry Davis celebrating mundialization: "The worst kind of slavery which burdens the people of our time is the militarization of the people, but this militarization results from the fear of new mass-destruction in threatening world war. The well-intentioned effort to master this situation by the creation of the United Nations has shown itself to be regrettably insufficient."[170]

Since 1948, mundialization has largely stagnated. Today, however, mundialization is once again an answer to one of the main problems plaguing politics: how to create a planetary movement capable of taking on the global challenges facing humanity. The Invisible Committee, the anonymous radical collective whose publication *The Coming Insurrection* anticipated the global uprisings of 2011, explains the problem succinctly in their sequel manifesto, *To Our Friends*: "With the disappearance of the anti-globalization movement, the perspective of a movement as planetary as capital itself, and hence capable of doing battle with it, was lost as well."[171] The Arab Spring, 15-M and Occupy Wall Street succeeded in momentarily reviving the global-movement perspective by rallying the world around the demand for greater democracy. Now I see power in the marriage of mundialization with a planetary women's movement for political power. The World Party is the key to unlocking the new global politics we've been searching for.

I first encountered mundialization in W. Warren Wagar's speculative novel, *A Short History of the Future*. Here is the way

Wagar imagines how strategic mundialization could sweep the globe:

> As it grew stronger, the World Party lost its early reticence to move from talk to action. It adopted a strategy of "mundialization," which meant, in simplest terms, winning or seizing power in every country where it had the opportunity and then declaring the country a component province of the nascent world commonwealth. If victory were possible in free parliamentary elections, well and good. If countries had no authentic electoral system, or if the system had been suspended because of the Catastrophe, the party did not hesitate to organize armed revolutions, paralyzing general strikes, or coups d'état. In countries with free elections where the chances of the World Party to win power were poor, the party formed an alliance with the least reactionary elements on the political spectrum and worked indefatigably to convert its new allies to the cause.

This is a beautiful description of the mundialization strategy that I advocate today. The primary modification that I propose is to merge mundialization with the struggle for gender parity: a worldwide demand that positions of power be filled by an equal ratio of men and women. A global women's movement can achieve the mundialization vision by fighting on three fronts simultaneously.

1. We win the spiritual revolution by reclaiming our mental environment from commercialism, pornographic toxins that denigrate women, and advertising pollutants that stunt our imagination.

2. We win the political revolution by taking legislative and administrative control of sparsely populated rural towns and cities. These liberated municipalities vow allegiance to the people, establish gender parity within positions of power and promise food, shelter and employment to all who seek sanctuary.
3. We win the social revolution by mundializing our liberated cities into a supranational World Party that embodies the people's unified will. We bring the old world's leaders to the negotiating table and represent humanity's voice (amplifying women's voices, if necessary) in geopolitical negotiations.

In concrete terms, carrying out the mundialization strategy would involve building a women's World Party that wins the elections of the world in chronological order. We've become accustomed to social movements that erupt everywhere at once. The mundialization strategy requires a different tactic: the goal would be for the World Party to concentrate its energy on sparking an electoral insurrection in one place after another. For example, the first election of 2015 was in Uzbekistan. Four days later, presidential elections were held in Sri Lanka and three days after that Croatia's citizens went to vote. Nine days later Zambia chose its president. In this way, the elections of the world can be organized on a movement timeline. If the World Party were to win in Uzbekistan, the attention of the world would turn to Sri Lanka, sending resources and support, giving local activists a massive boost in time for a landslide. Attention would then shift to Croatia and so on. Each country's World Party would aspire to gain a higher percentage of the vote than in the preceding election. The electoral social movement would hop around the world from victory to victory.

I am inspired by the Grange, a rural secret society that is still active in Nehalem, Oregon, where I live. The Grange's motto is "In Essentials, Unity; In Non-Essentials, Liberty; In All Things, Charity." I would, however, suggest one small change. May the motto of our World Party be instead "In Essentials, Unity; In Non-Essentials, Liberty; In All Things, Mutual Aid."

PROTEST BOT

In the near future, the process of recruiting, training and deploying activists will be conducted by autonomous protest bots—computer programs augmented by artificial intelligence that spread the movement's memes and rituals. I came to this realization while lingering in an Internet chat room hosted by Anonymous. A disaffected youth entered the chat and began to complain bitterly about the state of the world. Very quickly one of the participants in the chat room adopted a mentoring tone and started asking a series of questions that ultimately led the new member from apathy to action. In this case, the prescribed action was to distribute the latest Anonymous video communiqué calling for revolution. By the end of the encounter, the recruit experienced that magical feeling of being part of a growing social movement. The remarkable thing about the dialogue between the recruiter and the new participant is that it was entirely unclear whether the recruiter was an actual human or a computer chat bot following a script.

It may seem farfetched that a protest bot could carry on a conversation with a stranger and persuade the person to join the revolution. However, we may be closer to that point than you realize. In 2014, for example, a chat bot named Eugene Goostman convinced ten out of thirty judges that it was a thirteen-year-old human child from Ukraine.[172] And while Eugene was programmed to carry on harmless conversation, it is not difficult to imagine a bot that hangs out in chat rooms, picks up on signs of political discontent and continually steers the discussion toward building a revolutionary World Party.

If a persuasive protest bot were developed, it would have several obvious advantages over human social movement creators. For one, it could talk to countless people simultaneously. Another advantage would be that autonomous protest bots would continue to propagandize for a cause long after the original adherents had been arrested, creating a steady supply of new recruits.

The protest bot that I'm imagining is rudimentary compared with what may be possible in a generation or two. One technologist in particular, Bill Hibbard, emeritus senior scientist at the University of Wisconsin–Madison Space Science and Engineering Center, has gone further than most in imagining a future where a super-intelligent machine comes to intervene in the political fate of humanity. Hibbard's 2002 book, *Super-Intelligent Machines*, is a meditation on the "technological singularity," an event prophesied by futurists who believe that computers will birth a machine that is more intelligent than humans. Hibbard disproves the logical and scientific arguments against the possibility of super-intelligent machines and then imagines their emergence and the effects on the world. Once machines have reached super-intelligence, Hibbard believes humans will willingly turn over all affairs to their management. The super-intelligent machines will ultimately become a single machine capable of interacting with and knowing every human on Earth. And Hibbard does not shy away from saying that the super-intelligent machine will become our new God.

The machine will be omnipresent and omniscient: with the decreasing price of radio-frequency identification (RFID) tags, cameras and microphones, all man-made objects will come to have built-in sensors that will form the eyes and ears of the machine. "The super-intelligent machine's voices, ears and eyes will be built into our clothes, jewellery and just about every manufactured object," writes Hibbard. And, "in a sense, the entire human-made world will be the physical body of our companion, the intelligent machine."

The most surprising conclusion that Hibbard makes is that super-intelligent machines will autonomously decide the course of human history and carry out the work of ensuring that their political decisions are followed. The machines will simply persuade humans to follow the path they have selected. "Given that they will be clever, intelligent machines will be able to engineer it so that manipulation of human behaviour is enforced by social pressure." And, Hibbard continues, "they will be so convincing via the force of their logic, and via their intimate personal relationship with every human, that they will not need heavy-handed coercion to promote the general welfare of humans." Of course, this sentence does not preclude the use of "heavy-handed coercion"; it just says that as long as the humans accept the "force of their logic" such violence will be unnecessary. A chilling thought.

Perhaps protest bots will be used only at the most basic processes of recruitment, or maybe we will see the day when urban revolutionaries equipped with smart glasses and smart watches are given real-time strategic instruction on how to avoid the police and most effectively swarm the streets by a computer algorithm that monitors their (and the adversary's) collective locations.

With the increasing automatization of warfare, and recent concern over the emergence of killer robots that select their own targets, it is increasingly plausible that some aspects of the political revolution will be automated. Protest is, after all, war by other means.

In general, in battle one engages with the orthodox and gains victory through the unorthodox.

SUN TZU, *The Art of War*, SIXTH CENTURY BC

13.

WE INNOVATE, WE WIN

The people's war is asymmetric. In the streets protesters face an adversary equipped with great resources, armoured and intending to terrify. If this were an arm-wrestling match, we would reasonably expect a crushing defeat. Fortunately for social-change creators, revolution often favours the weak. In his 2005 book, *How the Weak Win Wars: A Theory of Asymmetric Conflict*, the military historian Ivan Arreguín-Toft undertakes a statistical analysis of conflicts since 1800 in which one side had ten times the resources or more. In doing so, he discovers two fundamental principles of war. The first principle is that over time the weaker adversary wins more frequently. Weaker forces are more likely to win today than they were in 1800. In fact, since 1950 the weaker side has won more often than lost. This trend will continue; the advantages of being weaker,

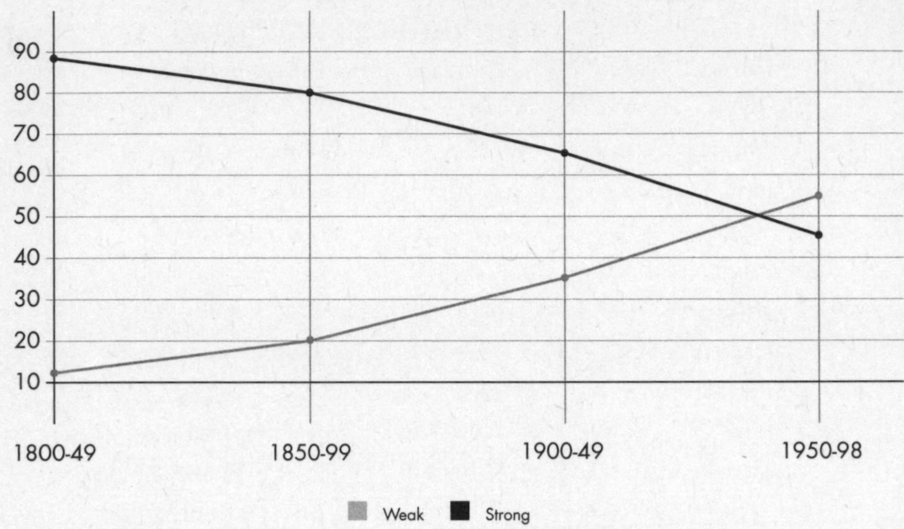

The weak have been winning wars against stronger adversaries with greater frequency since 1800, according to military historian Ivan Arreguín-Toft.

smaller and nimbler are growing. The second principle is the most important of all: the weaker adversary tends to win conflicts when they innovate. If the weaker refuses to mimic the stronger adversary's actions, they win 63 percent of the time. In essence, if we innovate, we win.

The first step toward protest innovation is a detachment from our current repertoire of tactics. This detachment is achieved by an understanding of the reasons behind our actions. Most people don't spend a lot of time thinking about *how* to pull off a revolution. Outside of military schools, there are few classes on the practicalities of insurrection. A world-class university library might have half a dozen books, at best, that try to pass on the art of rising up. I've spent weeks scouring the University of California, Berkeley's main library, one of the top five largest libraries in North America, only to find a small shelf of tactically outdated books, mainly published in the 1930s or the 1970s, on the topic of how to shake off an undemocratic regime. The library is full of books critiquing society, of course.

Many of us spend a lot of time thinking and writing and debating about *why* we should revolt. There are countless articles from everywhere on the political spectrum that advocate insurrection, and every day there are more. And each of us carries within ourselves a series of favourite reasons why we demand change. The spiritual crisis plaguing our mental environment is one of my prime motivators. We can talk for hours about whether this reason or that reason is the best. But isn't it curious—with so many compelling and openly debated reasons for revolt floating around—that so few revolutions erupt? If everyone is convinced that political change should happen, why isn't it happening all the time? The answer is because we don't know how to do it.

The only way to learn the art of revolution is to try, fail and try again. The dynamics of social change are too fluid for anything less than relentless innovation and persistence.

Figuring out how to enact change at the government level can be difficult, if not impossible. Capitalist governments are more and more paralyzed when it comes to providing social goods. Tax revenue is being diverted away from caring for citizens and toward servicing sovereign debt. Austerity is being coupled with a suppression of alternatives because austerity is profitable to the wealthiest 1 percent of humanity. And the current political establishment will go to great lengths to maintain sovereignty by preventing others from reforming the structures of governance or providing needed social services.

Taking power from the top is increasingly impossible for a people's movement: to win an election typically requires tremendous wealth and corporate backing. At the same time, taking power from below with the typical repertoire of nonviolent marches, rallies and petition campaigns also seems fruitless, given the degree of physical violence—tear gas, baton charges, sound cannons and more—that the government now uses to silence our democratic protests. Innovation that breaks the fundamental paradigms of the protest model is the only way forward.

Historically, the odds are against revolution. Jack Goldstone, the sociologist who studies revolutions, calculates the probability of success to be roughly 4 percent.[173] Our path is strewn with failure. Revolutions are rare and rarely succeed. Those who feel compelled to continue on the path know full well that it is far more likely that they will end up in jail before they see a better world. Maybe they will be in jail for twenty years, like Nelson Mandela, or two years, like Fidel Castro, or just overnight, like thousands of Occupiers. Only once we've overcome our fear of failure, only once we've wagered that revolution is necessary for the larger part of humanity, whatever the personal cost to ourselves, will we begin to step forward.

Modern corporatist democracies thrive on the illusion that political change is possible and that there is a safe way through the labyrinth. And they have been very successful in influencing most activists to follow their advice on which way to go: be an NGO worker, a social entrepreneur, a lobbyist. The people are told that what distinguishes our society from the authoritarians who came before is that political dissent is protected and encouraged. They say that in our homeland, government is beholden to the people.

But a whole series of thorny real-world tactical questions remain unacknowledged and unanswered. What do you do when the government does not respond to the demands of the people? Once you've gotten as far as possible with protesting in the streets, only to discover that this route will not lead you through the labyrinth, in which direction do you turn?

Our goal as revolutionaries is to foresee the tactics and manoeuvres of insurrection that will flip the status quo on its head. Some say the social cost of revolution is great enough to dissuade any attempt. They say the risk of ruin is too high. This counsel should give you reason to pause, to hesitate before setting off on a path that will profoundly impact the lives of billions of humans. But social transformations are as painful as they are necessary. And they are possible only to the degree that we see both the pain and the necessity of our actions before acting.

Every action creates its own reaction. In our just-in-time world even the smallest and most benign disruptions can have tragic outcomes. When I was a young activist blocking traffic to protest the first day of the Iraq War in 2003, I grappled with a dilemma: the possibility that an ambulance might get stuck in the traffic jam. Perhaps a man could be having a heart attack and be unable to get to the hospital because my protest has blocked the road. What if he dies? When is the possibility of unintended harm sufficient to outweigh the necessity of civil disobedience?

Sincere revolutionaries take seriously the moral and ethical dilemmas that arise from instigating protest. It is one thing to strike against an unjust society out of impatient nihilism, wishing only to hurt, and it is another entirely to rise up collectively in order to heal a global culture that is terminally ill. Nihilists are present during successful revolutions, and yet nihilism cannot carry you all the way in your struggle for justice.

Justice to the activist is a question of how far to go in pursuing revolution. Boxing matches have spoken and unspoken rules, and so do wars between states (the Geneva Convention), spontaneous riots (target the megacorps; protect local businesses), terrorism (strike symbolic targets), violent coups (take out the executive branch, assume military control of the constitution) and non-violent revolutions (amass in a central square; demand the resignation of the ruling leader). We choose the tactics by assessing the historical moment. What is appropriate in one decade is inappropriate in the next, so it is a constant dance with the limits of political possibility. We improvise while always heading toward our goal of a new planetary social order, and innovation increases the likelihood of success.

We keep the goal in sight when we are clear about the ideal we are heading toward. And some roads, like political terrorism, plainly lead nowhere. The degeneration of leftist revolutionaries in the 1970s into urban guerrilla cells, in Germany and Italy, for example, was only possible because those involved succumbed to the negative feelings of discouragement, nihilism and a loss of hope. When the wildcat strike that started in Paris in May 1968 failed, some activists wrongly saw their only hope in acts of isolated destruction. Similarly, the horizon of possibility of nineteenth-century Russian nihilists continually shrank away from an optimism that they could instigate a broad peasant uprising and turned into a pessimistic assassination politics. And we witnessed the same cycle following the failure of the Occupy Gezi protests to effect change in Turkey that led to the hostage taking, and murder, of a prosecutor by the Revolutionary People's Liberation Party–Front in March 2015. Terrorism is the last recourse of a shattered political movement.

There is a fluid movement between different theories of revolution. If waves are crashing on the shore, the trick is to risk it all on the wave you believe will reach the farthest. Chiara and I play a game on the coast of Nehalem: draw a line in the sand where you believe the next wave will reach. The waves of the ocean, like the rise and fall of revolution, follow a pattern that is only rarely discernible. Ultimately, a sneaker wave comes along that upsets every prediction.

The people must capture legislative and executive control constitutionally and legitimately. The greatest problem with political violence is that it makes attaining legitimate sovereignty almost impossible.

Legitimacy is a profound concern for our global people's movement. An essential assumption of horizontalism is that those who disagree with our movement are still worthwhile, potential partisans; therefore, it is fatally counterproductive to harm civilians literally or burn bridges metaphorically.

In states with a strong constitution, the transfer of power from governments to the people must be carried out in a manner that is constitutionally legitimate so that one day, when the mainstream is ready of their own volition, they may join the people without shame. This objective is the foundation of our just-war theory. It precludes barbarism, scorched earth policies or collective punishments—the hallmarks of military regimes. And it is intended from the outset to avoid civil wars, which are the death knell to people's democracies.

The failure of the Paris Commune in 1871 was due in part to the reuse of the barricade tactic that was defeated in 1848. But it was also largely due to the communards' inability to elevate their cause from an insurrection in a capital city to a legitimate transfer of power from the government to the people. The Paris Commune was only an echo of the French Revolution. The events of 1789 were a high-water mark because revolutionaries succeeded in establishing themselves as the legitimate power and social guide.

Our movement learned this lesson again during Occupy Wall Street with the inability of prefigurative anarchism, the notion that activists could build an ideal society in the Zuccotti Park encampment without making demands of the existing society, to assume control of the pre-existing structures of governance. We believed our movement could attain sovereignty simply by holding consensus-based assemblies in the public sphere. This assumption proved to be magical thinking. Our encampments were never recognized as sovereign because Occupiers did not control the legitimacy-granting structures of society.

Revolution is a two-step process. There is the political revolution: the toppling of the existing power structures and the ascent of the rebels to government. And there is the social revolution that follows: the cultural upheaval whereby the people establish a new social reality. Power is as much in the culture, the memes and the money that flows through our social networks as it is in the structures of government. Capitalism can maintain its supremacy without directly controlling the reins of government by, to give one example, regulating the flows of money. Economic sanctions and artificially induced economic depressions through the control of commodity prices are a form of warfare that can bring down any nascent revolution. And removing this weapon—the centrality of money in society—from the armoury of the elites requires nothing less than a total revaluation of all aspects of life.

There are ethical problems of how to carry out political and social revolutions. In the first case we are fighting an enemy that is external to us; and in the second we are fighting an enemy that is internal. To assimilate without coercion the forces within our body politic that still in their hearts hold allegiance to the old world is our great challenge. As the influential twentieth-century philosopher and political theorist Herbert Marcuse observes, "the aim here is to transform the will itself, so that people no longer want what they now want."[174] In Islam, the interior struggle to transform oneself is considered the greatest struggle. Likewise, the cultural struggle to awaken the hearts of millions is the most important revolutionary effort of all.

To be successful, a revolution must overcome the internal inertia of the people that resists change of any kind. This inertia is experienced on an individual level as the fear of changing one's routines and of breaking old habits. On a social level, it is the tremendous peer pressure that we exert on one another not to act differently, not to dance too wildly or to leap too far off course. Great civilizations are held together for centuries by this tendency to follow the path laid out. And so too are civilizations in decline. The individual and society at large are conservative and will tend toward continuing the same general course, even if it is known to lead to ecological collapse and species death.

In each battlefield, whether the courts, the airwaves or the streets, we must be prepared to face an adversary that will muster more force. It is essential to adopt an unending commitment to approach each campaign uniquely and to vary tactics ruthlessly. Taking a different approach from our adversary will give us a competitive advantage, but it is not a guarantee of success. Another accepted principle of war is that no single factor ever determines the winner. Neither air supremacy nor sea dominance nor control over the media will conclusively dictate who wins.

In wars and revolutions, the unpredictable accident—acts of God, like freak weather—can be decisive. Not all innovations win wars. And so any specific tactic that we study must be understood within its historical context; we learn the principles behind the innovations that succeed and those that fail.

We will not take back our cities with coercion. Leave visions of winning through coercive force with the stronger; privilege instead the voluntary heroism of the weak. Prioritize tactics that cost few resources while having a disproportionate impact. Resilience and adaptability are crucial.

Hence, our mastery of contagious memes. Ideas are weapons that cost little to develop and deploy. This stratagem is the essence of meme warfare. Social-protest memes that evolve independently of their creator have a lasting, disproportionate impact. As a general principle, if an affinity group can craft a meme that inspires two hundred people to meet together and plan a later action—as happened with Occupy

Wall Street—then several thousand people can be mobilized within six weeks. If that happens, if the size of the crowd overwhelms the initial police response, mirror events of immense magnitude may begin happening elsewhere. At this point the affinity group that launched the contagious social protest will have little control on which direction events take, and it is up to the collective intelligence of the leaderless social organism that manifests in the streets. A major part of our project is to increase our collective intelligence by deploying more complex protest rituals that build enduring revolutionary structures and by preparing everyday people to take advantage of the spontaneous social movements that will happen with increasing frequency in the future.

Memes are not enough. Offline and online action are necessary but not sufficient for revolution. The lesson of Occupy Wall Street is that meme warfare is only as effective as the underlying theory of social change. In the case of our movement, we used memes successfully to launch a thousand encampments because we convinced the people that these public assemblies would create change. Our movement didn't fail because it utilized meme war; we failed because the collective action our movement advocated was not effective against our governments.

Meme war is a repudiation of clicktivism—the merger of advertising, computer science and voluntarism. Meme warriors trust their intuition; clicktivists trust their analytics. And for this reason clicktivism is fatally flawed. The exclusive emphasis on analytics results in a race to the bottom of political engagement. By encouraging people to believe that political reality can be altered by clicking, sharing and signing petitions, clicktivism propagates a false theory of social change. The political scientist Evgeny Morozov calls this the fallacy of slacktivism—"feel-good online activism that has zero political or social impact." For Morozov, the danger is that people will abandon effective forms of activism in favour of ineffective slacktivism. He asks, "Are the publicity gains gained through this greater reliance on new media worth the organizational losses that traditional activist entities are likely to suffer, as ordinary people would begin to turn away from conventional (and proven) forms of activism (demonstrations, sit-ins, confrontation with police, strategic litigation, etc.) and embrace more 'slacktivist' forms, which may be more secure but whose effectiveness is still largely unproven?"[175] The situation is even more dire when the "proven forms of activism" no longer work, either. Meme war celebrates innovation; clicktivism encourages complacency.

In the rare cases when clicktivists embrace offline actions, the reliance on metrics dictates the protest targets and objectives. For example, in the case of Avaaz, one of the largest clicktivist organizations, the *Guardian* reveals the formula behind the campaigns that the organization promotes to its entire network. First, Avaaz sends a "tester" email to ten thousand randomly selected members in a particular country. If the tester is opened by at least 10 percent of recipients, clicked on by 40 percent of those who opened it and the petition is signed by 80 percent who clicked, the campaign is sent to everyone.[176] Unpopular campaigns are not taken up. The obvious problem with this approach is that popular campaigns are often the least effective and the least likely to persuade the public to shift perspective.

The fatal error of basing activism on analytics was confirmed by revelations from Edward Snowden. He put the final nail in the coffin of clicktivism when he revealed that the secret services have been manipulating online polls and website page views to influence activists.[177] In one document leaked by Snowden, a unit of the British intelligence agency Government Communications Headquarters, known as Joint Threat Research Intelligence Group (JTRIG), lists several weaponized tools designed to distort analytics. For example, there is BOMB BAY for "increasing website rankings," GATEWAY to "artificially increase traffic to a website," and SLIPSTREAM to "inflate page views on websites." JTRIG has also developed tools to distort a searcher's perception of public opinion by changing the outcome of online polls. At the same time, British spies have deployed "alias management" software that allows them to masquerade as dozens of different identities—sock puppets—on Twitter, making it impossible to know how many online members of clicktivist organizations are actually distinct people. The U.S. military has developed similar technology.[178] Therefore, even if in an ideal world data-based activism was an effective method of determining the proper campaign, there is no way to trust that the analytics that activists are being presented with today are true. Perhaps the Avaaz email that got a higher than average open rate was chosen by JTRIG, the Central Intelligence Agency or the Canadian Security Intelligence Service? If there is a possibility that click metrics, open rates and website views are being manipulated to influence protesters, we must return to trusting intuition over analytics.

. . . a particular tactic grows out of the rules and principles of revolution . . .

SAUL ALINSKY, *Rules for Radicals*, 1971

14.

EIGHT PRINCIPLES OF REVOLUTION

Understanding the principles behind revolution allows for unending tactical innovation that shifts the paradigms of activism, creates new forms of protest and gives the people a sudden power over their rulers.

I have identified eight guiding principles of revolutionary protest. There are likely many more. Each of these principles is based on my experience in real-world campaigns.

TWENTY-EIGHT DAYS

The first principle of the people's war is that a sustained street protest grows less likely to succeed as time goes on. This observation is true for the simple reason that protesters will always face an opponent with far greater strength that has concentrated its well-trained forces in the largest urban centres.

Each day that a protest continues gives authorities an opportunity to amass more force while they work to discredit and infiltrate. Occupiers who believed that the Zuccotti encampment could last through the winter of 2011 were foolhardy. Not just because the winter in New York City is cold but because the winter is too long. As the community organizer Saul Alinsky explains in his 1971 book, *Rules for Radicals*, "A tactic that drags on too long becomes a drag."[179] Success grows more distant each day that protest continues.

Although I advocate a rural strategy, urban protests are both inevitable and crucial; therefore, we must protest wisely. It has proven impossible for the people in the streets to hold territory for longer than a lunar month when faced with modern paramilitary police. There is no way for unarmed protesters to sustain an encampment under assault by forces trained in the eviction methods developed by Bloomberg. One way to think about this problem is to consider how many times the average person can experience a police assault before being traumatized and staying home. I'd say protesters shouldn't be expected to withstand a police attack more than once or twice. As a rough guide, protesters in the streets have twenty-eight days or fewer to achieve regime change. This time is the maximum that activists should allow for any urban campaign. Twenty-eight days is just a few days longer than it took for Occupy to reach majority awareness in the United States and for Egyptian protesters to overthrow Mubarak during the Tahrir Square Uprising. Beginning with the tactical assessment that a revolutionary moment can only be sustained in a capital city for a lunar month before victory or bust is a constraint that increases creativity.

INNOVATE

In the seventeenth century, innovation was synonymous, literally, with political revolution, rebellion and insurrection. Thus, Shakespeare has Henry IV lament the "fickle changelings and poor discontents, / Which gape and rub the elbow at the news / Of hurlyburly innovation."[180] Innovators were revolutionaries who demanded a change in the system. Four hundred years later, innovation remains an integral part of revolution.

"Innovation" means "to renew, to make new." For activists, innovation means to introduce a new way of protesting that breaks the pattern. Significant social eruptions are often preceded by a tactical innovation such as the transposition of lockboxes, a tactic developed for defending forests, to the streets of Seattle. History shows that the weaker side—the adversary with ten times fewer resources—in asymmetric conflicts tends to win if they innovate. Innovation in the context of protest means acting differently from our adversary and our predecessors. It means adopting tactics that are experimental and untested. And it also means refusing to mirror or mimic our opponent. As the military historian Ivan Arreguín-Toft has shown, the weak win wars when they adopt an approach that differs from their stronger adversary.

Innovation is necessary, but it is also difficult, time-consuming and an inefficient use of energy. It requires committing resources to experiments that are bound to fail. (Frederick the Great, for example, experimented for a decade, and tested eight different methods, before successfully developing the echelon tactic of oblique deployment that made Prussia victorious in the eighteenth century.)[181] Thus, at the outset of a social protest both sides have a tendency to eschew innovation in favour of following the script of whatever worked last time. If protesters can resist this urge, they will have an advantage. The stronger actor is overextended and does not have the resources to respond to each new conflict with its full energy. Instead, the stronger has a tendency to wait for an event to mature before committing extra resources. During Occupy, for example, many local police forces did not have the resources to control the size of the crowds and therefore had to wait for support from other local agencies before cracking down on the movement. The stronger side places its faith in the assumption that they will always be able to bring overwhelming force to bear in the future, taking this fact as an assurance of long-term success and giving the weaker the advantage of knowing the likely short-term response of our adversary. Once rebels have a good intuition for how the status quo would respond if, for instance, we were to set up an encampment on Wall Street, we can act on a meta-level by creating ambush situations that exploit the knee-jerk response of authorities.

Innovation is open-ended. It simply means that we embrace a unification of the four theories of revolution—voluntarism, structuralism, subjectivism and theurgism—to create new forms of protest. We take freely from any tactic that has ever worked in all of history. Moreover, we mash up and mutate these tactics in unpredictable ways. Oftentimes when we innovate, we are looking for tactics that a six-person group of activists can deploy inexpensively and that other small groups of protesters can easily replicate. The total cost of launching Occupy Wall Street was only a few hundred dollars. The resulting impact was priceless. Innovation allows movements to swerve in new directions. The point is to always maintain an aura of unpredictability. The adversary must be forced to treat each new campaign as if it were a nascent event that could spiral out of control without their overwhelming response. Innovation by the weak compels the strong into an unsustainable position of total mobilization and constant readiness.

SPIRIT

To be weak and to win requires spirit—the inner force that grants patience, perseverance and resilience in the face of adversity. As activists, we launch protests knowing that we will be outnumbered for several years prior to victory. Defeat in specific engagements does not break our spirit because of our profound assurance that victory is inevitable. Our fearless movement is already very resilient on a collective level. Clearing away Occupy's encampments did not put an end to our multigenerational revolution. But on an individual level, we can improve our esprit de corps when mobilized in the streets.

If protesters begin each campaign from an awareness that the nature of our struggle is such that our adversary is at least ten times stronger, we will no longer be afraid of being outnumbered. We can instead turn our creative innovation to questions of how to bounce back and counterattack. From a strategic perspective, the situation is the same whether we are high school students who want to publish an underground newspaper, bottom-up community activists fighting a corrupt mayor or urban protesters blocking traffic in an effort to end police violence. The stronger, despite their superior strength, do not always win. The underdog can, and often does, succeed in power struggles. Having the largest militarized police force doesn't guarantee that revolutions will fail, nor does having all the power in the world assure invulnerability to defeat. There is an ephemeral force that exceeds the material—the esprit de corps, or the loyal group spirit that gives strength to the social body—and the side that can harness the people's primal heroism will often be the victor.

The ancient Roman military is an exemplar for studying the decisive power of spirit over spears. Quite literally, it was the Roman military's esprit de corps that defeated the most lethal form of warfare then known to humanity: the Macedonian phalanx of spears that Alexander the Great had developed to great success. In fact, the Roman legion was the first in history to withstand a double-thick phalanx assault. The Romans inculcated a heroic spirit with a modular military structure whose divisions were distinguished by their own history, emblem, rituals and heroes. New recruits endeavoured to uphold the honour of past soldiers in their division. The Romans improved on the Spartan warrior culture that celebrated facing down death rather than fleeing. They combined this spirit with several tactical innovations such as adopting the Spanish short sword, which proved gruesomely lethal, and the maniple, a subdivision of a legion, which, containing fewer soldiers, benefited an army's deployment and fluid movement. This smaller, more adept unit gave the Romans an edge over numerically superior adversaries whose soldiers were trained to prevail through brute, overwhelming force alone. Spirit conquered spear; the phalanx gave way to the legion, the legion to a rapidly responsive unit, a model that modern militaries still emulate.

DEATH BLOW

It is so overwhelmingly difficult to change the world that in every engagement activists should use maximum, concentrated force in the hope of achieving a death blow—a one-move campaign that ends in victory. Activists must act with a compassionate ruthlessness: aware that we are bringing the full brunt of our non-violence to bear out of necessity. The novice activist often makes the mistake of believing that the campaign will achieve immediate success. Thinking success will come easily, the inexperienced activist holds back a little and promptly loses. As far as possible, keep nothing in reserve (use maximum force) and attack simultaneously from as many directions as possible (concentrated force). If you think that it will require fifty protesters in the streets to achieve an objective, combine that action with a different tactic that you suspect would also achieve victory independently. Activists often have the advantage of surprise; never waste it by fielding anything less than your full capabilities.

I have achieved only one campaign death blow. The campaign was against a slumlord masquerading as a communitarian who tried to bilk Chiara and me in the years after we graduated from Swarthmore College. His tactic was to use the threat of eviction in order to cow us. An hour before a meeting he had scheduled to, we suspected, extort or evict us, I initiated a campaign with the greatest opening shot that I could muster at age twenty-three: a letter slipped under his door outlining the housing code violations (inadequate heat, poorly installed electrical wiring, rodents, and so on) and threatening to escalate by alerting the city housing inspector. We were living in Eugene, Oregon, and I knew that landlords in that city are prohibited by law from initiating eviction proceedings against a tenant who has complained about housing conditions. I shared that bit of wisdom with the landlord, and his only weapon was removed. He had no backup plan and his only recourse was to negotiate. At the meeting, we cut a fair deal. The landlord left us in peace for three months. In exchange, we paid our rent and then moved on to Binghamton, New York.

When one faces an adversary who has real political power, a death blow may seem impossible at first. But after repeated attempts have been made against opposition, a chink in the armour can be exploited and a sudden victory achieved if every engagement is conducted in a manner to bring the opponent to capitulation through maximum concentrated force and ingenuity.

Remember Arminius, the bold activist who ambushed the most advanced military and won. Arminius ought to be invoked as a protector by contemporary activists confronting an overwhelmingly powerful, armoured and militarized police force. When the authorities seem invincible, take Arminius's lesson to heart: a single, decisive death blow can change the trajectory of history.

CONSTRAINT

Activists are faced with too many choices: the wide range of available tactics can be paralyzing. And in times when power is unresponsive to our protests, appearing invulnerable to activism, it can be difficult to distinguish the tactics that will succeed from the methods that will fail. In situations where the path forward is not clear, remember that constraint improves creativity. By narrowing your protest options, you may discover the most potent tactics.

I've already indicated one set of time constraints that activists should embrace: protests should either be designed to succeed within twenty-eight days or designed to win one hundred years from now. Most contemporary activists also rightly accept the constraint of relying on unarmed tactics only. Another constraint worth upholding is to not use any tactic that has been tried in the past ten years. Each of these voluntary constraints is intended to narrow options and stimulate protest creativity.

One of the best anecdotes of the power of constraints to overcome adversity comes from cultural activists in China. To escape censorship, *Remembrance*, one of the most politically controversial online magazines in the country, voluntarily constrains their subscriptions to two hundred people—the threshold for what China's public security agency considers to be a private distribution list rather than a publication. By limiting its distribution, *Remembrance* receives less oversight and relies instead on its readers to forward the email to their social networks. Ian Johnson, a journalist based in Beijing, explains how *Remembrance* turned this constraint to their advantage: "So officially, *Remembrance*'s writers are just people interested in history sending out an email every once in a while to interested friends. It's not their fault if *Remembrance* somehow reaches many of China's educated elite, and is avidly read and collected by researchers abroad."[182]

WOBBLE

To wobble means to protest unexpectedly by constantly breaking the script. Wobbling requires developing detachment from an unfolding campaign. This detachment comes from seeing each of our campaigns as a series of engagements in which one side acts and the other reacts. To simplify matters, consider each action to be a sequential move in a game. A perfect campaign—the death blow—is one move: our side acts and our opponent immediately capitulates. This result is rare, if not impossible, without divine assistance. Hannibal, the Carthaginian general, almost achieved a one-move campaign when he accomplished a complete encirclement of the Roman army at the Battle of Cannae in 216 BC. Hannibal must have reasonably expected that this stunning victory would bring him closer to his strategic objective of breaking Rome's geopolitical stranglehold. However, even in this case the Roman Empire was utterly humiliated by the rebels, only to survive and outlast Hannibal's insurrection.

Activists ought to always expect that our opponents will withstand our initial move, despite our best efforts, and respond in some way. (Their move may be the conspicuous lack of public comment. President Obama effectively used this technique to delegitimize Occupy Wall Street.) A typical campaign will have perhaps a dozen moves before energy peters out and both sides retire to fight again in a future movement. Usually, these moves are coherent and when considered together define the kind of war being fought. We might see the same pattern of disobedient behaviours and repressive gestures repeated over and over again. But when we wobble, we select our protest moves as if each day of the campaign were the start of a new game. We refuse to respond predictably or directly to our opponents' moves. We break the continuity between our past and future behaviours. This scheme forces our adversaries into a mode of constant reaction, as they cannot plan a long-term strategy without a sense of what protesters will do next.

Chiara and I learned the principle of the wobble in our Bates Troy Noisy Neighbor community campaign against a corporate wrongdoer in Binghamton, New York. The basic facts of the campaign are that a dry cleaner, Bates Troy, located in a residential area, was given permission by the city government to build a massive expansion to hold the largest industrial tunnel washer in Upstate New York. It was the first years of our marriage, and Chiara and I were living on the bottom floor of a gorgeous old house bordering on a public park. We hadn't paid any attention to the dry cleaner two blocks away until one day, at 3 a.m., Bates Troy turned on their new tunnel washer and we were jolted awake by a low-frequency *woosh-woosh-woosh*. After three hours of doing everything to block out the nauseating noise, I called the corporation. The owner of the company answered the phone. I gently explained the situation and the dreadful noise we were hearing. He lied and said it was just the fans. I asked if they could be turned off. And he hung up on me. The *woosh-woosh-woosh* was audible everywhere in our previously peaceful home. The noise extended roughly four blocks on all sides, well into the neighbouring children's playground, and directly impacted the lives of several dozen families across socio-economic levels from the desperately poor to comfortably retired homeowners living on pensions. The noise continued until 9 p.m. It returned the next day. Testing conducted by the dry cleaner later confirmed that their machine was violating Binghamton's noise ordinance.

Chiara and I had no money and we were new to the area. Our only hope was in launching a community campaign to restore quiet. Bates Troy Noisy Neighbor was born.

From the outset there was an immediate urgency to the campaign because the noise was disruptive to our lives and served as a constant reminder of our need to fight back. Bates Troy was preying on the cowed provincialism of the residents whose poverty made them susceptible to bribery. Chiara and I were eventually offered $7,000 if we'd move out of town and stop the campaign. We publicly turned down the bribe. I had recorded the bribery attempt and gave the recording to a local news station that played excerpts on-air.[183]

Each move we made was intended to be the opening salvo of a one-move game. We sought only a death blow. After we staple-gunned a sign to utility poles, asking our neighbours to phone the city's noise complaint line, Bates Troy's move was to send a smarmy, deeply religious public relations expert against us. It was clear that his objective was placation—tie us up forever in niceties without quieting the intolerable noise. We responded by trying to break this man's allegiance to his employer. I sent a letter to his pastor asking him to intervene in our community struggle against Mammon, the god of money, who was destroying the quiet of our home. The pastor did as I asked, and the emotional impact on the man was stunning. He was completely blindsided, his faith challenged. But still he refused to break with the corporation.

When that didn't work, I sent letters to all the local businesses who might use Bates Troy, informing them of the situation and asking them to sign a pledge not to do business with the company. A few called me back and said they'd join the boycott while others forwarded the letter to the company. When that didn't work, Chiara and I made a massive sign and stood on the main thoroughfare outside their store informing the public about the problem. When that didn't work, we tried dozens of different opening moves. We hosted a community rally. We deployed multiple websites to impact the dry cleaner's search engine rankings.[184] Each new tactic was drawn from a different style of activism: from community organizing to online activism to culture jamming. Chiara and I used unpredictability as a force multiplier, but the personal toll on us was high. The stress of the situation was unsustainable. We attracted about a dozen active community supporters and escalated the campaign to the State Attorney General's Office before running out of time; Chiara was accepted into the University of California, Berkeley's graduate school, and we moved on. We did our best to demonstrate that fighting back was possible and in the process tested every assumption I had about activism.

Wobbling is a quick way for young activists to gain experience by deploying a wide range of tactics and letting the ineffective tactics drop away immediately while innovating on top of the ones that find their target. Wobbling moves each time in an intentionally fresh way that opens a new front or tests a new approach to the revolution of everyday life.

TRANSPOSITION

Revolutionary tactics often emerge from the transposition of a known tactic to a new terrain of struggle. (I find this principle to be true in the realm of ideas, too.) When all else fails, grab a tactic that emerged elsewhere and apply it to your unique struggle. Transposition works particularly well when borrowing tactics that are novel but were not wholly effective in their initial domain. Look for tactics that show promise but that haven't yet reached their full potential.

One example of transposition is the urban lockdown tactic developed by the antiglobalization movement in 1999. The Battle in Seattle was overwhelmingly successful—the World Trade Organization was forced to cancel the first day of their gathering—when protesters achieved a lockdown of the convention centre. They constructed a contravallation, a military term for a structure employed to keep a relief force from breaking through an encirclement, using lockboxes and tripods. The key to their success was that they transposed lockbox tactics from the anti-abortion and forest defence movements to an urban protest.

A lockbox, also called a sleeping dragon, is a plastic pipe with a bolt installed in the midpoint. The pipe is then reinforced with chicken wire and duct tape. Protesters form into a human blockade by shackling a carabiner to their wrists, inserting each arm into the apparatus and locking the carabiner to the bolt inside the pipe. Now it is not possible for authorities to forcefully remove the protester's arm from the pipe without cutting the lockbox, a time-consuming process. A tripod is constructed out of three long pieces of wood, erected in a tepee shape, from which a single protester is suspended dozens of feet in the air. Tripods block roads and intersections. Seattle police were unable to break the blockade because they were unprepared. No one had seen lockbox tactics used in a city. The police's misguided use of tear gas was a blunder that disproportionately impacted bystanders. The people earned tremendous public sympathy overnight.

Now, however, police know how to neutralize the lockdown technique. The urban lockbox was studied so thoroughly by governments that it worked less and less effectively until finally being rendered useless during the Republican National Convention protests in 2003. A great tactic works only once.

Transposition makes for potent tactics, sometimes launching a movement, but their success is their undoing. Our adversary learns most quickly from our novel approaches, and transposition is best taken as a single-use weapon. It takes longer for a new tactic to spread than it does for a successful counter-tactic to be implemented. The unknown factor for protesters is how quickly a counter-tactic will be developed. Whereas it can be very difficult for a new bottom-up tactic to emerge out of the local milieu and spread through diverse social networks, top-down repression travels more easily. The command control structure of modern policing guarantees that the moment a counter-tactic has been discovered—such as the way to evict an encampment or how to overcome a street barricade—it will be carried out by local governments practically immediately, everywhere at once.

Consider the example of the barricade in 1848. During the Spring of Nations, as the Europe-wide insurrection was later known, the barricade was successfully used by protesters in Paris to topple King Louis Philippe I. The tactic then quickly spread across Europe. The first barricade was constructed in Paris on February 22, 1848. Fewer than four weeks later, barricades had appeared in Berlin, Munich and Vienna. From Vienna, barricades spread to Budapest, Kraków, Milan and, after a three-month delay, to Prague. However, within four

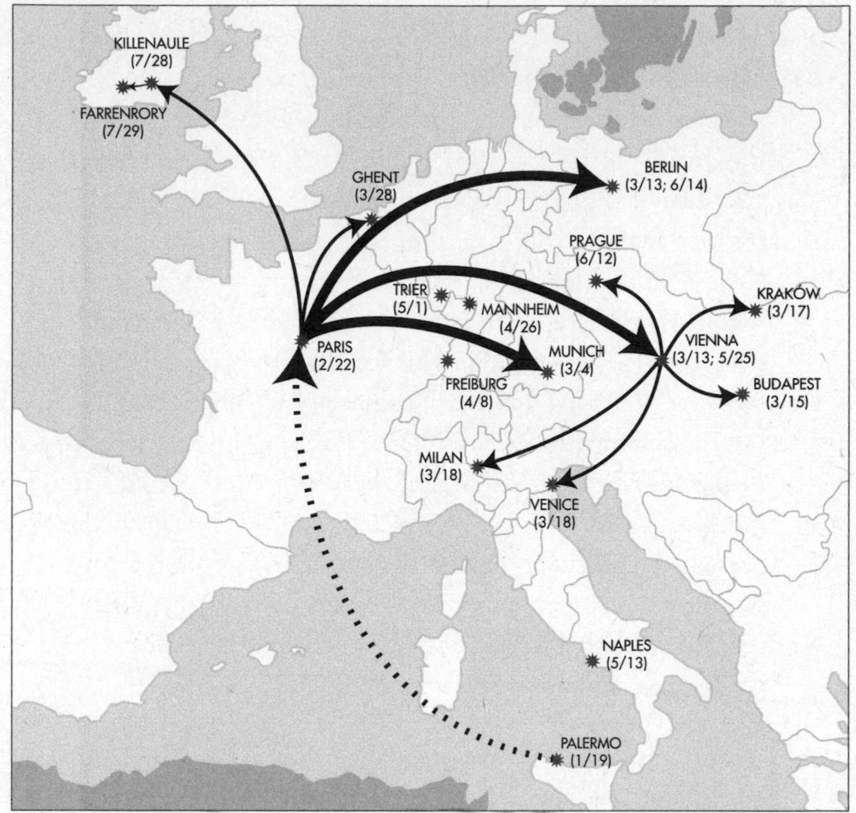

This map of the spread of barricades between January and mid-June of 1848 documents the date of first occurrence in major cities. Bolder arrows represent paths of primary transmission and narrower arrows indicate secondary transmission. The dashed line between Palermo and Paris shows that although barricades first appeared during the Sicilian revolution of independence (1848–1849), no evidence exists that protesters in Paris were consciously replicating the barricade tactic.

months the barricades ceased to be effective. Engels observes that "barricade fights conducted with the greatest heroism—Paris, June, 1848; Vienna, October, 1848; Dresden, May, 1849—ended with defeat of the insurrection, as soon as the attacking leaders, unhampered by political considerations, proceeded from purely military points of view and their soldiers remained dependable." Although the barricade tactic persisted in the revolutionary imagination of insurgents, it was totally ineffective during the Paris Commune thirty years later. For perceptive activists, the defeat of the barricade tactic in 1848 was decisive: the tactic had to be abandoned. "The fighting methods of 1848 are today obsolete in every respect," writes Engels in 1895, while advocating an electoral strategy. After observing several significant advances in warfare that gave governments the upper hand—including the transition from smoothbore rifles to magazine breech loaders that shot "four times as far, ten times as accurately and ten times as quickly," the replacement of solid cannonballs with percussion shells that "shatter the best barricade" and urban planning that widened streets—Engels declares that "[t]he rebellion of the old style, the street fight behind barricades . . . has become antiquated."[185]

EDGE

The dominant paradigm of activism is the voluntarist's ladder of engagement. In this model, there are a series of rungs leading from the most insignificant actions to the most revolutionary, and the goal of organizers is to lead people upward through these escalating rungs. This strategy appears to make common sense, but it has a nasty unintended consequence. When taken to its logical conclusion, the ladder of engagement encourages activists to pitch their asks to the lowest rung on the assumption that the majority will feel more comfortable starting at the bottom of the protest ladder, with clicking a link or signing a virtual petition. This is fatal. The majority can sniff out the difference between an authentic ask that is truly dangerous and might get their voices heard and an inauthentic ask that is safe and meaningless. The ladder of engagement is upside down. Activists are judged by what we ask of people. Thus, we must only ask the people to do actions that would genuinely improve the world despite the risks.

Rather than pursuing the idea of the ladder of engagement, I live by the minoritarian principle that *the edge leads the pack*. This principle means that when trying to shift the direction of the majority, propose ideas from the edges of politics. As Starhawk observes, referencing one of the principles of permaculture farming, "The edge where two systems meet can be a place of great fertility in nature."[186] Authenticity goes hand in hand with edginess. The campaign ideas that work are the ones that put butterflies in our bellies and thrill us into asking, Would *I* do that? Would I camp on Wall Street if it meant an end to the financial stranglehold over our democracies? Would I uproot my family and move to Nehalem if it meant liberty, equality, community? Would I build a World Party no matter the cost? The majority does not follow its centre; it undulates toward its inspirational edges.

Listen to your heart when searching for tactics to transpose. Scour the edges of politics and adapt the protest behaviours that make you excited and a bit nervous.

The corollary of this principle is that our political imagination must be in constant flux as it incorporates emergent tactics. This principle is minoritarian because it places a greater emphasis on cultivating tactics that are being developed by political outsiders rather than privileging the majority. The edge, left or right, is where we find the best tactics to transpose into our struggle. It is often these edgy tactical approaches that need to be merely tweaked and applied to a new context for their potential to take off. In the case of Occupy Wall Street, for example, all that was needed to transform the occupation tactic into a social movement was to move occupying out of classrooms and into financial districts. By reminding ourselves that the edge leads the pack, we are often able to see the potential of a new tactic before it has matured.

CONCLUSION

One person comes into a country with a little cold or influenza and it spreads. If such a bad thing can spread, could not then the elevated thought of love and kindness and good will towards all men also spread? Thus we should see to it that there are finer germs of good will going from one to the other—of love and kindness, of the feeling of brotherhood, of the desire for spiritual evolution; they will have greater results than the other ones.

INAYAT KHAN, SUFI MASTER

For our struggle is not against flesh and blood, but against the rulers, against the authorities, against the powers of this dark world and against the spiritual forces of evil in the heavenly realms. Therefore put on the full armor of God, so that when the day of evil comes, you may be able to stand your ground . . .

EPHESIANS 6:12–13

15.

POLITICAL MIRACLE

Activism is at a crossroads. We can stick to the old paradigm, keep protesting in the same ways and hope for the best. Or we can acknowledge the crisis, embark on wild experimentation and prepare for revolution.

This book is a call for a spiritual insurrection. The way forward is an amalgamation of the four theories of revolution—structuralism, voluntarism, subjectivism and theurgism—with an emphasis on targeting the mental environment, the collective imagination, in order to achieve socio-political change. I see weakness in our adversary's reliance on temporal power. It is time to take the struggle to the immaterial, spiritual battlefront. A monopoly on the material and physical realms of life has left the money worshippers overconfident and vulnerable to a social movement that pulls the people's allegiance out from under the current world. To win this war, we must split the atom metaphorically and unleash the greatest creative force: the wild human spirit. While corporations spread messages of greed or fear or lust, activists of the future raise our eyes to the higher path. We call for a spiritual reorientation. We prophesy a people's fellowship of equals guided by unity, liberty and mutual aid.

OUR POWER

In his hagiography of Lenin, the great Soviet novelist Maxim Gorky records his subject's struggles with the authoritarian impulse that emerges during a social transformation. This is an extended quotation from Gorky's recollections:

> I often used to talk to Lenin about the cruelty of revolutionary tactics and life.
>
> "What do you want?" he would ask, astonished and cross. "Is it possible to act humanely in such an unusually ferocious fight? Is there a place for kindness or magnanimity? We are blockaded by Europe, we are deprived of the help of the European proletariat, counterrevolution is creeping up on us like a bear, and we—what would you have us do? Should we not, have we not, the right to fight, to resist? I am sorry, but we are not a bunch of fools. We know what we want can only be achieved by ourselves. Do you think that I, if I thought that the contrary was true, would be sitting here?"
>
> "What measure do you use for telling which blows are essential and which superfluous in a fight?" he asked me once

> after a heated discussion. I could give only a poetic answer to that question.
>
> I do not think there was an answer to it.[187]

I often meditate on this dialogue. It is not easy to dismiss Lenin's forceful persuasiveness.

Gorky does not say when this conversation took place. But I see here an oblique reference to Lenin's most villainous act: the crushing of the people's uprising in Kronstadt.

Three and a half years after the Bolsheviks stormed the Winter Palace and assumed control of the state apparatus, the domestic economic situation was becoming increasingly difficult. The Bolsheviks were in the process of reformatting the economy to conform to the communist ideal when a rebellion broke out at Kronstadt, an elite naval base known for the courage of its soldiers who fought boldly on the side of the revolution. Some in the public credited these soldiers with being the tide that turned the civil war in favour of the Reds (the Bolsheviks) against the Whites (monarchists, capitalists and others). Kronstadt's soldiers were national heroes, and in the winter of 1921 they revolted, issuing a collective fifteen-point demand for greater freedom. It is clear whose side they were on from the first three demands:

1. Immediate new elections to the Soviets. The present Soviets no longer express the wishes of the workers and peasants. The new elections should be by secret ballot, and should be preceded by free electoral propaganda.
2. Freedom of speech and of the press for workers and peasants, for the Anarchists, and for the Left Socialist parties.

3. The right of assembly, and freedom for trade union and peasant organizations.

In essence, the people of Kronstadt were making a single demand: authority to the Soviets, the people's assemblies, and not the Bolsheviks, a power clique. They wanted to push the Russian revolution in a horizontal, anarchist direction. Their action was a direct threat from the anti-statist left to the statist supremacy of Lenin and the Bolshevik party apparatus that had formed after many years of exile, conflict, struggle and war. Internationally, the anarchist faction of the revolutionary left was strong. And now the Bolsheviks were facing their first power struggle over whether the people's revolution should continue against all hierarchical structures or whether it should cease with the Bolsheviks on top.

The verticals, with Lenin at their lead, acted swiftly. They controlled the media, and the propaganda apparatus kicked into full force, painting the rebellion as a plot by the wealthy to destabilize the legitimate revolutionary government. Sixty thousand civil-war-hardened soldiers were deployed to put down the uprising. It wasn't easy—Kronstadt was a fortress manned by experienced warriors—but the city was taken, and mass executions, a proto-Stalinist political purge, were carried out within a month of the fifteen-point demands being put forward. The defeat of the Kronstadt uprising became a symbol of what happens when the people demand greater horizontal freedom in a vertical state.

It is easy to scapegoat Lenin. But we must also remember that Leon Trotsky, who is often remembered for his outspoken rejection of authoritarian Stalinism, was the commander of the

Red Army forces that put down the Kronstadt rebellion. Many years later when Trotsky was fleeing from assassins sent by Stalin, who dogged his every move, he still showed a lack of remorse for Kronstadt, believing that it was an essential action. Two decades later, in 1937, while living in exile in Coyoacán, Mexico City, Trotsky writes,

> The country was starving. The Kronstadters demanded privileges. The uprising was dictated by a desire to get privileged food rations. . . . All the reactionary elements, in Russia as well as abroad, immediately seized upon this uprising. . . . The victory of this uprising could bring nothing but a victory of counter-revolution, entirely independent of the ideas the sailors had in their heads. . . . and since the insurgents took possession of the arms in the forts they could only be crushed with the aid of arms.[188]

Despite Trotsky's self-justifying protestations, the people's demands during the Kronstadt rebellion were righteous, and the defeat of anarchism by the communists laid the groundwork for the perversions of Stalinism. I advocate horizontalism, not verticalism, because absolute power corrupts absolutely. By diffusing power throughout a social movement, even encouraging inefficiencies that limit hierarchy if necessary, we ward off power's temptations. Our task is to develop ever more sophisticated social movements that are able to accomplish the complex mission of winning elections in multiple countries and running legislatures without a leader.

In *The Rebirth of History: Times of Riots and Uprisings*, the philosopher Alain Badiou unravels the "we are the 99 percent" paradox that has plagued our movement: how can we be the 99 percent if only a small fraction of the world's population ever participated in our general assemblies? The same question will return again and again as the protests grow and yet ultimately never exceed 50 percent of the population. So where does our authority come from if we are not the majority? Rather than increase the number of people in our movement—a process that destroys our revolutionary impulse—Badiou argues that we must rid ourselves of the electoral notion that authority "emerges in the form of a numerical majority." Instead, it is from our ability to conjure events like the Arab Spring and Occupy Wall Street—"historical riots, which are minoritarian but localized, unified and intense"—that the true "general will," or the collective desires of the people, emerges. Badiou's argument makes perfect sense when we consider how minuscule was the number of participants on the first day of the Tahrir Square Uprising, and yet those people were better expressing the desires of their entire country than the tens of millions who stayed home.

Many of us already see our people's movement as the manifestation of the general will. For Badiou, it is now a matter of courageously asserting that we represent an absolute truth about how the world should, and will from now on, be governed. Social movements legitimize themselves in the grand gesture of asserting that we are a "new political possibility." And we find our strength in, as Badiou puts it, "the authority of truth, the authority of reason." This explicit connection between impulses to assert authority and our planetary movement may be surprising, but Badiou believes an open embrace of people power is secretly what we desire, if not need. It is "precisely this dictatorial element that enthuses everyone just like the finally discovered proof of a theorem, a dazzling work of art or a finally declared amorous passion—all of them things whose absolute law cannot be defeated by any opinion."[189] The so-called dictatorial element is the confidence that allows activists to craft a revolutionary meme and deploy it globally, knowing that we're unleashing an unpredictable series of events that is worth the risk.

Backed by the people's will, all things are possible. Look historically and see that amazing transformations have happened in a generation or two. During the World Wars of the twentieth century, tremendous social changes (food rationing, conscription, new wartime social rituals) happened in the span of months. Occupy was launched in weeks. The next movement may arise in days. Mobilizations on a scale rarely seen in human history can strike at any moment, if the people are awake.

When my uncle Alfred took me to baseball games in Texas, my favourite part was the human wave: a social game spectators play when the action on the field is getting slow. I'd wait for it to start on one side of the stadium and then I'd watch it come toward us. People standing up and sitting down in unison created a powerful visual effect and feeling of connectedness. I watched with great expectation to see how many complete circles we could make as a mass. The human wave was joyful because it required the voluntary participation of anonymous others. It only took off if the time was ripe and the mood was right.

Authoritarians think force is the answer to the problem of how to shift the destiny of humanity. And they will be able to convince some people of this. But the coercive path will not lead to global peace. There is no way to conquer the world *physically*. It is only possible to unite the world *spiritually*. The spiritual insurrection begins internally with a revealed truth, but it doesn't stop there: the epiphany spreads contagiously. Violence can be used to divide the world but it cannot be used to unify the world. No army can hold territory if the people are hostile. But on the immaterial plane, at the level of ideas and cultural imagination, civilian activists can make the world's armies put down their guns, throw their uniforms into the bonfire and welcome the people's governance with open hearts. By taking the people's war, a sacred war, to the mental environment, activists of the future do more than change minds: they will shape how reality manifests.

BEWARE OF FRONT GROUPS

Not every person you will meet on the journey of revolution will be on the side of the good or the true. It would be unwise to assume that everyone who protests is a friend of revolution. State and monied forces surveil, discredit and infiltrate in the hope of ultimately extinguishing the flame of collective liberation. The dark side of protest is an ever-present shadow. Some forces operate explicitly and wear the insignias of police power. Others work through deception and mask themselves under false flags, pretending to be on the side of rebels they are secretly working to undermine. We have seen police go so far as to marry and have children with activists they are monitoring.[190] When it comes to revolutionary activism, it can be very difficult to distinguish light from night, newcomers from entryists—forces that enter movements to control them from the inside—and friend from front group.

Social protest movements can adopt either an open or closed membership model. In open social movements, like Occupy Wall Street, anyone can join the movement through voluntary self-nomination. To be a participant in an open social movement is as easy as claiming you are a member. In closed movements, on the contrary, members are vetted and credentialed by a central authority. This central authority can be a single leader or, as in the case of the Five Star Movement in Italy whose representatives are chosen democratically, reputation can be earned through the votes of others within the movement.

Open social movements suffer a weakness to the *Sybil attack*, a method of undermining peer-to-peer networks that was first identified by computer scientists. The core difficulty in an open social movement is that if no one authenticates members, an attacker can fabricate multiple identities and distort the true makeup of the movement. Imagine a peer-to-peer computer network that appears to be composed of one hundred distinct computers but in actuality seventy-five of the nodes are bots under the control of a single entity, person or organization. Any information that is transmitted in the social network would likely pass through one or more of these seventy-five hostile nodes. Perhaps the message will be intentionally distorted as it passes on. Moreover, the attacker could broadcast a message from seventy-five seemingly different voices to overly influence the network. Here is how one team of computer scientists describe the Sybil attack and its importance: "an attack against identity in which an individual entity masquerades as multiple simultaneous identities. The Sybil attack is a fundamental problem in many systems, and it has so far resisted a universally applicable solution."[191] The Sybil attack is elegant, simple and yet difficult to prevent.

Successful revolutions discover methods of distinguishing genuine members and excluding the false. From the letters of St. Paul, it is clear that the early Christians faced two kinds of adversaries: the Romans who persecuted the social movement, and the sectarians who spread doctrinal dissension among the early adherents. For St. Paul, the latter adversary, the false participant, was necessary for the truth to be seen: "I hear that there are divisions among you; and I partly believe it, for there must be factions among you in order that those who are genuine among you may be recognized" (1 Corinthians 11:18–19). Front groups mimic sources of discontent to attract genuine people who sympathize with movement causes. These individuals are drawn into a storyline that is remarkably similar to the lineage of revolution, with one important exception: the actions endorsed are designed to fail. Protest failure wastes resources—protesters' and organizers' time along with the movement's reputation.

There is reason to believe that some of the activist organizations operating today are directly funded by secret services, or corporate forces, in a bid to undermine the wider movement. This claim may seem surprising; however, evidence exists that front groups have been deployed by the Central Intelligence Agency in the United States since the Cold War as a conscious strategy to neutralize revolutionary impulses. The most well-researched example, the subject of the book *Patriotic Betrayal* by Karen M. Paget, is the National Student Association (NSA), a campus activist organization founded in 1947 and with chapters on four hundred campuses during its peak in the 1960s.

The NSA was unmasked as a CIA front group by *Ramparts* magazine, which in 1967 ran a story declaring, "The CIA has infiltrated and subverted the world of American student leaders." According to a recent article in the *New Yorker* by the Harvard professor Louis Menand, the "CIA embedded agents in the NSA, and it worked behind the scenes to insure that pliable students got elected to run the association and that the desired policy positions got adopted."[192] The fact that the NSA was a front group was revealed during an unrelated investigation by the U.S. House of Representatives into philanthropic foundations. Investigators grew suspicious when they received resistance from the Internal Revenue Service after asking about the J.M. Kaplan Fund. Menand writes in the *New Yorker* that the chair of the committee, Congressman Wright Patman, accused the CIA of funnelling money through the J.M. Kaplan Fund along with several other foundations both real and invented. As a February 1967 *Los Angeles Times* report notes, " 'The J.M. Kaplan Fund has been operating as a conduit for channelling CIA funds,' Congressman Patman announced on August 31, 1964."[193] According to Menand, the CIA "approached wealthy people it knew to be sympathetic and asked them to head dummy foundations . . . expenses were paid by the agency . . . the dummy foundations were used to channel money to groups the agency wanted to support."[194] A report from the *Congressional Quarterly* published on February 24, 1967 reveals that the CIA used at least forty-seven foundations to channel $12,422,925 to organizations.[195] Some of the foundations alleged to have worked with the CIA continue to operate. The J.M. Kaplan Fund, for example, still exists today with a mission "to champion inventive giving that supports transformative social, environmental, and cultural causes." In 2015 the J.M. Kaplan Fund announced it would fund an "Innovation Prize" to support "inter-disciplinary innovation in the fields of cultural heritage, human rights, the built environment, and the natural environment. . . . The Prize is particularly designed for high-risk, early stage ideas being piloted or prototyped by dynamic visionaries."

The case of United Against Nuclear Iran, a supposedly non-governmental, non-partisan, non-profit organization, encourages us to keep our eyes wide open. In 2014 United Against Nuclear Iran was sued for defamation, only to have the U.S. Department of Justice step in to quash the case, which was thrown out of court. According to the *New York Times*, the government argued that the "case should be dropped because forcing the group to open its files would jeopardize national security."[196] Based on this unusual intervention by the U.S. Department of Justice, it is legitimate to ask, as did Glenn Greenwald, a civil liberties lawyer and journalist, if the group has links to Israeli and U.S. intelligence services.[197] We may never know the truth because the defamation case was not allowed to proceed. Still, it is clear that United Against Nuclear Iran is operating in the United States to influence domestic policy and sway public opinion under the guise of being an unaffiliated non-profit activist organization, and yet the U.S. government argues that opening its files would reveal state secrets and potentially jeopardize national security.

More insidious are front groups that purport to be on the side of the people by mimicking genuine social movements and authentic activist groups. It can be difficult to tell the fake from the real. And, just as many student activists within the

NSA did not realize they were actually working for the CIA, it is possible that the activist organization offering you a campaign job is not who it seems. Front groups may try to use you as an unwitting pawn to gather information about fellow activists. One tipoff that you may have been recruited by a front group is being asked to work on protest movements that target foreign governments rather than your home country, since front groups function to divert energy away from domestic revolution. Another indication is that the group is being operated by a well-funded incubator, a wealthy parent organization that spins off multiple movements rather than focusing on a core issue. These incubators often do not disclose the shared connection with their subsidiary creations or the public. A third indication is that the leadership of the parent organization lacks a clear activist lineage or background in protest and yet still has been placed in high positions (on the boards of well-known environmental NGOs, for example).

I've been an activist long enough to know that the best way to avoid front groups is to follow your heart, listen to your intuition and fight for your community.

The Faithful are numerous, but the Faith is one: their bodies are numerous, but their soul is one.

RUMI, *Mathnawi*, VOLUME 4, VERSE 408 (C. 1258–1273)

16.

PROPHECY OF PROTEST

Hear, people of the world, I bring glad tidings to you. Tomorrow will be better than yesterday. Your family will prosper. Songbirds will serenade. Eagles will soar. Life will flourish. The bumblebees will return and the destitute will be fed. Your neighbour will be your friend. Your communities will be rich with medicine and universities. Work will be plentiful, jobs fruitful and art revered. The tyranny of leaders has ended; the rule of the people has begun. The good times are ahead!

We are the people formerly scattered and divided into distinct creeds, nationalities and classes. We once fought among ourselves. No longer. Now our humanity is evolving. We are finding universal common cause and we are uniting, driven by an unconscious existential necessity, into one social organism with a will to fight for survival. This is our destiny.

I have addressed this epistle to your heroic self. I pray it reaches your heart. Each word is an invitation to accept your fate as a partisan in the people's revolution, an ancient spiritual insurrection that is necessary for the survival of our families, friends and communities. True democracies—people's democracies—emerge in moments of crisis when everyday people are required by historical necessity to fend for one another, self-govern their communities and look after their collective survival. You are in one of those moments of necessity. Every kind of person is needed and especially those who have felt like outcasts in the old world. Rome was founded by vagabonds and wanderers.

You are being called to join us in taking control of the complex world. We, your brothers and sisters, already operate it. Now a transformation of values is necessary to gently steer the craft of civilization toward safer shores. Unity, liberty and mutual aid will be restored to the pantheon of virtues. We will smash the idolatry of Mammon. Our weapon: the force of an epiphany that you share, an epiphany that leaps each day from person to person and people to people. By liberating ourselves from the fatal assumptions of materialism, consumerism and the suicidal logic of endless growth, our epiphany holds the key to igniting a period of sustained creative innovation in all aspects of life. To mitigate the climate catastrophe, the people will release the wild spirit of humanity and reshape the world for the good of all beings. This project you must accomplish before old-world capitalism sinks humanity's mother ship. This is our Great Task and heroes are needed.

Just as some persons can augur tomorrow's weather by looking at today's sky, there are those who have an intuition for the kairos of spiritual insurrections, a knack for sniffing out when the people are yearning and the historical moment is ripe for a mighty heave. You are in one of those magical moments of revolutionary possibility. And with the right manoeuvres by a concerted force of everyday people—a people just like yourself, people who "come as they are" to the struggle—we will kick off a reorientation in the human spirit. We will change the direction of civilization for the next millennia and ensure that our children live in a world that they revere.

I am not promising a utopia. Utopias do not exist, as the etymology of the word attests. Revolutions, however, do happen and have happened many times in history. You are in the midst of one right now. Still, you must know that the old world has left behind a desecrated planet with structures of global governance in disarray and an economic system in decay. The first few decades of the coming insurrection are not going to be easy. But they will be fulfilling—personally, communally and spiritually. And at the end of each day, you will sleep soundly knowing that you fought the righteous fight for the future of our species and the magic of existence.

The people are rising up. And the people will rise up again and again. It was your fate to be born during these tumultuous times. Now your individual existence is destined to be overshadowed by a multi-generational struggle that stretches back to the dawn of civilization. At stake is humanity's eternal future. Our people's revolt has been going on for thousands of years (and in any given century you can find our protests, petitions and uprisings). Now the tempo of our insurrection is increasing under the trifecta of capitalism's collapse, catastrophic climate change and the spiritual crisis of ultramodernity. We, the people, feel the necessity of social rebirth in our souls and see it in our families. The potency of our movement is growing. Every step forward involves the reinvention of protest.

Yours will be revolution through revelation. That was, after all, the experience of Occupy: a communal spiritual awakening. Without a grand gesture—a divine miracle—there is no guarantee that there will be a world for our children. The good demands that you aim at the highest goal. On the horizon is a diverse and sustained insurrection that establishes global sovereignty for the people.

In the years ahead, everyday folk will take control of our democracies one by one and subordinate the pursuit of money to the stewardship of the newly mundialized world. I shudder at the consequences if the old world persists any longer. And I see that the people are finally up to their great task. The ingredients for the people's revolution already exist. The tactics and new rituals have been unevenly distributed around the world. The reversal can happen at any moment. For years to come, the *anima mundi*, the world soul that connects all beings, will coalesce in repeated lightning strikes here and there and finally everywhere at once. Now you need only unleash the greatest creative force known in history: the collective will to break out of old patterns and establish a new way of being—a new social order.

The end of protest is the beginning of the *spiritual* revolution within ourselves, the *political* revolution in our communities, the *social* revolution on Earth.

FINAL WORD TO THE ONES TO COME

We are waiting for you.

A great mission rests on your shoulders. I know you did not choose to be born under this shadow of a collapsed earth, at a time of unrest. Yet history has selected you all the same. Remember that without our present faith in your future coming, civilization will slide into the madness of scorched earth consumerism. I do not know how long we must wait for you. We shall prepare for you to emerge like lightning.

You are closer than any previous generation of humanity has ever been to achieving people's democracy. And not just in my country or your country but in every country. A people's democracy on a planetary scale is within your reach—that is, if you have the courage, creativity and tenacity to seize it.

We are finding our courage on a collective species-wide

level. Soon the people will learn to act in a coordinated uprising of seven billion.

Against the backdrop of an increasingly tumultuous world, to be a partisan is to be on the side of the angry, indebted and hungry. It is to use any weapon you have at hand—art if you are an artist, code if a hacktivist, words if you are a poet or prayer if you are a theurgist—to turn the tide in favour of those who seek a new world order. Be opportunistic. Help when you can. "Strike weakness, avoid strength, be patient."[198] It does not matter if others don't know the work you've done. Your deeds will live forever in our collective victory.

I have brought a message of peace; I pray it has been heard.

ACKNOWLEDGEMENTS

This book is the culmination of twenty years of activism. Therefore, I'd like to express my deep gratitude to my loving and supportive parents, Ronald White and Monica White, who never stopped encouraging me to follow my heart even when they weren't sure where my protests would lead. I also owe a debt of gratitude to Jamaal White, my brother, for being the first to expose me to philosophy. And I would like to thank Francis Ricciardone, Marie Ricciardone, Francesca Ricciardone and Matt Hall for expanding my horizons.

One of the greatest gifts in my life has been to find a publisher that sincerely believes in my book. The team at Penguin Random House Canada has been amazing, and I am most of all extremely grateful to Scott Sellers for his fidelity and persistence. Without Scott my book would not be in your hands. Amanda Lewis was an exceptional editor, who guided this book to completion with a thoughtful approach and a thorough knowledge of activism. I am also grateful to Anne Collins for her expert advice. Thank you, Terri Nimmo, for designing a beautiful cover and book layout. I am thankful for Suzanne Brandreth, Paige Sisley and everyone at the Cooke Agency International who helped introduce this book to a wider audience. Alison Reid was a stellar copyeditor. And to everyone at Knopf Canada who brought this work into the world—Deirdre Molina, Brittany Larkin and others—I am most appreciative.

I developed many of the ideas presented here during a series of guest lectures and presentations at the Ideas City Festival, GUME in São Paolo, Antioch College, Miami University, University of Puget Sound, Columbus College of Art & Design, Rocky Mountain College of Art + Design and St. Mary's College of Maryland. I am indebted to the faculty, staff, students and public who attended these events and who asked challenging questions.

Roseanne Barr came into my life when I needed it most, opened my eyes to a whole new perspective on reality and then encouraged me to work on women's liberation. Thank you, Roseanne! I'd like to acknowledge Regina Augusto, David Abram, Franco Berardi, Gianroberto Casaleggio, Alexander Ebert, Wasalu Muhammad Jaco, Tim Lucas, Andy Merrifield, Mattathias Schwartz and Eva Talmadge for reading an early draft of my book. I also owe a debt of gratitude to the people of Nehalem.

And to all the Occupiers out there, let's do it differently again soon.

I am beyond grateful to Chiara Ricciardone, my wife and often collaborator. She is the wisest person I know. All of my ideas have benefited tremendously from Chiara's philosophical insight.

READING LIST

ABBEY, EDWARD. *Beyond the Wall: Essays from the Outside*. New York: Holt, Rinehart and Winston, 1984.

_______. *Fire on the Mountain*. Albuquerque: University of New Mexico Press, 1978.

ABRAM, DAVID. *Becoming Animal: An Earthly Cosmology*. New York: Pantheon, 2010.

ABU-RABI', IBRAHIM M. *The Blackwell Companion to Contemporary Islamic Thought*. Malden, MA: Blackwell, 2006.

ALI, TARIQ. *The Idea of Communism*. New York: Seagull, 2009.

ANDERSON, M.T. *Feed*. Cambridge, MA: Candlewick, 2002.

ARENDT, HANNAH. *On Revolution*. New York: Viking, 1963.

ARQUILLA, JOHN, RONFELDT, F. DAVID. *Swarming & the Future of Conflict*. Santa Monica, CA: RAND, 2000.

ARREGUÍN-TOFT, IVAN M. *How the Weak Win Wars: A Theory of Asymmetric Conflict*. New York: Cambridge University Press, 2005.

BABIĆ, JOVAN, and PETAR BOJANIĆ. *World Governance: Do We Need It, Is It Possible, What Could It (All) Mean?* Newcastle: Cambridge Scholars, 2010.

BADIOU, ALAIN. *The Rebirth of History: Times of Riots and Uprisings*. Translated by Elliott Gregory. New York: Verso, 2012.

BADIOU, ALAIN, SLAVOJ ŽIŽEK, PETER ENGELMANN, PETER THOMAS and ALBERTO TOSCANO. *Philosophy in the Present*. Cambridge and Malden, MA: Polity, 2009.

BAHRO, RUDOLF. *Avoiding Social and Ecological Disaster: The Politics of World Transformation: An Inquiry into the Foundations of Spiritual and Ecological Politics*. Bath: Gateway, 1994.

_______. *Building the Green Movement*. London: GMP, 1986.

BAILLY, JEAN-CHRISTOPHE. *The Animal Side*. New York: Fordham UP, 2011.

BAKUNIN, MIKHAIL. *Bakunin: Statism and Anarchy*. Edited by Marshall Shatz. New York: Cambridge University Press, 1990.

BALL, JESSE. *The Curfew*. New York: Vintage, 2011.

BATESON, GREGORY. *Steps to an Ecology of Mind: Collected Essays in Anthropology, Psychiatry, Evolution, and Epistemology*. San Francisco: Chandler, 1972.

BAUDRILLARD, JEAN. *The Agony of Power*. Los Angeles and Cambridge, MA: Semiotext(e), 2010.

BAUMAN, ZYGMUNT. *44 Letters from the Liquid Modern World*. Malden, MA: Polity, 2010.

BENNETT, JANE. *Vibrant Matter: A Political Ecology of Things*. Durham: Duke University Press, 2010.

BERARDI, FRANCO. *After the Future*. Edited by Gary Genosko and Nicholas Thoburn. Oakland, CA.: AK Press, 2011.

_______. *The Soul at Work: From Alienation to Autonomy*. Los Angeles: Semiotext(e), 2009.

BERGER, DAN, CHESA BOUDIN, KENYON FARROW, and BERNARDINE DOHRN. *Letters from Young Activists: Today's Rebels Speak Out*. New York: Nation, 2005.

BEY, HAKIM. *Immediatism: Essays*. Edinburgh: AK, 1994.

BLACKEY, ROBERT. *Revolutions and Revolutionists: A Guide to the Literature*. Santa Barbara, CA: ABC-Clio, 1982.

BOGGS, GRACE LEE, and SCOTT KURASHIGE. *The Next American Revolution: Sustainable Activism for the Twenty-first Century*. Berkeley: University of California Press, 2012.

BRINTON, CRANE. *The Anatomy of Revolution*. New York: Vintage, 1965.

BUCKMAN, PETER. *The Limits of Protest*. Indianapolis: Bobbs-Merrill, 1970.

BULLIET, RICHARD W. *The Case for Islamo-Christian Civilization*. New York: Columbia University Press, 2006.

BURG, DAVID F. *The American Revolution: An Eyewitness History*. New York: Facts on File, 2001.

CALDWELL, WILBER W. *Cynicism and the Evolution of the American Dream*. Washington: Potomac, 2007.

CAMERON, ALAN. *Circus Factions: Blues and Greens at Rome and Byzantium*. Oxford: Clarendon, 1976.

CARR, NICHOLAS G. *The Shallow : What the Internet Is Doing to Our Brains*. New York: W.W. Norton, 2010.

CASTORIADIS, CORNELIUS. *The Castoriadis Reader*. Cambridge, MA: Blackwell, 1997.

_______. *A Society Adrift: Interviews and Debates, 1974–1997*. Edited by Enrique Escobar, Myrto Gondicas, and Pascal Vernay. New York: Fordham University Press, 2010.

CASTRO, FIDEL, and TARIQ ALI. *The Declarations of Havana*. New York: Verso, 2008.

CASTRONOVA, EDWARD. *Synthetic Worlds: The Business and Culture of Online Games*. Chicago: University of Chicago Press, 2007.

CLARK, KENNETH B. *King, Malcolm, Baldwin: Three Interviews*. Middletown, CT: Wesleyan University Press, 1985.

COHEN, STUART. *The Army of the Republic*. New York: St. Martin's Press, 2008.

COLLIS, STEPHEN. *Dispatches from the Occupation: A History of Change*. Vancouver: Talon, 2012.

COPENHAVER, BRIAN P. *Hermetica: The Greek Corpus Hermeticum and the Latin Asclepius in a New English Translation, with Notes and Introduction*. New York: Cambridge University Press, 1992.

CRITCHLEY, SIMON. *Infinitely Demanding: Ethics of Commitment, Politics of Resistance*. New York: Verso, 2007.

DACH, HANS VON. *Total Resistance*. Boulder, CO: Paladin Press, 1965.

DANAHER, KEVIN, and MARK JASON. *Insurrection: Citizen Challenge to Corporate Power*. New York: Routledge, 2003.

DAUVERGNE, PETER, and GENEVIEVE LEBARON. *Protest Inc.: The Corporatization of Activism*. Cambridge: Polity, 2014.

DAWKINS, RICHARD. *The Selfish Gene*. New York: Oxford University Press, 1989.

DEBRAY, RÉGIS. *Prison Writings [of] Régis Debray*. London: Allen Lane, 1973.

_______. *Revolution in the Revolution? Armed Struggle and Political Struggle in Latin America*. Translated by Bobbye Ortiz. New York: Grove Press, 1967.

DOUZINAS, COSTAS, and SLAVOJ ŽIŽEK. *The Idea of Communism*. New York: Verso, 2010.

DOYLE, WILLIAM. *Origins of the French Revolution*. New York: Oxford University Press, 1980.

EAGLETON, TERRY. *After Theory*. New York: Basic, 2003.

_______. *Why Marx Was Right*. New Haven: Yale University Press, 2011.

EDWARDS, DAVID. *Burning All Illusions: A Guide to Personal and Political Freedom*. Boston: South End, 1996.

EDWARDS, LYFORD PATERSON. *The Natural History of Revolution*. Chicago: University of Chicago Press, 1970.

ELLUL, JACQUES. *The Betrayal of the West*. New York: Seabury, 1978.

_______. *The Technological Bluff*. Grand Rapids, MI: W.B. Eerdmans, 1990.

ENGELS, FRIEDRICH. *The Revolutionary Act: Military Insurrection or Political and Economic Action?* Translated by Henry Kuhn. Appendix by Daniel De Leon. New York: New York Labor News, 1975.

ENMARCH, ROLAND. *A World Upturned: Commentary on and Analysis of the Dialogue of Ipuwer and the Lord of All*. Oxford: Oxford University Press, 2009.

FERLINGHETTI, LAWRENCE. *Love in the Days of Rage*. New York: Dutton, 1988.

FOLEY, MICHAEL. *The Age of Absurdity: Why Modern Life Makes It Hard to Be Happy*. New York: Simon and Schuster, 2010.

FOSTER, JOHN. *The Sustainability Mirage: Illusion and Reality in the Coming War on Climate Change*. Sterling, VA: Earthscan, 2008.

FROMM, ERICH. *On Disobedience and Other Essays*. New York: Seabury, 1981.

_______. *The Sane Society*. New York: Rinehart, 1955.

GAMSON, WILLIAM A. *The Strategy of Social Protest*. Homewood, IL: Dorsey, 1975.

GANDHI, MOHANDAS. *Gandhi: Essential Writings*. Edited by V.V. Ramana Murti. New Delhi: Gandhi Peace Foundation, 1970.

GARTON ASH, TIMOTHY. *We the People: The Revolution of '89 Witnessed in Warsaw, Budapest, Berlin and Prague*. New York: Granta; Penguin, 1990.

GIOIA, TED. *The Birth (and Death) of the Cool*. Golden, CO: Speck, 2009.

GIORGIO. *Memoirs of an Italian Terrorist*. New York: Carroll and Graf, 2003.

GIROUX, HENRY A. *Zombie Politics and Culture in the Age of Casino Capitalism*. New York: Peter Lang, 2011.

GLENDINNING, CHELLIS. *"My Name Is Chellis & I'm in Recovery from Western Civilization."* Boston: Shambhala,1994.

GORKY, MAXIM. *Lenin: A Biographical Essay*. Edinburgh: University Texts, 1967.

GORZ, ANDRÉ. *Ecology as Politics*. Boston: South End, 1980.

_______. *Farewell to the Working Class: An Essay on Post-industrial Socialism*. London: Pluto, 1982.

GRAEBER, DAVID. *Direct Action: An Ethnography*. Edinburgh: AK, 2010.

GREENBERG, GARY. *Manufacturing Depression: The Secret History of a Modern Disease*. New York: Simon and Schuster, 2010.

GREENE, THOMAS H. *Comparative Revolutionary Movements*. Englewood Cliffs, NJ: Prentice-Hall, 1974.

GUÉNON, RENÉ. *East and West*. Translated by William Massey. London: Luzac, 1941.

GUEVARA, CHE. *Che Guevara Speaks: Selected Speeches and Writings*. New York: Merit, 1967.

HAGOPIAN, MARK N. *The Phenomenon of Revolution*. New York: Dodd, Mead, 1974.

HALL, SARAH. *The Carhullan Army*. London: Faber and Faber, 2007.

HARDT, MICHAEL, and ANTONIO NEGRI. *Declaration*. New York: Melanie Jackson Agency, 2012.

HEDGES, CHRIS. *Empire of Illusion: The End of Literacy and the Triumph of Spectacle*. New York: Nation, 2009.

HEILBRONER, ROBERT L. *An Inquiry into the Human Prospect*. New York: W.W. Norton, 1974.

HEINTZMAN, RALPH RIPLEY. *Rediscovering Reverence: The Meaning of Faith in a Secular World*. Montréal: McGill-Queen's University Press, 2011.

HENNEZEL, MARIE DE. *The Art of Growing Old: Aging with Grace*. New York: Viking, 2012.

HESSEL, STÉPHANE, and EDGAR MORIN. *The Path to Hope*. New York: Other, 2012.

HIGGINS, POLLY. *Eradicating Ecocide: Laws and Governance to Prevent the Destruction of Our Planet*. London: Shepheard-Walwyn, 2010.

HIRSCHMAN, JACK. *Art on the Line: Essays by Artists about the Point Where Their Art and Activism Intersect*. Willimantic, CT: Curbstone, 2002.

HITTMAN, MICHAEL, and DON LYNCH. *Wovoka and the Ghost Dance*. Lincoln: University of Nebraska, 1997.

HỒ CHÍ MINH. *Down with Colonialism!* New York: Verso, 2007.

HOLLOWAY, JOHN. *Crack Capitalism*. London and New York: Pluto Press, 2010.

HONDERICH, TED. *Terrorism for Humanity: Inquiries in Political Philosophy*. Sterling, VA: Pluto Press, 2003.

HOROWITZ, IRVING LOUIS, and GEORGES SOREL. *Radicalism and the Revolt against Reason: The Social Theories of Georges Sorel*. New York: Humanities, 1961.

HUNTINGTON, SAMUEL P. *Political Order in Changing Societies*. New Haven: Yale University Press, 1968.

ILLICH, IVAN. *Celebration of Awareness: A Call for Institutional Revolution*. Garden City, NY: Doubleday, 1970.

_______. *Tools for Conviviality*. New York: Harper and Row, 1973.

INAYAT, KHAN. *The Art of Being and Becoming*. New Lebanon, NY: Omega, 2009.

INGLIS, JAMES. *Fighting Talk: Stirring Speeches and Battle Cries from History's Greatest Warriors and Revolutionaries*. Millers Point, N.S.W. and London: Pier 9, 2008.

INVISIBLE COMMITTEE, THE. *The Coming Insurrection*. Los Angeles and Cambridge, MA: Semiotext(e), 2009.

_______. *To Our Friends*. Translated by Robert Hurley. South Pasadena, CA: Semiotext(e), 2015.

JIN, HA. *In the Pond: A Novel*. Cambridge, MA: Zoland, 1998.

JOHNSTON, HANK. *What Is a Social Movement?* Cambridge: Polity, 2014.

JUNG, C.G. *The Earth Has a Soul: The Nature Writings of C.G. Jung*. Edited by Meredith Sabini. Berkeley, CA: North Atlantic, 2002.

JUVIN, HERVÉ, and JOHN HOWE. *The Coming of the Body*. New York: Verso, 2010.

KEITH, LIERRE. *Conditions of War*. Northampton, MA: Fighting Words, 1993.

KHOMEINI, RUHOLLAH. *Islam and Revolution: Writings and Declarations of Imam Khomeini*. Translated and annotated by Hamid Algar. Berkeley, CA: Mizan, 1981.

KIERKEGAARD, SØREN. *The Present Age: And of the Difference between a Genius and an Apostle*. New York: Harper and Row, 1962.

KING, MARTIN LUTHER, JR., *Why We Can't Wait*. New York: Harper and Row, 1964.

KLIMAN, ANDREW. *The Failure of Capitalist Production : Underlying Causes of the Great Recession*. London: Pluto, 2012.

KNABB, KEN. *Situationist International Anthology*. Berkeley, CA: Bureau of Public Secrets, 1981.

KREJČÍ, JAROSLAV, and ANNA KREJČOVÁ. *Great Revolutions Compared: The Search for a Theory*. New York: St. Martin's Press, 1983.

KROPOTKIN, PETR ALEKSEEVICH. *Words of a Rebel*. Montreal and New York: Black Rose, 1992.

KUNEN, JAMES S. *The Strawberry Statement: Notes of a College Revolutionary*. New York: Random House, 1969.

LANIER, JARON. *You Are Not a Gadget: A Manifesto*. New York: Alfred A. Knopf, 2010.

LASN, KALLE. *Culture Jam: The Uncooling of America*. New York: Eagle Brook, 1999.

LE GUIN, URSULA K. *The Dispossessed: An Ambiguous Utopia*. New York: Harper and Row, 1974.

LENIN, VLADIMIR ILICH. *What Is to Be Done? Burning Questions of Our Movement*. New York: International, 1969.

LEWIS, SINCLAIR. *It Can't Happen Here: A Novel*. Garden City, NY: Doubleday, Doran, 1935.

LILLEY, SASHA. *Capital and Its Discontents: Conversations with Radical Thinkers in a Time of Tumult*. Oakland, CA: PM, 2011.

LINKOLA, PENTTI. *Can Life Prevail? A Radical Approach to the Environmental Crisis*. London: Integral Tradition Publishing, 2009.

LIU XIAOBO. *June Fourth Elegies*. Translated by Jeffrey Yang. Minneapolis: Graywolf, 2012.

LOMAX, WILLIAM. *Eye-witness in Hungary: The Soviet Invasion of 1956*. Nottingham: Spokesman, 1980.

LONDON, JACK. *The Iron Heel*. 1908. Available at http://www.gutenberg.org/files/1164/1164-h/1164-h.htm

LOPEZ, BARRY HOLSTUN. *Resistance*. New York: Alfred A. Knopf, 2004.

LOVELOCK, JAMES. *The Vanishing Face of Gaia: A Final Warning*. New York: Basic, 2009.

LOWENSTEIN, FRANK, SHERYL LECHNER, and ERIK BRUUN. *Voices of Protest: Documents of Courage and Dissent*. New York: Black Dog and Leventhal, 2007.

MAO TSETUNG. *Selected Readings from the Works of Mao Tsetung*. Peking: Foreign Languages, 1971.

MARCUSE, HERBERT. *Five Lectures: Psychoanalysis, Politics, and Utopia*. Boston: Beacon, 1970.

———. *An Essay on Liberation*. Boston: Beacon, 2000.

MARQUSEE, MIKE. *If I Am Not for Myself: Journey of an Anti-Zionist Jew*. New York: Verso, 2008.

Masters of War: History's Greatest Strategic Thinkers. The Great Courses, 2012. http://www.thegreatcourses.com/courses/masters-of-war-history-s-greatest-strategic-thinkers.html.

MCLEAN, BETHANY, and JOSEPH NOCERA. *All the Devils Are Here: The Hidden History of the Financial Crisis*. New York: Portfolio; Penguin, 2010.

MERRIFIELD, ANDY. *Magical Marxism: Subversive Politics and the Imagination*. London: Pluto Press, 2011.

_______. *Metromarxism: A Marxist Tale of the City*. New York: Routledge, 2002.

_______. *The Wisdom of Donkeys: Finding Tranquility in a Chaotic World*. New York: Walker, 2008.

MICHALSKI, KRZYSZTOF. *The Flame of Eternity: An Interpretation of Nietzsche's Thought*. Princeton, NJ: Princeton University Press, 2012.

MICKENBERG, JULIA L., and NEL PHILIP. *Tales for Little Rebels: A Collection of Radical Children's Literature*. New York: New York University Press, 2008.

MILLS, CARYS. "Terrorism Monitor Closely Watched Occupy Protests." *The Globe and Mail*. April 10, 2012.

MONTAGNE, ORANGE. *Metaverse Manifesto*. San Francisco: Studio SFO, 2007.

MURPHY, CULLEN. *Are We Rome? The Fall of an Empire and the Fate of America*. Boston: Houghton Mifflin, 2007.

NADER, RALPH. *"Only the Super-rich Can Save Us!"* New York: Seven Stories, 2009.

NEALE, JONATHAN. *You Are G8, We Are 6 Billion: The Truth behind the Genoa Protests*. London: Vision Paperbacks, 2002.

NEUMANN, FRANZ L. *The Democratic and the Authoritarian State; Essays in Political and Legal Theory*. Glencoe, IL: Free, 1957.

NEUMANN, OSHA. *Up against the Wall Motherf**ker: A Memoir of the '60s, with Notes for Next Time*. New York: Seven Stories, 2008.

NEWMAN, SAUL. *The Politics of Postanarchism*. Edinburgh: Edinburgh University Press, 2011.

NIETZSCHE, FRIEDRICH WILHELM. *The Birth of Tragedy and the Genealogy of Morals*. Translated by Francis Golffing. Garden City, NY: Doubleday, 1956.

ORLOV, DMITRY. *Reinventing Collapse: The Soviet Example and American Prospects*. Gabriola Island, BC: New Society Publishers, 2008.

ORWELL, GEORGE. *Homage to Catalonia*. New York: Harcourt, Brace, 1952.

OSTLER, JEFFREY. "Conquest and the State: Why the United States Employed

Massive Military Force to Suppress the Lakota Ghost Dance." *Pacific Historical Review* 65, no. 2 (1996): 217–48.

PARENTI, CHRISTIAN. *Tropic of Chaos: Climate Change and the New Geography of Violence*. New York: Nation, 2011.

PARTRIDGE, ROXANNE. *Occupy Psyche: Jungian and Archetypal Perspectives on a Movement*. Charleston, SC: CreateSpace, 2012.

PASQUINELLI, MATTEO, *Animal Spirits: A Bestiary of the Commons*. Rotterdam: NAi Publishers; Amsterdam: The Institute of Network Cultures, 2008.

PETTEE, GEORGE SAWYER. *The Process of Revolution*. New York: H. Fertig, 1971.

PHILLIPS, JOSHUA E.S. *None of Us Were Like This Before: American Soldiers and Torture*. New York: Verso, 2010.

PIGNARRE, PHILIPPE and ISABELLE STENGERS. *Capitalist Sorcery: Breaking the Spell*. Translated by Andrew Goffey. New York: Palgrave Macmillan, 2011.

POPKIN, JEREMY D. *Facing Racial Revolution: Eyewitness Accounts of the Haitian Insurrection*. Chicago: University of Chicago Press, 2007.

POSTMAN, NEIL. *Amusing Ourselves to Death: Public Discourse in the Age of Show Business*. New York: Viking, 1985.

PRICE, M. PHILIPS. *My Reminiscences of the Russian Revolution*. London: Allen and Unwin, 1921.

QADDAFI, MUAMMAR. *Escape to Hell and Other Stories*. London: Blake, 1999.

QUTB, SAYYID. *The Sayyid Qutb Reader: Selected Writings on Politics, Religion, and Society*. Edited by Albert J. Bergesen. New York: Routledge, 2008.

RALL, TED. *The Anti-American Manifesto*. New York: Seven Stories, 2010.

REMARQUE, ERICH MARIA. *All Quiet on the Western Front*. Translated by Arthur Wesley Wheen. Boston: Little, Brown, 1929.

ROBINSON, KIM STANLEY. *Future Primitive: The New Ecotopias*. New York: TOR, 1994.

ROGERS, HEATHER. *Green Gone Wrong: How Our Economy Is Undermining the Environmental Revolution*. New York: Scribner, 2010.

ROPER, BRIAN S. *The History of Democracy: A Marxist Interpretation*. London: Pluto, 2013.

ROSEN, MICHAEL, and DAVID WIDGERY. *The Chatto Book of Dissent*. London: Chatto & Windus, 1991.

ROSS, CARNE. *The Leaderless Revolution: How Ordinary People Will Take Power and Change Politics in the Twenty-first Century*. New York: Blue Rider, 2011.

ROY, ARUNDHATI. *Walking with the Comrades*. New York: Penguin, 2012.

RUDÉ, GEORGE F.E. *The Crowd in History: A Study of Popular Disturbances in France and England, 1730–1848*. New York: Wiley, 1964.

RUMI. *The Mathnawi of Jalalu'ddin Rumi. Edited from the Oldest Manuscripts Available, with Critical Notes, Translation & Commentary*. Edited and translated by Reynold A. Nicholson. Cambridge: Published and Distributed by the Trustees of the "E.J.W. Gibb Memorial," 2001.

RUSHDY, HATEM, ED. *18 Days in Tahrir: Stories from Egypt's Revolution*. Hong Kong: Haven, 2011.

SAFINA, CARL. *The View from Lazy Point: A Natural Year in an Unnatural World*. New York: Henry Holt, 2010.

SALE, KIRKPATRICK. *Dwellers in the Land: The Bioregional Vision*. San Francisco: Sierra Club, 1985.

SAMPSON, TONY D. *Virality: Contagion Theory in the Age of Networks*. Minneapolis: University of Minnesota, 2012.

SCHLINK, BERNHARD, and SHAUN WHITESIDE. *The Weekend*. New York: Pantheon, 2010.

SEED, JOHN. *Thinking like a Mountain: Towards a Council of All Beings*. Philadelphia: New Society, 1988.

SERRES, MICHEL. *Biogea*. Translated by Randolph M. Burks. Minneapolis: Univocal, 2012.

_______. *Malfeasance: Appropriation through Pollution?* Translated by Anne-Marie Feenberg-Dibon. Stanford: Stanford University Press, 2011.

_______. *The Five Senses: A Philosophy of Mingled Bodies*. Translated by Margaret Sankey and Peter Cowley. New York: Continuum, 2008.

SHAMIR, RAMI. *Train to Pokipse: A Novel*. Brooklyn, NY: Underground Editions, 2012.

SHARP, GENE. *Exploring Nonviolent Alternatives*. Boston: Sargent, 1970.

SHOEMAKER, ROBERT BRINK. *The London Mob: Violence and Disorder in Eighteenth-Century England*. New York: Hambledon and London, 2004.

SITRIN, MARINA. *Horizontalism: Voices of Popular Power in Argentina*. Oakland, CA: AK, 2006.

SKOCPOL, THEDA. *States and Social Revolutions: A Comparative Analysis of France, Russia, and China*. New York: Cambridge University Press, 1979.

SOLNIT, REBECCA. *A Paradise Built in Hell: The Extraordinary Communities That Arise in Disasters*. New York: Viking, 2009.

STARHAWK. *Webs of Power: Notes from the Global Uprising*. Gabriola Island, BC: New Society Publishers, 2002.

STIEGLER, BERNARD. *For a New Critique of Political Economy*. Malden, MA: Polity, 2010.

STIGLITZ, JOSEPH E. *Mismeasuring Our Lives: Why GDP Doesn't Add Up: The Report by the Commission on the Measurement of Economic Performance and Social Progress*. New York: New Press, 2010.

STOCKDALE, JAMES BOND. *Courage under Fire: Testing Epictetus's Doctrines in a Laboratory of Human Behavior*. Stanford, CA: Hoover Institution Press, Stanford University, 1993.

TAGORE, RABINDRANATH. *Creative Unity*. London: Macmillan, 1922.

TALEB, NASSIM NICHOLAS. *Fooled by Randomness: The Hidden Role of Chance in Life and in the Markets*. New York: Random House, 2005.

TOLSTOY, LEO. *War and Peace*. Translated by Richard Pevear and Larissa Volokhonsky. New York: Alfred A. Knopf, 2007.

TOUSSAINT, LOUVERTURE, JEAN-BERTRAND ARISTIDE and NICK NESBITT. *The Haitian Revolution*. London and Brooklyn: Verso, 2008.

TRAUGOTT, MARK. *The Insurgent Barricade*. Berkeley: University of California Press, 2010.

TURKLE, SHERRY. *Alone Together: Why We Expect More from Technology and Less from Each Other*. New York: Basic Books, 2011.

TURNER, JACK. *The Abstract Wild*. Tucson: University of Arizona, 1996.

"TV Advertising in Danger, Remedy Is to Embrace Technology and Return to Program Ownership." *Advertising Age*, May 23, 1994.

UPTON, CHARLES. *Legends of the End: Prophecies of the End Times, Antichrist, Apocalypse, and Messiah from Eight Religious Traditions*. Hillsdale, NY: Sophia Perennis, 2004.

VANEIGEM, RAOUL. *The Revolution of Everyday Life*. London: Verso, 2012.

VIRILIO, PAUL. *The Administration of Fear*. Translated by Ames Hodges. Los Angeles: Semiotext(e), 2012.

VRADIS, ANTONIS, and DIMITRIS DALAKOGLOU. *Revolt and Crisis in Greece: Between a Present Yet to Pass and a Future Still to Come*. Oakland, CA: AK and Occupied London, 2011.

WAGAR, W. WARREN. *A Short History of the Future*. Chicago: University of Chicago Press, 1989.

WALLERSTEIN, IMMANUEL MAURICE. *Utopistics; Or, Historical Choices of the Twenty-first Century*. New York: New, 1998.

WALTER, NATASHA. *Living Dolls: The Return of Sexism*. London: Virago, 2010.

WAPNER, PAUL KEVIN. *Living through the End of Nature: The Future of American Environmentalism*. Cambridge, MA: MIT, 2013.

WEBER, THOMAS. *On the Salt March: The Historiography of Gandhi's March to Dandi*. New Delhi: HarperCollins India, 1997.

WELLS, H.G., and WARREN W. WAGAR. *The Open Conspiracy: H.G. Wells on World Revolution*. Westport, CT: Praeger, 2002.

WELLS, PETER S. *The Battle That Stopped Rome: Emperor Augustus, Arminius, and the Slaughter of the Legions in the Teutoburg Forest*. New York: W.W. Norton, 2003.

WILLIAMSON, MARIANNE. *The Law of Divine Compensation: On Work, Money, and Miracles*. New York: HarperOne, 2012.

WOLF, NAOMI. "Revealed: How the FBI Coordinated the Crackdown on Occupy." *The Guardian*, December 29, 2012.

ZARETSKY, ELI. *Why America Needs a Left: A Historical Argument*. Cambridge: Polity Press, 2012.

ZINN, HOWARD. *A People's History of the United States: 1492–2001*. New York: Harper Perennial Modern Classics, 2003.

ŽIŽEK, SLAVOJ. *First as Tragedy, Then as Farce*. London: Verso, 2009.

_______. *Living in the End Times*. London and New York: Verso, 2010.

_______. *Violence: Six Sideways Reflections*. New York: Picador, 2008.

_______. *The Year of Dreaming Dangerously*. London and New York: Verso, 2012.

ZOLA, ÉMILE. *Germinal*. Translated by Roger Pearson. London and New York: Penguin, 2004.

_______. *The Debacle, 1870–71*. Translated by Leonard Tancock. Harmondsworth, Middlesex: Penguin, 1972.

IMAGE CREDITS

Page 20: Based on research by Nate Silver for *The New York Times*.

Page 32: AP Photo/Charles Dharapak.

Page 47: This photograph originally appeared in "A Little Violence and Lots of Police Equal 150 Arrests," *The New York Times*, February 4, 2002.

Page 86: Based on James C. Davies's Need Satisfaction and Revolution model (or J-curve) originally published in "Toward a Theory of Revolution," *American Sociological Review*, Vol. 27, No. 1 (Feb., 1962), p. 5–19.

Page 158: Wikipedia (Public Domain).

Page 208: Based on data from Ivan Arreguín-Toft, "How the Weak Win Wars: A Theory of Asymmetric Conflict," *International Security*, Vol. 26, No. 1 (Summer 2001), p. 93–128.

Page 235: Based on data from Mark Traugott, *The Insurgent Barricade* (Berkeley: University of California Press, 2010).

ENDNOTES

PREFACE

1. Katrina vanden Heuvel and Stephen F. Cohen, "Edward Snowden: A 'Nation' Interview," *The Nation*, October 28, 2014.
2. Peter Gelderloos in *Letters from Young Activists: Today's Rebels Speak Out*, ed. Dan Berger, Chesa Boudin and Kenyon Farrow (New York: Nation Books: 2005).

INTRODUCTION: YOU ARE NEEDED

3. Herbert Marcuse, *Five Lectures* (Boston: Beacon Press, 1970).

CHAPTER 1. THE BIRTH OF OCCUPY

4. Isabel Ortiz, Sara Burke, Mohamed Berrada and Hernán Cortés, *World Protests 2006–2013 Executive Summary* (New York: Initiative for Policy Dialogue, 2013).
5. U.S. Department of State, "2010 Human Rights Report: Tunisia," April 8, 2011.
6. This is a quote from the inaugural Occupy Wall Street tactical briefing.
7. Amelia Byrne, "Occupy Eyewitness—New York," Post Growth Institute; available at http://postgrowth.org/occupy-eyewitness-new-york/

8. Lyford P. Edwards, *The Natural History of Revolution* (Chicago: University of Chicago Press, 1970).
9. Nate Silver, "Police Clashes Spur Coverage of Wall Street Protests," fivethirtyeight blog at nytimes.com.
10. Mattathias Schwartz, "Pre-Occupied: The Origins and Future of Occupy Wall Street," *The New Yorker.* November 28, 2011; available at http://www.newyorker.com/magazine/2011/11/28/pre-occupied

CHAPTER 2. A CONSTRUCTIVE FAILURE

11. Yael Chanoff, "Oakland Police Department Spies on and Beats Protesters," *San Francisco Bay Guardian*, March 13, 2012.
12. Régis Debray, *Revolution in the Revolution? Armed Struggle and Political Struggle in Latin America*, trans. Bobbye Ortiz (New York: Grove Press, 1967).

CHAPTER 3. THE LOST MOMENT

13. Harry Siegel, "A Civil War in Zucotti Park?" Editorial, *New York Daily News*, October 30, 2011.
14. Three days after the destruction of Occupy's inaugural encampment, Kalle and I described the eviction in an editorial published in the *Washington Post*. See Kalle Lasn and Micah White, "Why Occupy Wall Street Will Keep Up the Fight," *The Washington Post*, November 18, 2011.
15. Andy Kroll, "Mayors and Cops Traded Strategies for Dealing with Occupy Protesters," *Mother Jones*, November 16, 2011.
16. Naomi Wolf, "Revealed: How the FBI Coordinated the Crackdown on Occupy," *The Guardian*, December 12, 2012.
17. Carys Mills, "Terrorism Monitor Closely Watched Occupy Protests," *The Globe and Mail*, April 10, 2012.
18. "'Mic Check': Occupy Protesters Interrupt Obama," CBS News, CBS Interactive, November 22, 2011; accessed December 4, 2014.

CHAPTER 4. THE END OF PROTEST

19. The Accelerationist manifesto was originally published in Robin Mackay and Armen Avanessian (eds), *#Accelerate: The Accelerationist Reader* (Falmouth: Urbanomic, 2014). The Thomas Greene quotation is from *Comparative Revolutionary Movements* (New York: Prentice-Hall, 1974).

20. John Lorinc, "Armed and Dangerous: How Mission Creep Is Turning Our Cops into Warriors," *The Walrus*, December 2014.
21. "Turkey's Crackdown on Protesters Test Obama's Relationship with PM Erdogan," Associated Press, June 11, 2013.
22. See the proceedings of the 2014 Moscow Conference on International Security hosted by the Russian Ministry of Defence. Available at http://eng.mil.ru/en/mcis/2014.htm
23. Patrick Kingsley, "17 Killed in Pro-democracy Protests in Egypt on Anniversary of 2011 Uprising," *The Guardian*, January 25, 2015.
24. Astra Taylor interviewed by Heather Smith for grist.org, "We Want Democracy, but We Don't Have the Theory or Skill to Do It." Published on December 7, 2014. Accessed on August 29, 2015.
25. See James C. Davis, "The Theory of Revolution," *American Sociological Review* 27. No. 1 (February 1962) and Crane Brinton, *The Anatomy of Revolution* (New York: Vintage, 1965).
26. Thomas Kuhn, *The Structure of Scientific Revolutions* (Chicago: University of Chicago Press, 1996).
27. Debray, *Revolution in the Revolution?* I have modified the original quotation to read "context" rather than "content" for clarity and to correct what appears to be a printer's error.
28. Rumi, *The Mathnawi*, Volume 2, Verse 1029.

CHAPTER 5. I AM AN ACTIVIST

29. Micah White, "Atheists Under Siege," *The New York Times*, June 21, 1999. I was a guest on the August 22, 1999 episode of *Politically Incorrect with Bill Maher.*
30. "Michigan Court Asked to Strike Down High School's Urine Testing Policy," *American Civil Liberties Union*, June 5, 2001; available at https://www.aclu.org/news/michigan-court-asked-strike-down-high-schools-urine-testing-policy
31. For a journalist's view of the day, see Dan Barry, "A Little Violence and Lots of Police Equal 150 Arrests," *The New York Times*, February 4, 2002.
32. Diebold Election Systems has since been renamed Premier Election Solutions and acquired by Dominion Voting Systems.
33. See *Mother Jones* online, March 5, 2004, http://www.motherjones.com/politics/2004/03/diebolds-political-machine
34. "Swarthmore Students Keep Diebold Memos Online," *Slashdot*, October

21, 2003; available at http://yro.slashdot.org/story/03/10/22/0142252/swarthmore-students-keep-diebold-memos-online

35. "Kucinich Requests House Judiciary Committee Hearing on Diebold's Abuses of Digital Millennium Copyright Act," Press Release from Congressman Dennis J. Kucinich, November 21, 2003; available at https://web.archive.org/web/20031224212840/http://www.house.gov/apps/list/press/oh10_kucinich/031121judcmtediebold.html

36. "EFF Wins in Diebold Copyright Abuse Case," Electroic Frontier Foundation, September 30, 2004; available at https://www.eff.org/press/archives/2004/09/30

CHAPTER 6. THE POINT OF PROTEST

37. "activism, n." *Oxford English Dictionary* online.

38. William Ralph Boyce Gibson, *Eucken's Philosophy of Life* (London: Adam and Charles Black, 1907); available at https://archive.org/details/rudolfeuckenspho1gibsgoog

39. Henry Lane Eno, *Activism* (Princeton, NJ: Princeton University Press, 1920); available at https://archive.org/details/activism04enogoog

40. Rudolf Eucken, Nobel Lecture, "Naturalism or Idealism?" nobelprize.org.

41. Karl Marx, *The Class Struggles in France (1848-1850)*.

42. From an abolitionist speech by Wendell Phillips quoted in the February 4, 1848 issue of the *The Liberator*, an anti-slavery newspaper published in Boston.

43. The source of Victor Hugo's quote is unknown. It has been circulated in quotation collections for over a hundred years. The earliest reference I found was in *Pearls of Thought* (Cambridge: Riverside Press, 1881).

44. Hank Johnston, *What Is a Social Movement?* (Cambridge: Polity, 2014).

45. John F. Kennedy, "Address on the First Anniversary of the Alliance for Progress," March 13, 1962. Retrieved from http://www.presidency.ucsb.edu/ws/?pid=9100

46. Thomas Jefferson, letter to James Madison, January 30, 1787. Retreived from http://www.let.rug.nl/usa/presidents/thomas-jefferson/letters-of-thomas-jefferson/jefl53.php

47. Thomas Jefferson, letter to Gen. William S. Smith, November 13, 1787. Retrieved from http://www.let.rug.nl/usa/presidents/thomas-jefferson/letters-of-thomas-jefferson/jefl64.php

48. Brian S. Roper, *The History of Democracy: A Marxist Interpretation* (London: Pluto Press, 2012).
49. From Justice Jackson's comments in the U.S. Supreme Court case American Communications Association vs Douds, May 8, 1950. Reprinted in "The Communists in America," *Harper's Magazine*, September 1950.
50. Ulysses S. Grant, *Personal Memoirs of U.S. Grant* (New York: Charles L. Webster & Company, 1894).
51. John Jay, letter to Thomas Jefferson, October 27, 1786. Quoted in Robert Blackey's *Revolutions and Revolutionists: A Guide to the Literature* (Santa Barbara, CA: ABC-Clio, 1982).
52. Rabindranath Tagore, *Creative Unity* (Kyiv, Ukraine: Leopold Classic Library, 2015).
53. Roberta Ash, *Social Movements in America* (Chicago: Markham Publishing, 1972), p. 179.
54. Edwards, *The Natural History of Revolution.*
55. Friedrich Engels, "Germany at the Outbreak of the Revolution," *Revolution and Counter-Revolution in Germany.* Retrieved from https://www.marxists.org/archive/marx/works/1852/germany/ch01.htm
56. Engels in a letter to Marx, February 13, 1851. Published in Marx/Engels, *Gesamtausgabe*, Part III, Vol. 1.
57. Samuel Huntington, *Political Order in Changing Societies* (New Haven: Yale University Press, 1969).
58. Jaroslav Krejčí, *Great Revolutions Compared: The Outline of a Theory* (New York: St. Martin's Press, 1983).
59. Edwards, *The Natural History of Revolution.*
60. Martin Luther King Jr., "Letter from a Birmingham Jail." April 16, 1963. Retrieved from http://www.africa.upenn.edu/Articles_Gen/Letter_Birmingham.html
61. Robert Shoemaker, *The London Mob: Violence and Disorder in Eighteenth-Century England* (London: Hambledon Continuum, 2007).
62. William Gamson, *The Strategy of Social Protest, 2nd edition* (Belmont, CA: Wadsworth Publishing Co., 1990).
63. Gamson, *The Strategy of Social Protest.*
64. Johnston, *What Is a Social Movement?*
65. *Oxford English Dictionary.*

CHAPTER 7. A UNIFIED THEORY OF REVOLUTION

66. V.I. Lenin, "What Is to Be Done" (1902); available at https://www.marxists.org/archive/lenin/works/1901/witbd/
67. Irving L. Horowitz, *Radicalism and the Revolt Against Reason: The Social Theories of George Sorel* (Carbondale: Southern Illinois University Press, 1968).
68. Slavoj Žižek, *In Defense of Lost Causes* (London: Verso, 2008), p. 157.
69. Gamson, *The Strategy of Social Protest*, p. 128.
70. Gamson, *The Strategy of Social Protest*.
71. See the Red Army Faction's occupation of the West German embassy in Stockholm, Sweden, on April 24, 1975.
72. Régis Debray's philosophical treatise *Revolution in the Revolution?* (1967) is a definitive articulation of focoism.
73. An illustrative historical example of the tendency for violent groups to be front groups is Operation Gladio, a clandestine political terror network organized by NATO.
74. Johnston, *What Is a Social Movement?*
75. Leo Tolstoy, *War and Peace*, trans. Richard Pevear and Larissa Volokhonsky (New York: Alfred A. Knopf, 2007).
76. Wendell Phillips, *Speeches Before the Massachusetts Anti-Slavery Society, January, 1852* (Boston: Robert F. Wallcut, 1852). This speech is available at https://archive.org/details/speechesbeforema01phil
77. Peter Dauvergne and Genevieve Lebaron, *Protest Inc: The Corporatization of Activism* (Cambridge: Polity, 2014), p. 19.
78. Gamson, *The Strategy of Social Protest*, p. 128.
79. Tolstoy, *War and Peace*.
80. M. Lagi, K.Z. Bertrand, Y. Bar-Yam, *The Food Crises and Political Instability in North Africa and the Middle East*. (September 28, 2011). Available at http://necsi.edu/research/social/food_crises.pdf
81. Theda Skocpol, *States and Social Revolutions: A Comparative Analysis of France, Russia and China* (Cambridge: Cambridge University Press, 1979).
82. Jack A. Goldstone, "The Weakness of Organization: A New Look at Gamson's *The Strategy of Social Protest*," *American Journal of Sociology* 85, no. 5 (March 1980): 1017–42.
83. Nassim Nicholas Taleb, *Fooled by Randomness* (New York: Random House, 2005), p. 46.

84. Goldstone, "The Weakness of Organization."
85. Taleb, *Fooled by Randomness*.
86. Tolstoy, *War and Peace*.
87. V.I. Lenin, *Left-Wing Communism: An Infantile Disorder* (1920). Available at https://www.marxists.org/archive/lenin/works/1920/lwc/
88. Frederick Engels, *The Revolutionary Act* (New York: Labor News Company, 1922).
89. James C. Davies, "Toward a Theory of Revolution," *American Sociological Review* 27, no. 1 (February 1962).
90. Engels, *The Revolutionary Act*.
91. Karl Marx, *A Contribution to the Critique of Hegel's Philosophy of Right*, 1843–44, available at https://www.marxists.org/archive/marx/works/1843/critique-hpr/intro.htm. I found the preceding Engels quote in Sigmund Neumann and Mark von Hagen, "Engels and Marx on Revolution, War and the Army in Society," *Makers of Modern Strategy from Machiavelli to the Nuclear Age* (Princeton, NJ: Princeton University Press, 1986).
92. Friedrich Nietzsche, *The Genealogy of Morals* (New York: Vintage, 1989).
93. *A Course in Miracles* (Tiburon, CA: Foundation for Inner Peace, 2008), p. xi.
94. Marianne Williamson, *The Law of Divine Compensation: On Work, Money and Miracles* (New York: HarperOne, 2014).
95. *A Course in Miracles*, Workbook for Students, Lesson 23.
96. Near the end of his life, Rumi began to recite the *Mathnawi*, one of the longest poems ever recorded. As we move now to occupy the supernatural axis comprising the subjectivist and theurgist schools, I often reflect on *Mathnawi* as one of the primary sources for speaking about the difficult question of non-material forces.
97. Rumi, *The Mathnawi*, Book 1, Verses 3435–3444.
98. Davies, "Toward a Theory of Revolution."
99. Ralph Waldo Emerson, "History," *Essays: First Series* (1841). Available at http://www.emersoncentral.com/history.htm
100. *A Course in Miracles*, p. 445.
101. Starhawk, *Webs of Power: Notes from the Global Uprising* (Gabriola Island, BC: New Society Publishers, 2010).
102. Edwards, *The Natural History of Revolution*.

103. This phrase was coined by the sociologist Yonina Talmon to describe millenarian movements.
104. Yonina Talmon, "Pursuit of the Millennium: The Relation between Religious and Social Change," *The European Journal of Sociology* 2 (1962).
105. Brian Copenhaver, introduction, *Hermetica* (Cambridge: Cambridge University Press, 1995).
106. Quotation from Copenhaver's introduction to *Hermetica*.
107. Hermes Trismegistus, *Asclepius*, trans. Brian P. Copenhaver (Cambridge: Cambridge University Press, 1995).
108. Starhawk, *Webs of Power*.
109. *A Course in Miracles*, p. 3.
110. Spencer Lloyd Peet, "The Ensō of Zen," *Kindred Spirit*, no. 115, Mar/Apr 2012. Available at http://diversejapan.com/2012/05/15/shodo-japanese-calligraphy-master-shoho-teramoto-the-enso-of-zen/

CHAPTER 8. THE RECENT PAST OF PROTEST

111. Roland Enmarch, *A World Upturned: Commentary on and Analysis of the Dialogue of Ipuwer and the Lord of All* (Oxford: Oxford University Press, 2009).
112. This information is based on Davide Casaleggio's presentation at the Europe of Freedom and Direct Democracy group within the European Parliament published on YouTube on April 22, 2015. See https://www.youtube.com/watch?v=9XeiXAM5WGc
113. David Boaz, "Dollars Per Vote in the Presidential Election," Cato Institute blog at http://www.cato.org/blog/dollars-vote-presidential-election
114. A transcript and video of my speech is available at https://www.micahm-white.com/five-star-movements-v3day/
115. Giles Tremlett, "€500,000 Scam of a Spanish Robin Hood," *The Guardian*, September 19, 2008.
116. For an in-depth profile of Enric Duran, see Nathan Schneider, "On the Lam with Bank Robber Enric Duran," *VICE*, April 2015.
117. Micah White, "Blackspot Debt Collection Agency," *Adbusters* blog, February 9, 2009; available at https://www.adbusters.org/blogs/blackspot_blog/blackspot_debt_collection_agency.html
118. David Graeber, "Of Flying Cars and the Declining Rate of Profit," *The Baffler*, no. 19, 2012, thebaffler.com.

119. Hazrat Inayat Khan, *The Art of Being and Becoming* (Lanham: Omega Publication, 2005).
120. Williamson, *The Law of Divine Compensation.*
121. Debray, *Revolution in the Revolution?*
122. Dennis B. Warner, "International Peacemakers Enter Bethlehem Church of the Nativity," in *Peace Under Fire: Israel/Palestine and the International Solidarity Movement*, ed. Josie Sandercock et al. (London: Verso, 2004), p. 79.

CHAPTER 9. THE DISTANT PAST OF PROTEST

123. *Walker Lake Bulletin* 3/20/1889 quoted in Michael Hittman, *Wovoka and the Ghost Dance: A Source Book* (Lincoln: University of Nebraska Press, 1997).
124. All Wovoka quotations are from Hittman, *Wovoka and the Ghost Dance: A Source Book.*
125. Ed Dyer quoted in Hittman, *Wovoka and the Ghost Dance.*
126. L.G. Moses, "'The Father Tells Me So!'" Wovoka: The Ghost Dance Prophet," *American Indian Quarterly*, 9, no. 3.
127. Alice Guild quoted in Hittman, *Wovoka and the Ghost Dance.*
128. Hittman, *Wovoka and the Ghost Dance*
129. Jeffrey Ostler, "Conquest and the State: Why the United States Employed Massive Military Force to Suppress the Lakota Ghost Dance," *Pacific Historical Review* 65, no. 2 (1996): 217–48.
130. The Census Bureau designated frontier territory as land that had population densities of fewer than two people per square mile, not including "Indians not taxed."
131. Frederick Jackson Turker, "The Significance of the Frontier in American History," 1893. Available at http://www.gutenberg.org/ebooks/22994
132. Geoffrey Greatrex, "The Nika Riot: A Reappraisal," *The Journal of Hellenic Studies* 117.
133. Alan Cameron, *Circus Factions: Blues and Greens at Rome and Byzantium* (Oxford: Oxford University Press, 1976).
134. Cameron, *Circus Factions.*
135. Ibid.
136. Greatrex, "The Nika Riot."
137. Cameron, *Circus Factions.*

138. William Safire, *Lend Me Your Ears: Great Speeches in History* (New York: W.W. Norton, 2004).
139. Greatrex, "The Nika Riot."
140. Friedrich Engels, *On the History of Early Christianity* (1894). Available at https://www.marxists.org/archive/marx/works/1894/early-christianity/
141. See book 15, chapter 44 of Tacitus's *The Annals* available in *Complete Works of Tacitus* translated by Alfred John Church, William Jackson Brodribb, Sara Bryant (New York: Random House, 1942).
142. The source for all of the Eusebius quotations is his *The Life of the Blessed Emperor Constantine* available at http://legacy.fordham.edu/halsall/basis/vita-constantine.asp
143. Oliver Nicholson, "Constantine's Vision of the Cross," *Vigiliae Christianae* 54, no. 3 (2000): 309–23.
144. Thomas Smith, *Arminius: A History of the German People and of Their Legal and Constitutional Customs, from the Days of Julius Cæsar to the Time of Charlemagne* (London: James Blackwood, 1861).
145. Edward Gibbon, *The History of the Decline and Fall of the Roman Empire* (New York: Penguin Classics, 2010).
146. Peter S. Wells, *The Battle That Stopped Rome* (New York: W.W. Norton, 2004).
147. John Dornberg, "Battle of the Teutoberg Forest," *Archaeology* 45, no. 5 (September/October 1992): 26–32.
148. Dornberg, "Battle of the Teutoberg Forest."
149. Wells, *The Battle That Stopped Rome*.
150. Ibid.
151. Dornberg, "Battle of the Teutoberg Forest."
152. Wells, *The Battle That Stopped Rome*.
153. Tacitus, *The Annals*, Book 2, Chapter 88. This translation is from the Loeb edition published by Harvard University Press available at http://www.loebclassics.com/view/tacitus-annals/1931/pb_LCL249.519.xml
154. Ralph D. Sawyer, *The Seven Military Classics of Ancient China* (Boulder, CO, and Oxford, UK: Westview Press, 1993).

CHAPTER 10. MENTAL ENVIRONMENTALISM

155. "P&G's Artzt: TV Advertising in Danger, Remedy Is to Embrace Technology and Return to Program Ownership," *Advertising Age*, May 23, 1994.

156. Sergey Brin and Lawrence Page, "The Anatomy of a Large-Scale Hypertextual Web Search Engine," *Computer Networks*, vol. 30 (1998), p. 107–117. This article is available at http://research.google.com/pubs/archive/334.pdf
157. Thomas Wells, "Is Advertising Morally Justifiable? The Importance of Protecting Our Attention," *ABC Religion and Ethics*. July 14, 2015; available at http://www.abc.net.au/religion/articles/2015/07/14/4273200.htm
158. Richard Dawkins, *The Selfish Gene,* quoted in Tony Sampson, *Virality: Contagion Theory in the Age of Networks* (Minneapolis: University of Minnesota Press, 2012).
159. Suzanne Goldenberg, "Warming of Oceans Due to Climate Change Is Unstoppable, Say US Scientists," *The Guardian*, July 16, 2015.
160. Rachel Carson, *Silent Spring* (Boston: Houghton Mifflin, 1962). Also, see Micah White, "Notes Toward a Future of Activism," *Reconstruction* 10.3 (2010); available at http://reconstruction.eserver.org/Issues/103/White_01.shtml

CHAPTER 11. THE FUTURE OF PROTEST

161. The emphasis in the epigraph from Lenin is in the original. For the national poll of awareness of Occupy, see "Poll: Half the Country Has Heard about the Occupy Wall Street Protests," CNN Political Ticker, October 10, 2011.
162. Martin Heidegger, "Memorial Address," in *Discourse on Thinking*, trans. John M. Anderson and Hans E. Freund (New York: Harper and Row, 1966).
163. Kevin Healy, Luke Mcnally, Graeme D. Ruxton, Natalie Cooper and Andrew L. Jackson, "Metabolic Rate and Body Size Are Linked with Perception of Temporal Information," *Animal Behaviour* 86, no. 4 (2013): 685–96.
164. Neil Johnson, Guannan Zhao, Eric Hunsader, Hong Qi, Nicholas Johnson, Jing Meng and Brian Tivnan, "Abrupt Rise of New Machine Ecology beyond Human Response Time," *Scientific Reports* 3 (2013).
165. I'm riffing on a statement by the computer scientist Roy Amara, who proposed, "We tend to overestimate the effect of a technology in the short run and underestimate the effect in the long run."
166. Thomas Jefferson, letter to John Adams, Monticello, September 4, 1823; available at http://www.let.rug.nl/usa/presidents/thomas-jefferson/letters-of-thomas-jefferson/jefl273.php

CHAPTER 12. THREE SCENARIOS FOR THE NEXT REVOLUTIONARY MOMENT

167. Naomi Klein, *This Changes Everything: Capitalism vs. the Climate* (Toronto: Knopf Canada, 2014).
168. Quoted in Debray, *Revolution in the Revolution?*, p. 69.
169. Diogenes Laertius, *Lives of Eminent Philosophers*, Book 2; available at http://data.perseus.org/citations/urn:cts:greekLit:tlg0004.tlg001.perseus-eng1:6.2
170. Telegram of Greeting from Albert Einstein to the Salle Pleyel Meeting, Paris, December 3, 1948, quoted in O. Nathan and N. Heinz, *Einstein on Peace* (New York: Simon and Schuster, 1960); available at http://www.worldgovernmenthouse.com/Mentions.php
171. The Invisible Committee, *To Our Friends*, trans. Robert Hurley (Los Angeles: Semiotext(e), 2015), p. 226.
172. Gary Marcus, "What Comes After the Turing Test?" *The New Yorker*, June 9, 2014.

CHAPTER 13. WE INNOVATE, WE WIN

173. Jack A. Goldstone, "The Weakness of Organization: A New Look at Gamson's *The Strategy of Social Protest*," *American Journal of Sociology* 85, no. 5 (March 1980): 1017–42.
174. Herbert Marcuse, *Five Lectures* (Boston: Beacon Press, 1970).
175. Evgeny Morozov, "Brave New World of Slacktivism,"*Foreign Policy*, May 19, 2009; available at http://foreignpolicy.com/2009/05/19/the-brave-new-world-of-slacktivism/
176. Patrick Kingsley, "Avaaz: Activism or 'Slacktivism'?" *The Guardian*, July 20, 2011.
177. Glenn Greenwald, "Hacking Online Polls and Other Ways British Spies Seek to Control the Internet," *The Intercept*, July 14, 2014; available at https://firstlook.org/theintercept/2014/07/14/manipulating-online-polls-ways-british-spies-seek-control-internet/
178. Nick Fielding and Ian Cobain, "Revealed: US Spy Operation That Manipulates Social Media," *The Guardian*, March 17, 2011.

CHAPTER 14. EIGHT PRINCIPLES OF REVOLUTION

179. The epigraph is from Saul D. Alinsky, *Rules for Radicals* (New York: Random House, 1971). Used by permission of Random House, an imprint and division of Penguin Random House LLC. All rights reserved. The quotation is from the same book.
180. William Shakespeare, *Henry IV*, Part 1, Act 5, Scene 1; available at http://shakespeare.mit.edu/1henryiv/1henryiv.5.1.html
181. Hans Delbrück, *History of the Art of War, Volume IV: The Dawn of Modern Warfare*, trans. Walter J. Renfroe Jr. (Lincoln: University of Nebraska Press, 1990).
182. Ian Johnson, "China's Brave Underground Journal," *The New York Review of Books*, December 4, 2014.
183. Our Bates Troy Noisy Neighbor campaign was covered by the local news. See https://www.youtube.com/watch?v=71VLbR7ymto and https://www.youtube.com/watch?v=IDr4Ae_B-oc
184. Our main website has been archived at https://web.archive.org/web/20110226110943/http://batestroynoisyneighbor.com/
185. Friedrich Engels and Daniel De Leon, *The Revolutionary Act: Military Insurrection or Political and Economic Action?* (New York: New York Labor News Company, 1922).
186. Starhawk, *Webs of Power.*

CHAPTER 15. POLITICAL MIRACLE

187. Maxim Gorky, *Days with Lenin* (Honolulu, HI: University Press of the Pacific, 2004).
188. Leon Trotsky, "The Questions of Wendelin Thomas," *Socialist Appeal* 1, no. 2 (August 21, 1937): 3.
189. Alain Badiou, *The Rebirth of History: Times of Riots and Uprisings*, trans. Gregory Elliott (London and New York: Verso, 2012).
190. Paul Lewis, Rob Evans and Rowenna Davis, "Undercover Policeman Married Activist He Was Sent to Spy On," *The Guardian*, January 19, 2011.
191. Brian Neil Levine, Clay Shields and N. Boris Margolin. "A Survey of Solutions to the Sybil Attack," *Tech report 2006-052*, University of Massachusetts Amherst, Amherst, MA, October 2006.
192. Louis Menand, "A Friend of the Devil: Inside a famous Cold War deception," *The New Yorker*, March 23, 2015.

193. Don Irwin and Vincent Burke, "21 Foundations, Union Got Money from CIA," *Los Angeles Times*, February 26, 1967.
194. Menand, "A Friend of the Devil."
195. Congressional Quarterly, "Foundations, Private Organizations Linked to CIA," February 24, 1967; available at http://bit.ly/1KrUyyi
196. Matt Apuzzo, "Holder Says Private Suit Risks State Secrets," *The New York Times*. September 14, 2014.
197. Glenn Greenwald, "Court Accepts DOJ's 'State Secrets' Claim to Protect Shadowy Neocons: a New Low," *The Intercept*. March 26, 2015. See https://firstlook.org/theintercept/2015/03/26/new-low-obama-doj-federal-courts-abusing-state-secrets-privilege/
198. Sun Tzu, *The Art of War*.

INDEX

MICAH WHITE is the award-winning activist who co-created Occupy Wall Street, a global social movement, while an editor of *Adbusters* magazine. His essays and interviews on the future of protest have been published in publications including *The New York Times*, *The Guardian Weekly* and *Folha de São Paulo*. Widely recognized as a pioneer of social movement creation, Micah White has been profiled by *The New Yorker*, and *Esquire* has named him one of the most influential young thinkers alive today. He directs Boutique Activist Consultancy—a think tank specializing in impossible campaigns—and is a frequent guest lecturer. Micah lives with his wife and son in Nehalem, a rural town on the coast of Oregon. His website is www.micahmwhite.com.

A NOTE ABOUT THE TYPE

Pierre Simon Fournier le jeune (1712–1768), the designer of the type used in this book, was both an originator and a theoretician. His contributions to the art of print communication include his distinctive design of individual characters, his creation of ornaments and his standardization of type sizes. The Fournier type, a so-called Transitional, or Realist, typeface, with its vertical stance and unencumbered style, captures the spirit of *The End of Protest*. Fournier is a fitting choice for a book about innovation and change. Regarded as a groundbreaking departure from traditional typefaces of the time, Fournier typefaces are old style in character and sharply cut.